Multilateral
Activities in
South East Asia

Pacific
Symposium
1995

Multilateral Activities in South East Asia

Edited by
Michael W. Everett
and
Mary A. Sommerville

National Defense University Press
Fort Lesley J. McNair
Washington, DC

National Defense University Press Publications

To increase general knowledge and inform discussion, the Institute for National Strategic Studies, through its publication arm the NDU Press, publishes McNair Papers; books based on of University- and Institute-sponsored symposia; books relating to U.S. national security, especially to issues of joint, combined, or coalition warfare, peacekeeping operations, and national strategy; and a variety of briefer works designed to circulate contemporary comment and offer alternatives to current policy. The Press occasionally publishes out-of-print defense classics, historical works, and other especially timely or distinguished writing on national security.

Portions of this book may be quoted or reprinted without permission, provided that a standard source credit line is included. NDU Press would appreciate a courtesy copy of reprints or reviews.

NDU Press publications are sold by the U.S. Government Printing Office. For ordering information, call (202) 512-1800 or write to the Superintendent of Documents, U.S. Government Printing Office, Washington, DC 20402.

Library of Congress Cataloging-in-Publication Data
Pacific Symposium (National Defense University) (1995)
   Multilateral activities in South East Asia : Pacific Symposium,
1995 / edited by Michael W. Everett and Mary A. Sommerville.
      p.   cm.
   Symposium sponsored by the National Defense University.
   Includes bibliographical references.
   1. Asia, Southeastern—Economic conditions—Congresses.
   2. National security—Asia, Southeastern—Congresses. I. Everett,
Michael W. II. Sommerville, Mary A., 1944-   . III. National Defense
University. IV. Title.
   HC441.P3   1995
   337.1'59—dc20   95-19569
                                                                 CIP

First printing, August 1995

For sale by the U.S. Government Printing Office
Superintendent of Documents, Mail Stop: SSOP, Washington, DC 20402-9328
ISBN 0-16-047999-1

CONTENTS

Part I
A SOUTH EAST ASIA PERSPECTIVE

Part II
THE SOUTH EAST ASIA ENVIRONMENT:
View from the Peripheral Nations

FOREWORD

For many years, bilateral arrangements to support national security among Asia-Pacific nations were the only framework; recently, this foundation has been shifting to support a gradual development of complementary multilateral arrangements. This development has been focused, so far, on South East Asia. The growth of ASEAN, with its commitment to "preventive diplomacy," clearly symbolizes the development of multilateralism in South East Asia. Papers in this volume reflect the views of many Asia-Pacific nations regarding the rise of multilateralism in that area.

Parts I and II present the view from experts from the Philippines, Indonesia, and Malaysia, then the views of analysts from Australia, China, India, and Japan—those large nations on the periphery. The middle section of the book addresses the relationships of AFTA, APEC, and the WTO, and predicts future developments in South East Asia as a result of the influence of these economic-oriented institutions. Parts IV and V offer the views of distinguished writers from South East Asia, other Asian nations, and the United States about the sorts of multilateral arrangements that exist and likely scenarios for the future.

The stability in South East Asia holds great promise for improvements to environmental, health, education, and social programs as well as to the national economies of the region. Vietnam's recent inclusion into ASEAN and our subsequent diplomatic recognition are major steps that add to long-term South East Asian stability. But areas of potential instability remain—chief among them the Taiwan-China dispute, the fragile Cambodian peace, conflicting claims over the Spratly Islands, and the division of Korea. The next 20 years will be an era of almost phenomenal change across the Pacific. This book, with its discussions of the vital economic, political, and military perspectives of multilateralism in South East Asia, will help us understand part of the coming change.

ERVIN J. ROKKE
Lieutenant General, U.S. Air Force
President, National Defense University

ix

SUMMARY

The yearly Pacific Symposiums sponsored by the National Defense University have covered many topics, such as evolving strategic priorities, the new Pacific security environment, cooperative security in the Pacific Basin, and cooperative engagement and economic security—and nearly all concerned security issues. With the threat of the Cold War gone, it's almost as if the Asia-Pacific region has breathing room to advance more domestic interests such as economic development and social programs. Indeed, to that end, the 1995 symposium took a different tack—"Multilateral Activities in South East Asia."

Five subtopics allowed the many participants several opportunities to explore all facets of this rather large topic: The South East Asia Perspective; The South East Asia Environment: View from the Peripheral Nations; AFTA, APEC, and the WTO: How Do They Fit Together?; How Much and What Kind of Multilateralism?; and A Look Toward the Future. The common thread among all, however, was economic security, with an emphasis on doing business the Asian way. Discussions focused on the importance of marketing and selling goods to other than Western nations and the effect on world economics.

This book begins with a personal observation by Admiral Richard C. Macke, Commander in Chief, U.S. Pacific Command, who views strategic security to be a strong concern. He emphasizes that long-term stability, as fostered by credible U.S. security assurances, promotes market advances and technical services. Admiral Macke believes the future provides the real excitement. While it's true that multicultural dialogues will face challenges, and there's the North Korea problem and the overwhelming presence of China, plus the territorial disputes and myriad other problems, it's also significant that APEC will invest $1.1 trillion in the region over the next 6 years—the equivalent of building 15 Santa Monica freeways everyday! It would seem that South East Asia believes in itself.

The thoughts of Sheldon Simon follow. Taking a long-term view, Dr. Simon sees multilateralism as a two-track action comprising politico-economic and security components. He believes economic regionalism in the Asia-Pacific is driven by market forces rather than politics, as in Europe. This economic regionalism is also motivated by fear of being shut out of other regionalisms—a condition that could lead to a decline in the U.S. marketing position in the area. On the security front, Mr. Simon sees the region attempting to create its own security mechanisms in line with Asian political developments, which are not necessarily in step with U.S. foreign policy goals.

The first part, *The South East Asia Perspective,* contains three papers. The first, by Dr. Carolina G. Hernandez, of the Philippines, stresses that, although the Asia-Pacific nations may want the United States to remain committed to regional safeguarding, these countries wish to set their own course, without outside interference. To that end, the current notion is to expand ASEAN to no more than 10 members. They also believe they are natural economic partners, that rapid economic development leads to increasing political openness, and that domestic reforms lead to regional stability. The second paper, from the Indonesian perspective, presents the austere views of Dr. J. Soedjati Djiwandono, who feels that ASEAN has no economic clout but acknowledges that it has been able to maintain peace among the South East Asian countries. Thus ASEAN countries should bear primary responsibility for peace and security in the region; outsiders should be there only to maintain military balance, not to provide security. The last paper, a view from Malaysia, is by Dr. Rajmah Hussain, who believes in the power of ASEAN and ARF, because these organizations stress that comprehensive security is not based solely on military issues but must include economic, cultural, political, and social issues as well.

Part II, *The South East Asia Environment,* offers pbservations from peripheral nations, beginning with some interesting observations by Rory Steele, from Australia. Mr. Steele believes that by 2010, Indonesia and Thailand will be in the top 15 countries economically. Australia is proud of APEC, an Australian initiative, which appears to be working for all parties, and ARF, which it views as a preventive diplomacy forum. Further, Australia sees itself as part of South East Asia, not a peripheral nation, especially since it exports 14% of its trade exports to the South East Asia region.

Senior Colonel Peng Guangquian, of the PRC, believes that Asian nations should focus quickly on economic development, because economic competition will intensify in the region. He also stresses that there will be no return of the Cold War, and thus U.S. military presence in the region is no longer necessary.

Presenting the Indian viewpoint is Dr. C. Raja Mohan, who assures us that although India has secluded itself the South East Asia in the past, it has recently taken steps to become trading partners with nations of the Asia-Pacific area. Dr. Mohan does express concern about the balance of security in the region, especially the Russia/China connection; the impact of Islam; the fate of ICBMs in the area; and China's rising power. Overall, he believes that multilateralism will transform South East Asia into something good.

The view from Japan, is presented by Professor Akio Watanabe, who says that Japanese regional interests include stability in South East Asia and maritime safety of the sea lines of communications. Japan does not see failed states as a major issues in the region, and indeed has shifted a significant portion of its investments in the West to countries in the Asia-Pacific region.

Part III, *AFTA, APEC, and the WTO: How Do They Fit Together?*, presents some very solid ideas in three papers. The first, from Wisern Pupphavesa, discusses the interlocking concepts of the three bodies. He stresses that the ASEAN style of trading (informal, nonbinding) is very different from the western tradition (formal, with binding agreements), and the commonly shared factors of ASEAN countries are stable growth and development and emphasis on open trade. He also mentions that the United States needs to pay more attention to South East Asia, the fastest growing area in the world.

The second paper, by Pearl Imada-Iboshi, discusses NAFTA, AFTA, and APEC and also emphasizes the Asian way of trading. She notes that regional solutions to trade have become popular and that there can be rapily increasing trade without trade arrangements and institutional frameworks, indicating a preference for evolutionary integration rather than formal integration.

Ambassador Joun Yung Sun, from Korea, presents the third view, the impact of APEC on the Asia-Pacific region. He believes that economic considerations are assuming greater importance in international relations, as nations are finding it difficult to separate economic from political ties. Further, economic interaction is expected to pave the way for future diplomatic and political cooperation.

How Much and What Kind of Multilateralism is the fourth group of papers, which begins with Dr. Kwa Chong Guan's reflections on multilateralism. He, too, discusses "the Asian way" of developing organizations, by recognizing the differences of values, norms, and practices among the nations, emphasizing the search for commonalities and understanding, working toward shared objectives step by step, rather than developing blueprints. He also recognizes that a primary cause of regional instability and insuecruity is power rivalry and intervention, thus the region would be better off if isolated from the broader international system. Dr. Kwa suggests all this may be achieved through confidence and security building measures, underscoring again the Asian way.

Ambassador Dao Huy Ngoc follows this paper with his views on regional security cooperation. He recognizes that each country in the region is facing many domestic economic changes; potential interstate conflict still exists; and that the relationship among the United States, Japan, China, and Russia is crucial for stability and peace in the region. Ambassador Ngoc also acknowledges that whereas in the past political and military power were in the forefront, today economic priorities, historical background, and Asian culture and values are increasingly becoming instrumental forces in the evolution of international politics.

Making multilateralism work is the theme of Dr. Amitav Acharya's paper. He believes that attitudes toward multilateralism shifted dramatically with the end of the Cold. Dr. Acharya stresses that although ARF faces significant challenges and constraints, it will be the great contributor to regional security, by using the very norms that have already committed ASEAN members to peaceful conduct and facilitated its evolution toward a regional security community. Indeed, he believes there is no viable alternative to ARF. It cannot, of course, address the full range of security problems that could arise in the region, but the security dialogues envisioned under ARF could, over time, promote transparency, confidence building, and other forms of security cooperation.

Paul Bracken wrote the final paper in this section from the U.S. perspective. Dr. Bracken notes that multilateralism will provide an arena of competition, and so one must look for robustness in ASEAN economies—i.e, how will each stand up during times of crises? And while he believes that the G-7 system should be preserved, he also recognizes that the United States must be flexible when it comes to adapting new thinking and rewriting scripts. Dr. Bracken says that predictions about the success of multilateralism is not possible at this time, but even with the potential for regional conflict, multilateralism will most likely prove a positive tact.

The final section, *A Look Toward the Future,* provides some startling and sometimes unsettling thoughts. Professor Kenneth Courtis states that the United States must *export* itself out of the next recession and that it will eventually be well behind its competitors in the world market because of its lack of reinvestment capital. He also envisions that the economic growth center of the world will be in Asia; calculates that Japan will run a trillion dollar surplus withing the next decade; and estimates that China must create 280 million jobs in the next 10 years to maintain employment stability.

Stephen Merchant predictions include an economic transformation in Asia; China emerging as an economic and military superpower; and Japan assuming a more active role in security arrangements in the area.

Richard Wilson concludes the book with his observations that ASEAN economic policy is strongly connected to global economy. Should the global economy collapse, ASEAN would be threatened also. He also notes that whereas in the beginning ASEAN countries supported no middle class and suffered internal insurgencies, it is now characterized by tolerance of societal changes, because of economic success, and pragmatism, which will win over competing ideologies.

Multilateral Activities in South East Asia

THE STRATEGIC VIEW

Richard C. Macke

I recently experienced traveling 130,000 miles throughout the Asia-Pacific region for the last 7 months—a "total immersion" course in political-military science—which allowed me to make some broad observations about the area.

The remarkable economic growth we see in the Asia-Pacific region is often characterized as an "economic miracle," but it is also a "security miracle." The extraordinary economic performance of the countries in my Area of Responsibility (AOR) rests on a foundation of stability and regional security underwritten by the visible forward presence of capable American forces and our credible security assurances, an opinion shared by every senior military and civilian leader I meet in the PACOM AOR. They all want to know: *will the United States stay engaged?* And of course I should clarify that I haven't traveled to North Korea yet; they may *not* want us to remain engaged!

The stability that underlies this security miracle in the Pacific is not simply "the absence of war." We seek long-term stability founded on shared regional confidence. Such confidence fosters market maturation and the demand for advanced technical services. This is a trade sector where the United States has

Admiral Richard Macke is the Commander in Chief, U.S. Pacific Command. He leads the largest of the unified commands and directs Army, Navy, Marine Corps, and Air Force operations across more than 100 million square miles. Previous assignments include Commander Carrier Group TWO and Commander Carrier Group FOUR. Admiral Macke also served as the Director for Command, Control, Communications and Computer (C4) Systems, Joint Staff. In 1991 he assumed the position of Director, Joint Staff.

exceptional strengths, and there is a huge market in the Asia-Pacific region. We talk excitedly about what our trade is *now,* but the real excitement lies in the future. The Asian Asia-Pacific Economic Cooperation members plan to invest $1.1 trillion in infrastructure over the next 6 years. I like President Clinton's reminder that in concrete terms, this is the equivalent of 15 Santa Monica freeways every day.

Because we want a security environment built on shared regional confidence, today's military forces must be prepared for more than "making people *not* do things" the deterrence of "threats" that characterized the Cold War. And military forces must be prepared for more than "making people *do* things," such as "leave Kuwait," a function we can call *"compellence."* Military forces must be able to directly reinforce the regional confidence essential for long-term stability. This is the function of military power that Michael Howard called reassurance.

Pacific Command executes all these security roles through the theater military strategy we call "Cooperative Engagement, a well-established, winning theater military strategy that guides the employment of the entire range of military resources provided to me by the American people. In crisis, we work to deter aggression and encourage cooperation with our friends and allies.   In peacetime, we pursue reassurance through the forward stationing and deployment of our military forces, the training and sustainment of capable forces, and a broad range of military activities. If necessary, we are prepared to win in conflict. In conflict, we remain ready for decisive "compellence" victory in combat; unilaterally, if necessary, but we prefer to act together with allies and coalition partners who have a common stake in regional security. It's better, of course, to deter conflict through effective crisis response. And it's best to prevent a crisis from even arising by a broad and sustained program of reassurance that reinforces that shared regional confidence essential for long-term security and stability.

I've already told you how important our forward military presence is to this strategy. Because of the tyranny of distance imposed by the size of the Pacific and Indian Oceans, any claim to be a legitimate Asia-Pacific power would ring hollow in the absence of a visible, tangible, and capable military presence. One of the most effective manifestations of U.S. military presence, and a key element of our strategy of Cooperative Engagement, is our extensive program of foreign military interaction. The Asia-Pacific region is marked by incredible diversity. Individuals have different cultures and different values. But military professionals have a shared bond of military experience, and communicate quite effectively. That was certainly my own personal experience, with Chinese military leaders, and when I went to Hanoi and dealt with former adversaries. We gain tremendous strategic leverage from low-cost, high-payoff military interaction programs employing our key strategic advantage: our people. I do not view these contacts as "nice-to-have," but rather as critical activities that are strategic, long-term investments of extraordinary potential.

One of the most important of these contacts is the International Military Education and Training (IMET) program. I really feel strongly about this. Over 60 Congressmen heard it from me last week during testimony in Congress, and now you're going to have to sit through it, too. You all know that IMET is the training of young foreign military and civilian leaders in the United States. It's impossible to overstate the long-term strategic value of this low-cost program. I can't think of anything with a more effective payoff for a very low cost. When I sit with General Wimol, the Royal Thai Army Commander in Chief, he's got seven generals lined up next to him, the present and future leadership of the Thai Army, and every one of them a graduate of IMET. You can look at so many of the major players in the very important area of Northeast Asia: former Defense Minister of South Korea, Mr. Rhee; Chairman of the Japanese Joint Staff Council Nishimoto; and Glenn Marsh, U.S. Commander of I Corps. They were classmates at the Army War College at Carlisle. As IMET students return home and ascend to positions of prominence in military and government positions, we simply cannot buy the mutual understanding generated by this type of program.

Consider Indonesia: an incredibly important country, the fourth largest nation in the world, the largest Muslim nation, Chair of the Non-Aligned Movement, with a dynamic economy, positioned astride major sea lines of communication. Our IMET program has been closed to Indonesia for the last 28 months. We may likely have a situation, several years from now, when we will face an extended period when the Indonesian military will be led by individuals who do not have a first-hand understanding of the United States. I offer my professional military opinion that it is a mistake to use the IMET program for short-term punishment of unfavorable behavior. We should use it to positively influence future behavior. We are using our best tool to teach leaders about human rights as a club for perceived human rights problems.

"Foreign military interactions," "military-to-military contacts," IMET—these reassurance actions are widely understood to be good things. Our presence and our peacetime military activities reinforce our relationships with friends and allies, reassuring them with respect to our long-term commitment, the effectiveness of our warfighting capability, and the values and quality of our people. I found Congress to be very receptive to my arguments for these programs. These programs are key to our Cooperative Engagement strategy, and they are also key to the future of that strategy . . . because if these activities are so effective in our important bilateral relationships, why can't they be equally effective in multilateral relationships? I hold it as my personal charter, therefore, to extend the Cooperative Engagement strategy by encouraging Multilateral Military Activities.

Now, let's talk about the fact that some folks say the word "multilateral" can't be used in the Asia-Pacific region. That it "can't be done," or that we "can't get there from here." We can't keep looking at the Asia-Pacific region as in the past, although of course, the past can be instructive. It's useful to consider the pessimism originally associated with the first ideas about a multilateral organization called "ASEAN." When ASEAN worked, the pessimism had to shift to the notion of an "ASEAN Regional Forum." In a very short time the ASEAN Regional Forum advanced far beyond initial projections. APEC was another idea that had no future, but it has done very well. The current trend in APEC pessimism is the total impossibility of the Bogor goals of free trade by the year 2020. Will that happen? I don't know, but I think back 25 years to what the world was like in 1970. I hesitate to claim I could predict today's world, and I refuse to claim to know what can or can't be done by 2020.

Does the advancement of multilateral dialogues face some challenges? Absolutely. In Northeast Asia, the Northeast Asia Security Dialogue is advancing slowly, with North Korea a stubborn nonparticipant. North Korea faces a faltering economy and international isolation and is undergoing the first hereditary transfer of Communist power. All indications are that Kim Jong Il is in charge, but the North Korean leadership remains isolated and unpredictable. The greatest concern of the North Koreans is survival of the regime, and we must be careful not to give them the perception that their survival is threatened. If that happens, they might lash out. The Agreed Framework with North Korea is a significant achievement that addresses a serious proliferation threat, not only for the region, but for the entire world. It caps the North Korean nuclear program and should reduce overall tensions, permitting North-South rapprochement to resume. So far, North Korea has complied with the agreement, but our experience with North Korea tells us to always "expect the unexpected." The Agreed Framework is based on reciprocal performance, a step by step approach, so we can ensure North Korean compliance. Significantly, implementation of the Agreement will require extensive multilateral cooperation.

Although their nuclear program is currently capped, the North remains a dangerous conventional threat, with over a million individuals under arms, and 65 to 70 percent of those forces within 100 km of the DMZ. They have deployed a tremendous artillery capability along the DMZ and within range of Seoul. We have to *deter* North Korea, and if necessary, be ready to *compel* it. If we can improve our relations, maybe over the long term we can move to *reassurance*. Certainly it is unwise to do anything that would undercut our current deterrent posture. We must maintain forces in Korea for the foreseeable future. Meantime, the Republic of Korea is an active player in the world. They have improved relations with Russia, China, and Japan. I can't emphasize enough the care we take to ensure total coordination with our close friend and ally, the Republic of Korea and how integral the ROK will be in the ultimate resolution on the Korean Peninsula.

Equally important to the North Korean situation and the future of multilateral efforts throughout the region, will be Japan. The Japan-U.S. Security relationship has long been held up as an example of one of the most successful bilateral relationships in the world, and rightfully so. In every respect, this is a global partnership and a remarkable demonstration of successful *reassurance,* in which the number one and number two economic powers in the world enjoy one of the closest treaty alliances in history. Our 1960 Treaty of Mutual Cooperation and Security with Japan remains a key factor to the broad sense of shared regional confidence we seek throughout the AOR. U.S. forces in Japan visibly demonstrate our commitment to the stability of the entire region, and they are available for short-notice deployment throughout the theater. They reinforce our deterrence of North Korea's conventional threat. Frequent combined U.S. and Japanese military exercises enhance professional interaction and interoperability between our militaries. The benefit of this cooperation was demonstrated in our readiness to respond to Japanese humanitarian needs during the recent tragedy in the Kobe earthquake. Japan contributes to overseas security through their overseas development assistance programs and is a regional power of extraordinary influence. Just as Japan has been and will continue to be one of our strongest bilateral partners, it is a vital member of any multilateral dialogue, especially in Northeast Asia.

In South East Asia, I have already mentioned the success of ASEAN and the ASEAN Regional Forum. I look forward to any questions you may have about South East Asia, because it is truly an exciting part of the world. I simply want to point out that if you are still "bearish" on multilateral approaches in the region, then I suggest you sell any stock you have in the Spratly Islands, because that is clearly a problem of multilateral dimensions, where the United States does not take a position on the claims of the many parties, but does advocate resolution without recourse to violence.

There's an element of commonalty to Northeast Asia and South East Asia, and that is China. With one-fifth of the world's population, strategic nuclear weapons, veto power on the United Nation's Security Council, and a dynamic economy, China is already a world power. China, however, faces some enormous challenges in the future. I firmly believe that an approach that emphasizes dialogue rather than isolation or confrontation offers the greatest promise for maintaining stability of the Asia-Pacific region. Most significantly for the topic at hand, China is of enormous significance to the issue of multilateral dialogues of any type in the Pacific. Although the Chinese say their military is not their central priority, the Peoples Liberation Army is clearly central to all their goals: internal stability, economic progress, and external respect. That is why our growing program of reassuring military contacts with the Chinese military is so important. As China's future unfolds, the PLA will play a pivotal role. China continues to increase the pace and scope of its military modernization program, and we fully recognize the concerns of many regional nations as China's power projection capability grows. But I do not see China's military as a near-term threat to the U.S. or to our interests in Asia. My assessment would change, however, if we choose to isolate, rather than engage and reassure China.

As I close, I want to caution everyone about my enthusiasm for multilateral military activities. Multilateral military activities is not a revolutionary idea; it is an evolutionary one, an extension of a well-proven concept of engagement and reassurance. It cannot and will not replace our key bilateral relationships and we are content to advance the progress of multilateral activities in the "Asian way"—gradually, with consensus, and at a pace that friends and allies in the region find comfortable.

THE PARALLEL TRACKS OF ASIAN MULTILATERALISM

Sheldon W. Simon

INTRODUCTION

As the Asia-Pacific approaches a new millennium, regional international relations are moving away from Washington-centered bilateralism to a more diffuse multilateral structure, consisting of both politico-economic and security components. Both are quite comprehensive in that almost all Asia-Pacific states are involved, though they are not completely inclusive. For example, Russia, North Korea, the Indochinese states, and Burma (Myanmar) are not yet members of economic regional groups, nor are North Korea, Taiwan, and Indochina members of the new regional security gathering. However, Vietnam, Laos, and Cambodia in all probability will join both types of Asia-Pacific organizations by the turn of the century.

Economic regionalism in the Asia-Pacific, in contrast to Europe, has been driven by market forces rather than politics. The European Community evolved over a 35-year period through top-down political decisions. Economies were linked through negotiations among Western European governments. In the Asia-Pacific region, economic regionalism has been a product of market forces through which capital from Japan, the United

Sheldon W. Simon is Professor, Political Science, Arizona State University. He is currently a Member, United States Council on Security Cooperation in the Asia-Pacific, and a Member, Fulbright Political Science Award Selection Committee. His previous position was as Principal Investigator, South East Asia Security Environment Project, Department of Defense. Dr. Simon has written numerous articles and books and is currently doing research on Chinese, Japanese, Soviet, American and Indochinese security policies.

States and Europe created links among Asian economies via transnational corporations and technology transfer. Again, unlike Europe, this market-led regionalism is open to interaction with states outside the Asia-Pacific on the basis of reciprocity. The European model is rejected as too rigid, institutionalist, and discriminatory.[1]

Open economic regionalism in East Asia is partially driven by fears that other regionalisms will be closed. Asian states fear being shut out of the North American Free Trade Agreement (NAFTA) as well as the European Union (EU). They are attracted, rather, to the concept of global free trade embodied in the General Agreement on Tariffs and Trade (GATT) and its successor World Trade Organization (WTO). Within their own region, Asian states have initiated policy consultations as well as some coordination to establish such common goals as the gradual elimination of trade barriers. They hope to accomplish these tasks through the Association South East Asian Nations (ASEAN) Free Trade Area (AFTA) negotiations and Asia-Pacific Economic Cooperation (APEC) forum plans. At this stage, however, no member state is willing to consider sharing authority with a supranational mechanism that could make binding decisions as in the EU.

One of the most striking features of Asian economic growth has been mutual economic penetration. In the aggregate, this has led to remarkable rates of economic growth in the Pacific over the past 15 years. But, it has also led to friction with respect to the distribution of trade benefits, particularly between the United States and Japan and the U.S. and the newly industrializing economies (NIEs). America has been running large annual deficits with the Asia-Pacific—currently around $80 to $90 billion—since the early 1980s. To meliorate this financial drain, Washington has pressed its Asian trading partners to open their markets further to U.S. products, in the Japanese case even insisting that some U.S. exports be guaranteed shares of Japan's market (government procurement, automobile parts, and computer chips). Bilateral negotiations with Japan, China, South Korea, and Thailand particularly have created political tensions that threaten to undermine the generally favorable U.S. relationship with Asia in the post-Cold War period.

Despite these frictions, Asia-Pacific economies are of vital importance to the United States. American trade across the Pacific is one and a half times its counterpart with Europe;

exports to APEC countries account for 2.6 million jobs in the U.S. economy; approximately 50 percent of U.S. exports are sent to Asia and about 60 percent of U.S. imports come from that region; and 30 percent of U.S. overseas investment goes to APEC countries.[2]

THE DECLINING U.S. POSITION IN THE ASIA-PACIFIC

As a declining hegemon, the United States plans to sustain important political/security and economic positions in the western Pacific. However, it can no longer accomplish these ends either unilaterally or exclusively bilaterally. Its allies now share the costs of maintaining forward deployed U.S. forces on their soil with Japan paying virtually all local costs after 1995 and the Republic of Korea (ROK) approximately 35 percent of these costs.[3]

Because trade drives American foreign policy toward the Pacific rim in the post-Cold War, the U.S. Department of Commerce and the Office of the U.S. Trade Representative seem to take precedence over both the Departments of State and Defense. Thus, the Clinton administration places the need to protect foreign patents, copyrights, and intellectual property at the top of its foreign policy agenda in dealing with Thailand, Indonesia, China, and the ROK. It also presses for more open markets throughout the region. The United States believes that the Pacific's economic dynamism is at least partly based on the export emphasis of virtually all its economies. Unlike Europe, so far Asia does not appear to be sliding toward protectionism or inward-looking regionalism. Washington hopes to ensure that this economic openness continues. The U.S. president has consciously used the American military presence as a lever to open regional markets further for U.S. products. At the November 1993 APEC summit in Seattle, he stated, "We do not intend to bear the cost of our military presence in Asia and the burdens of regional leadership only to be shut out of the benefits of growth that stability brings."[4] Thus, under Clinton, the United States has brandished its security role as a good for which improved trade and investment access should be exchanged.

Another point of contention between the United States and several of its Asian partners is Washington's emphasis on human rights as a condition for economic assistance and favorable political relations.   Increasingly, U.S. aid is allocated to nongovernmental organizations (NGOs) in recipient countries. Many of these NGOs are in conflict with their governments.   In Indonesia, for example, $320,000 was recently given to the Indonesian Legal Aid Institute, one of the country's leading NGOs in the promotion of democratic reform. Such actions, though small in scale and impact, are seen by some as interference in Jakarta's internal affairs.[5]

Further complicating this issue is the fact that the U.S. vision of human rights is derived from North American and European histories, which emphasize the rights of the individual vis-a-vis governments. Asian experiences reverse these priorities, insisting that benefits for the collective (society) must come ahead of the individual, and government's primary responsibility and a basic "human right" must be economic development. Additionally, U.S. efforts to link workers' rights and environmental issues to trade are challenged in Asia as a form of American protectionism. Better wages and working conditions are seen as a way of raising costs and lowering the competitiveness of Asian products.[6]

Finally, it should be noted that the ability to use access to the American market as leverage is declining. By the early 1990s, 43 percent of Asia's exports were sent to other Asian states. Relative dependence on the U.S. market declined from 30 percent in 1986 to only 21 percent in 1991.[7]   This is all the more reason for the United States to remember that "get tough" unilateralism will not fit in an era of economic globalization and regional multilateralism.

APEC AND OPEN REGIONALISM

APEC represents the culmination of a process of market-oriented, outward-looking policy reforms that began in the ASEAN economies in the 1980s. These reforms ultimately convinced the Association's most skeptical member, Indonesia, that an Asiawide economic consultative body had become a necessity. Because the market economies of East Asia are trade-dependent, APEC was launched in 1989 in support of the GATT process of *open regionalism*, a commitment to nondiscrimination or the offer of most favored nation (MFN) treatment to all trade partners either inside or outside APEC who are willing to reciprocate.   Thus,

APEC has been more concerned with the health of global trade than the creation of an East Asian trade bloc.[8]

Indeed, most APEC members, with the exception of the United States, Australia, Singapore, and possibly Indonesia, prefer that the organization confine its activities to discussions of trade and investment liberalization and related studies. There is little sentiment to institutionalize this forum by creating a permanent bureaucracy or allocating decisions on these matters to the membership as a group. Thus, APEC has no decisionmaking capability. Nevertheless, it has established 10 working groups capped by a distinguished array of well known economists and other intellectuals drawn from its members. This Eminent Persons Group (EPG) has taken 2 years to devise a free-trade blueprint for the region, a recommendation guaranteed to generate controversy. The other working groups are less controversial and have already produced useful reports on APEC investment patterns and a tariff database for all members.[9]

The United States may have a different agenda for APEC, however. The Clinton administration's concentration on opening Asian markets is seen by Washington as APEC's primary utility. If there is a regional commitment to trade liberalization through APEC, then U.S. efforts to deal with bilateral trade imbalances with Japan, China, and Thailand should be eased. However, any special U.S. bilateral trade arrangements may be at the expense of other APEC partners. This occurred in Japan's negotiations with both U.S. beef at the expense of Australia and American plywood at the expense of Indonesia and Malaysia.[10] U.S. behavior reinforces the apprehensions of the ASEAN countries that Washington is out to hijack APEC and turn it into a free trade area that will be dominated by the large economies.

Certainly, the August 1994, Second EPG Report for the November APEC meeting in Jakarta could be read in this light. It called for regionwide trade and investment liberalization in three phases, with industrial countries eliminating all barriers by 2010, the NIEs by 2015, and finally the less developed states by 2020. The EPG Report also took note of potential conflicts between APEC and the practices of such subregional groups as the AFTA and NAFTA, urging that these bodies equalize the preference arrangements they offer members of their subgroups with the larger APEC.[11] This is in keeping with the latter's commitment to open regionalism: equal benefits to outsiders providing they reciprocate. Parallel recommendations are being made for investment policy through a separate APEC committee report which requested that members provide nondiscriminatory treatment to foreign investments, that is, to treat foreign investors the same as domestic investors. This recommendation is also consonant with GATT principles.[12]

EPG free-trade proposals are interpreted as particularly advantagious to the United States because they call for reciprocity, a procedure the U.S. has advocated in bilateral negotiations with Asian trade partners. Reciprocity would require trade partners to open their markets to each other on an equal basis. As U.S. negotiators insist, this would level the playing field. Thai officials, reflecting the concerns of other ASEAN states, reacted cautiously, however, fearful that equal treatment for foreigners would drive some local industries out of business. Malaysia and the Philippines have openly criticized the EPG proposals, claiming that, if implemented, they would move APEC toward a trade bloc, diminishing ASEAN's importance within the larger Pacific group.[13] Nevertheless, with Indonesian President Suharto's support, the free-trade timetable could well prevail, even though it may be inconsistent with GATT principles against discrimination and despite Malaysian President Mahathir's objection to APEC becoming a trade bloc instead of a "loose forum."[14]

SUBREGIONALISM: AFTA AND THE EAEC

A major reason for ASEAN reticence over Pacific-wide free trade is the belief that it would supersede ASEAN's own free trade area. Similarly, Malaysia's East Asian Economic Caucus (EAEC) initiative has been stalled by Washington's objection that it would split APEC into Asian and non-Asian components. At its July 1994 Foreign Ministers meeting, the ASEAN communique virtually ignored the EAEC. This stalemate appears unresolvable because Japan has stated it cannot support the Caucus unless the United States removes its objection.[15]

The successful conclusion of the Uruguay Round of GATT negotiations has accelerated the AFTA timetable of tariff reductions in order to keep ASEAN consistent with the new WTO. AFTA negotiators have shortened the time from 15 to 10 years to that intra-ASEAN tariffs on industrial and agricultural goods will be reduced to a maximum of 5 percent by 2003. These reductions combined with new subregional economic cooperation, among Indonesia-Malaysia-Singapore, Philippines-Indonesia-Malaysia, and the Mekong River states of Thailand and Indochina should help to make South East Asia an attractive investment region. Moreover, the ASEAN economic ministers have also agreed to expand AFTA's coverage to include raw agricultural products and the services sector. This expanded AFTA should cover virtually all intra-ASEAN trade which currently accounts for 20 percent of the total trade of ASEAN members.[16]

The primary obstacle to harmonious American participation in Pacific economic regionalism remains the EAEC. Prime Minister Mahathir has downgraded his original 1990 proposal, which would have created a separate ASEAN-led bargaining group for Asia-Pacific economic diplomacy to a more modest consultative group within APEC. EAEC proponents have also sought to reassure North America and Australia that the Caucus would remain committed to an open multilateral trading system. Other potential EAEC members such as South Korea, Singapore, and, of course, Japan would also insure that the group did not create a protectionist bloc within APEC. Washington's continued objection, therefore, may be overdrawn. The United States could earn considerable good will within the region by endorsing the EAEC. Such an endorsement would be an effective followup to America's renewal of China's MFN status. Moreover, the real target for EAEC proponents may be less the United States than Japan. That is, the EAEC may well be a device to open Tokyo's market to Asian exporters rather than a way of diminishing the importance of the non-Asian members of APEC.

REGIONALISM AND ASIAN SECURITY

The second track of Asian-Pacific regionalism in the post-Cold War period lies in the political-security realm. Pacific-wide security discussions are a new phenomenon. They evolved in the aftermath of the Cold War and emerged from the U.S. military drawdown in the Pacific. While American forces remain at fixed bases in both Japan and Korea, they have left the Philippines in South East Asia, even though the ASEAN states did not desire a complete U.S. departure from the region. In fact, all six ASEAN states in varying degrees have become involved in helping the

United States maintain a low-profile air and naval presence in their vicinity through a relationship known as "places not bases."[17] Memoranda of understanding have been signed bilaterally with all ASEAN members, except the Philippines, through which U.S. ships and planes in small numbers have rights of access to specific ports and airfields for repair, provisioning, and joint exercises. Through these arrangements, the United States remains the dominant sea and air power throughout the western Pacific and not just in Northeast Asia where its only bases are located. The low-key U.S. presence in South East Asia is designed to alleviate local anxieties about putative regional threats without compromising sovereignty or offending nationalist sentiments. Nevertheless, U.S. efforts in late 1994 to discuss with the Philippines and Thailand the prospect of permanent offshore prepositioned military supplies in their vicinity were rejected as a vestige of the old Cold War dependence on outsiders for regional security. That era has ended.

Although a U.S. presence remains, it is no longer a sufficient guarantee of security nor is it appropriate for such concerns as territorial disputes, local arms buildups, and ethnic tensions. Only discussions among the region's members can address these effectively. These discussions seek to develop a habit of dialogue and transparency among regional actors, thus providing reassurance about intentions even as military capabilities increase.[18] South Korea's establishment of diplomatic relations with three of its former adversaries (China, Russia, and Vietnam) is an example of efforts to establish this new dialogue of reassurance even as the ROK gradually builds a military capacity for regional—not just peninsular—action.

ASEAN's decision to become the core of an Asian-Pacific security discussion forum emerged from two realizations:

- The region's economic linkages to Northeast Asia meant that developments in the North Pacific directly affected South East Asia.
- A desire to preempt the organization of a Pacific-wide security group in order to have some control over its agenda.

ASEAN feared the prospect of being subordinated to the United States, Japan, Korea, and China if any combination of the latter initiated regional dialogue before ASEAN could.

Initially through post-ministerial conferences (PMCs) and then through the ARF (discussed below), ASEAN and its dialogue partners have developed an Asiawide discussion agenda for the 1990s whose primary aim seems to be *transparency*. Information on arms transfers, acquisitions, and indigenous arms production; military deployments and exercises; and defense doctrines are all fair game for a cooperative security dialogue. This agenda was originally developed by government-funded think tanks in the ASEAN states, consisting primarily of academic researchers whose recommendations were then transferred for action to the official level.[19] The ultimate purpose of transparency is, of course, reassurance. Accumulated mutual confidence is a prerequisite to resolving harder issues such as territorial and resource disputes. That ASEAN, an organization which has assiduously avoided any semblance of security responsibilities since its inception, should emerge as the primary institution for wide-ranging Pacific security discussion is a real measure of how much change the post-Cold War world has induced in Asia. ASEAN is founding a new regional security order centered on itself to at least partially replace (some would say supplement) the old system based on bilateral security ties with the United States.[20] Emblematic of this new arrangement is the fact that the 1976 ASEAN Treaty of Amity and Cooperation has become the basis of security ties among neighbors. The Indochina states are adhering to it as a first step toward joining ASEAN itself.

An additional explanation for Asian decisions to create their own security mechanisms is a growing realization that America's post-Cold War foreign policy goals may not be entirely compatible with Asian political developments. The Clinton administration has placed democracy and human rights near the top of its global agenda. This means that Washington has become increasingly concerned with how Asian states are governed. From the target government's viewpoint, this comes perilously close to direct interference in its internal politics and a challenge to governing elites. Insofar as this human rights concern focuses on labor conditions, it is also seen as an effort to raise business costs in the region and/or justify U.S. protectionism against Asian products. Either way, Washington's human rights agenda is one more indication that the purely military security concerns of the Cold War have ended and a much more complex U.S. relationship with the Asia-Pacific has begun.[21]

The country whose security intentions seem the most imponderable in Asia is China. On the one hand even traditional adversaries such as Malaysia, Indonesia, and the ROK see the PRC as a newly awakened capitalist giant with which trade and investment provide mutual profitability. On the other, it is perceived to be a regional great power inexorably developing economic and military capabilities that will permit Beijing to restore its traditional influence over the region. In general, the Asian states have responded by trying to encourage China's outward looking commercial policies in hopes of nurturing a political-business elite with a strong stake in maintaining regional stability.

A litmus test for the PRC's intentions is its policy toward the future of the potentially oil rich Spratly archipelago in the South China Sea. China remains the only holdout among six claimants (PRC, Vietnam, Malaysia, Taiwan, Brunei, the Philippines) by refusing to endorse a pledge to refrain from using force to settle incompatible claims. Moreover, it has also refused to engage in multilateral discussions about creating a development regime for the Spratlys, though it appears to have endorsed the idea in principle.

China has focused its Spratly confrontation on Vietnam, thereby hoping not to antagonize the ASEAN states. However, Vietnam will soon join ASEAN (late 1995 is the projected date), and Hanoi immediately agreed to the 1992 ASEAN declaration on the South China Sea asking all parties to the dispute to exercise restraint and settle their differences peacefully. Therefore, China lost its diplomatic gambit with the Association, which sees Beijing and not Hanoi as a threat to the region. This alignment on the South China Sea reverses the situation of the 1980s, when Vietnam was the predator and China one of the region's protectors against a Moscow-Hanoi alliance.

Nevertheless, Chinese specialists insist Vietnam is at fault, having sunk 80 to 100 oil wells in the South China Sea area claimed by Beijing. Of the SRV's annual 35 million barrels of offshore crude production, China alleges that most come from disputed areas. To prevent further Vietnamese drilling in a block given by China to the U.S.-based Crestone corporation, the People's Liberation Army Navy has deployed warships to interdict resupply of Hanoi's rig.[22] Competitive exploration and drilling in overlapping blocks is one of the most dangerous features of the

Spratly conflict. Military confrontation between Hanoi and Beijing occurred in 1988 and could occur again.

TRENDS IN DEFENSE COOPERATION

China and Vietnam are not the only states along the Pacific rim with mutual suspicions of each other's intentions. Indeed, the single most important obstacle to the creation of a genuine Asia-Pacific security concert is a persistent absence of trust among neighbors. Illustrative of this anxiety was a recent complaint by an Indonesian parliamentary official that Malaysia's military exercises featuring the capture of an island by that country's new rapid deployment force could be interpreted to be an indirect threat to Indonesia because of island disputes between the two countries. Singapore and Thailand were also reported to express concern for they, too, have unresolved territorial claims against Malaysia.[23] All this despite the fact that these states are close collaborators within ASEAN on security issues.

Malaysian defense acquisitions are fairly typical of arms buildups throughout the Pacific over the past decade as economic prosperity has permitted the region's militaries to acquire modern air and naval components. Unlike the period through the early 1980s, East Asian armed forces are expanding their tasks beyond counterinsurgency and border protection to control of air and sea spaces in their vicinities. These new capabilities have become particularly important since the 1982 Law of the Sea Treaty was activated in November 1994. Under this new maritime regime, littoral states acquire a 200-mile exclusive economic zone (EEZ) whose protection depends on an oceangoing navy and long-range air force.

In this context, Malaysia has taken delivery of Russian Mig-29s and American FA-18D fighters as well as two new British frigates. In the pipeline are submarines, three-dimensional defense radars, and a new fleet of fast patrol boats. All are justified in terms of developing an EEZ defense capability. Malaysian officials do not stop there, however. Defense Minister Datuk Sri Najib Tun Razak notes that "our added capability means we are contributing to regional security. A stronger Malaysia in military terms means a stronger ASEAN." Moreover, similar upgrades by Singapore, Indonesia, Thailand, Australia, or further away, South Korea, are all acceptable so long as they exclude weapons of mass destruction. Minister Najib has also reiterated the importance of a continued American military presence and regular joint exercises with regional forces so that they can work together on a bilateral basis.[24]

Other forms of defense cooperation are emerging, too. A major breakthrough in Philippine-Malaysian relations has occurred, considerably easing the long-term enmity that had prevailed between the two countries over an unresolved Philippine claim to Sabah. Indicative of Malaysia's willingness to see the claim essentially as an issue in domestic Philippine politics rather than as a problem between the two states, Minister Najib and Philippine Defense Secretary Renato de Villa concluded a bilateral defense cooperation pact in September 1994. The agreement provides for regular joint military exercises, an exchange of military information to encourage transparency, and the possible joint use of each other's defense locations. The latter would include repair and service, thus providing for the repair of Philippine C-130 transport aircraft at Malaysian facilities.[25]

Japan, too, may be moving gradually toward a regional defense capability. A summer 1994 high-level advisory committee report to the Japanese government recommended not only a greater commitment to U.N. peacekeeping operations but also improved surface warfare, sealift, and air defense capabilities through the acquisition of air refueling tankers. These capabilities would provide Japan with longer range deployment opportunities.[26]

As if to underline these new considerations, for the first time, Japan and South Korea began to plan for training exchanges, and the two countries' navies exercised *jointly* for the first time in the six-nation RIMPAC exercises near Hawaii.[27]

THE ASEAN REGIONAL FORUM (ARF)

As the Cold War wound down in the 1980s, alternative security logics to Realism's confrontational approach began to be explored. The old idea of a *concert* of countries was resurrected, though on a regional rather than global basis. In Europe, the Conference on Security and Cooperation (CSCE) was revitalized as a device to bridge NATO and the now-defunct Warsaw Pact. In Asia, discussions were initiated in nonofficial think tanks to explore security arrangements *with* rather than against states.[28] These new dialogues, many of which included government participants in their private capacity, emulated such Track Two economic communities as the Pacific Economic Cooperation Conference (PECC) and Pacific Basin Economic Council (PBEC). That is, they conceptualized security in a broad manner, going beyond narrow military considerations to economic development and commercial links, all the while emphasizing cooperative approaches.

During the 1980s, as discussed above, East Asian states also experienced sustained economic growth. Resources became available to expand defense establishments beyond counterinsurgency and close-in territorial defense to the protection of adjacent sea and air space out to the 200 nautical miles EEZ enunciated in the 1982 Law of the Sea Treaty. Overlapping maritime jurisdictions and the need to collaborate on fishery poaching and antipiracy led to intense discussions in such Track Two regional groups as the ASEAN Institutes of Security and International Studies (ISIS).[29] These discussions included academic policy specialists from throughout the region, addressing issues that were considered too sensitive for official meetings. The ASEAN-based fora laid the groundwork for subsequent governmental negotiations on such issues as collaboration in the exploitation of South China Sea resources and peaceful settlement of the Spratly islands claims.

ARF evolved gradually from ASEAN-ISIS meetings to the ASEAN Post-Ministerial Conferences, which inaugurated security discussions in 1992. A Senior Officials Meeting in July 1993, in turn, announced the creation of an annual Regional Forum to begin the following year. Virtually every state along the Pacific rim was included with the exceptions of North Korea, Vietnam, Cambodia, and Burma. Particularly noteworthy has been Japan's enthusiastic participation; this marks the first time Tokyo has engaged in multilateral security discussions. This new policy may symbolize a break from the Yoshida Doctrine's exclusive reliance on the United States in all security matters. It may constitute the beginning of an independent Japanese voice in Asian security matters. Japanese security analysts have recently written of cooperative security arrangements that will supplement the Japan-U.S. Security Treaty: "Japan may need, for example, to provide such cooperation as transportation and rear support for the United States guarding the major shipping lanes."[30] Thus, the presence of U.S. bases in Japan will be seen more directly as a Japanese contribution to regional stability.

In its early stages, the ARF will probably not go much beyond a venue for the discussion of security transparency and confidence-building measures (CBMs). Regional problems that have been addressed by the ASEAN Senior Officers Meeting (SOM) in March 1994 prior to the July ARF included Cambodia, South China Sea issues, relations with Burma, and nuclear issues on the Korean peninsula. The SOM's recommendation to the ARF was to be as inclusive as possible, that is, to engage disputants in proactive negotiations when feasible to resolve international disputes. Singapore's *Straits Times* perhaps best articulated the Asia-Pacific's hope for the new Forum on March 2, 1994:

> What the region needs is a permanent forum to facilitate consultative processes, promote confidence-building measures, and whenever necessary, set up the machinery to investigate disputes. This implies, of course, constant dialogue and interaction so that members acquire a better appreciation of each other's security concerns.

The 1994 Bangkok ARF took several important steps: (1) it established the Forum as an annual event; (2) it endorsed ASEAN's Treaty of Amity and Cooperation as a code of conduct among ARF members, thus formalizing a kind of nonaggression undertaking among them. This was understood to be a CBM and a basis for political cooperation; and (3) studies were commissioned for the next ARF scheduled for 1995 in Brunei which included nuclear nonproliferation, further CBM prospects, the creation of a regional peacekeeping training center, exchanges of nonclassified military information, antipiracy issues, and preventive diplomacy.[31] These topics are so broadgauged that they could cover virtually all possible security issues along the Pacific rim.

Some countries proffered specific security issues, reflecting their own priorities. The ROK proposed consideration of a Northeast Asia Security Cooperation forum that would parallel South East Asian security discussions. Australia presented a paper on defense cooperation among the region's militaries that could induce "habits of cooperation" and lead to a "framework for regional security." An ASEAN report called for the exchange of defense white papers as a transparency measure. Japan and the Philippines proposed a regional arms register. And, while

Vietnam requested multilateral negotiations on the South China Sea, the Chinese contribution was limited to an expression of interest in scientific cooperation around the Spratly islands.[32]

Among the most important of these suggestions was the South Korean plan for a ministerial-level security forum for Northeast Asia that would include the two Koreas, Japan, China, Russia, and the United States. Like the Regional Forum, its Northeast Asia subgroup would first focus on CBMs and preventive diplomacy based on nonaggression and nonintervention agreements. With progress toward the settlement of the Korean nuclear standoff achieved in October 1994, prospects for a Northeast Asian security dialogue may be improving. It would provide a mechanism for bringing Russia back into regional security discussions as well as a way of linking Japan and both Koreas in political discourse for the first time. China may be the least interested in such an arrangement, however. Beijing has preferred to deal with security matters on a bilateral basis and has not responded positively to transparency proposals such as foreign observers at People's Liberation Army military maneuvers or joint exercises.[33]

Equally indicative of security problems facing the Asia-Pacific are those that were dropped from the Bangkok ARF statement because they were considered too controversial or premature. These included the creation of a regional security studies center, the exchange of military observers among neighbors, the sharing of defense white papers, and the establishment of a maritime data base which would facilitate the protection of sea lanes. Nor were the future of Cambodia or Burma mentioned in the final statement, though the situation in both countries was discussed in the ARF meeting. Dissensus prevailed, with Thailand opposing any effort to assist in the development of a more professional Cambodian army, while the United States and Australia argued that assistance to that army may be necessary if the Khmer Rouge are to be defeated and internal security restored.[34] For Thailand, a more stable Cambodia could mean a neighbor less susceptible to Thai economic interests and political pressure.

CONCLUDING OBSERVATIONS

The United States will remain an important player in Asia's political economy and security future. However, it will be seen increasingly to be an outsider as the nations of the Asia-Pacific turn more and more to each other for trade and investment. The U.S. market can no longer be the primary engine of growth for Asia-Pacific development. As a heavily indebted mature economy, it cannot absorb the export surpluses that characterized Asian development in the Cold War era. Thus, Asian states increasingly turn to one another as both suppliers and markets. Japan's trade surplus with the rest of Asia exceeded its surplus with the United States for the first time in 1993. Taiwan, the ROK, Singapore, and even Malaysia are becoming major investors in their neighbors' development. Japan's direct investment in South East Asia has soared in the 1990s as the strong yen has led a number of manufacturers to locate in other parts of the region. These economic dynamics are occurring outside the U.S. relationship with the Asia-Pacific.

Along the security dimension, while a U.S. naval and air presence in the Pacific remains welcome for its calming and deterrent effects, its importance for the settlement of local conflicts over South China Sea jurisdiction claims, Cambodia's future, Burma's fate, illegal migration among neighbors, and a host of other political tensions is marginal. Regional political/security disputes will be negotiated in regional fora, such as ASEAN, or handled exclusively among the disputants. Any American role in dispute settlement will, once again, be marginal. So, although the United States continues to be the number one Pacific power, its economic and security roles in the Asian portion of the Pacific are inexorably declining.

NOTES

1. For recent discussions of these distinctions, see Tsuneo Akaha, "Asia-Pacific Regionalism: The Economic Dimension" (a paper prepared for the International Studies Association--West meeting, The University of Washington, Seattle, October 15, 1994); and Richard Higgott, "Introduction: Ideas, Identity and Policy Coordination in the Asia-Pacific," *The Pacific Review* (7,4) 1994, 1-20.

2. *Asahi Shimbun* (Tokyo) July 8 and November 6, 1993.

3. For an extended assessment of the U.S. position in the Pacific, see Sheldon W. Simon, "U.S. Policy and the Future of Asian-Pacific Security," *The Australian Journal of International Affairs* (47,2) October 1993, 250-262.

4. Quoted by *Kyodo* (Tokyo) November 19, 1993, in FBIS, *Daily Report East Asia*, November 23, 1993, 4.

5.   Nigel Holloway, "Seed Money," *Far Eastern Economic Review*, August 18, 1994, 18.

6.   Statement by Singapore Foreign Minister S. Jayakumar as carried by *The Straits Times*, July 28, 1994.

7.   Sean Randolph's presentation to The Heritage Foundation's Asian Studies Center Symposium: *The New "Malaise": Clinton Adrift in Asia* (Washington, DC: The Heritage Lectures, June 21, 1994), 15.

8.   Richard A. Wilson, "APEC: The Next Step Toward A New Pacific Community," *CAPA Report No. 12* (San Francisco: The Asia Foundation, November 1993).

9.   Mohammed Ariff, "The Multilateralization of Pacific-Asia" (a paper prepared for the Fourth Defence Services Asia Conference, Kuala Lumpur, April 21-22, 1994), 3.

10.   Ibid., 11.

11.   "APEC Set to Consider Ambitious Plan to Create World's Most Open Trade Area," *The Asian Wall Street Journal Weekly*, August 8, 1994, 4.

12.   *Kyodo*, September 10, 1994, in FBIS, *Daily Report East Asia*, September 12, 1994, 2.

13.   *The Nation* (Bangkok) September 7, 1994, in FBIS *Daily Report East Asia*, September 7, 1994, 80; *Kyodo*, September 21, 1994, in ibid., September 21, 1994, 2-3; and *The Bangkok Post*, September 24, 1994, in ibid., September 26, 1994, 2.

14.   *The Asian Wall Street Journal Weekly*, September 26, 1994, 2.

15. *Kyodo*, July 23, 1994, in FBIS, *Daily Report East Asia*, July 25, 1994, 8-9.

16.   Adam Schwarz, "Local Heroes," *Far Eastern Economic Review*, October 6, 1994, 14-15.

17.   The evolution of this new U.S. security relationship with South East Asia is discussed by Donald K. Emmerson, "U.S. Policy Themes in South East Asia in the 1990s," in David Wurfel and Bruce Burton, eds., *South East Asia in the "New World Order": Rethinking the Political Economy of a Dynamic Region* (Basingstoke, England: Macmillan Press, 1995).

18.   Hee Kwan Park, "Multilateral Security Cooperation," *The Pacific Review* (6,3) 1993, 253.

19.   David Dewitt, "Common, Comprehensive, and Cooperative Security," *The Pacific Review* (7,1) 1994, especially 9-11.

20.   Donald Crone, "New Bilateral Roles for ASEAN," in Wurfel and Burton, eds., *op. cit.* Also see Sheldon W. Simon, "Realism and Neoliberalism: International Relations Theory and South East Asian Security," *The Pacific Review* 8, no. 1 (1995).

21.   See Sheldon W. Simon, "East Asian Security: The Playing Field Has Changed," *Asian Survey*, December 1994; and Charles McGregor, "South East Asia's New Security Challenges," *The Pacific Review* 6, no.

3 (1993): 269.

22.   "Dispute Over South China Sea Provides a Test for China's Regional Intentions," *The Asian Wall Street Journal Weekly,* July 25, 1994, 12.

23.   *Antara* (Jakarta) October 10, 1994, in FBIS, *Daily Report East Asia,* October 11, 1994, 84.

24.   Interview with Malaysian Defense Minister Najib in *The Sunday Times* (Singapore), July 24, 1994.

25.   *The Sunday Chronicle* (Manila), September 25, 1994.

26.   Kensuke Ebata, "More Active Security Role Urged for Japan," *Jane's Defense Weekly,* August 27, 1994, 4.

27.   *Kyodo,* June 14, 1994, in FBIS, *Daily Report East Asia,* June 14, 1994, 8-9.

28.   For a review of these security studies, see Paul Evans, ed., *Studying Asia-Pacific Security* (University of Toronto, York University Joint Centre of Asia-Pacific Studies, and the Centre for Strategic and International Studies, Jakarta, 1994).

29.   The most recent review of ASEAN ISIS activities may be found in Pauline Kerr, "Security Dialogue in Asia-Pacific," *The Pacific Review* 7, no. 4 (1994). This consortium of private, though often government-sponsored, think tanks was formed in 1988, and included all ASEAN states except Brunei.

30.   Satoshi Morimoto, "The Future of Japan-U.S. Security," *Secutarian* (Tokyo) July 1, 1994, in FBIS, *Daily Report East Asia,* October 20, 1994, 15-16.

31.   *Kyodo,* July 25, 1994, in FBIS, *Daily Report East Asia,* July 26, 1994, 9.

32.   These proposals are summarized in *The Bangkok Post,* July 25, 1994, in FBIS, *Daily Report East Asia,* July 25, 1994, 17-18.

33.   Nayan Chanda, "ASEAN: Gentle Giant," *Far Eastern Economic Review,* August 4, 1994, 16.

34.   A review of the ARF Cambodia debate was carried by *Kyodo,* July 26, 1994, in FBIS, *Daily Report East Asia,* July 26, 1994, 13.

Part I

A SOUTH EAST ASIA PERSPECTIVE

VIEW FROM THE PHILIPPINES

Carolina G. Hernandez

INTRODUCTION

South East Asia is coming of age. Colonized by western powers in the 16th century, dominated by them for hundreds of years, caught between superpower competition during the Cold War, South East Asia in the 1990s stands on the threshold of what could be a new era, one that has the potential of enabling this subregion to define its own future without undue interference by external powers. At the center of this subregion is ASEAN, consisting of Brunei, Indonesia, Malaysia, the Philippines, Singapore and Thailand. Before too long, it will be joined by Vietnam, followed in due course by Laos, Cambodia, and perhaps Myanmar.

New thinking is emerging among its various elites, thinking that is reflected in policy decisions of South East Asian leaders.[1] It is informed by the strategic calculation that the various countries in South East Asia need to forge closer ties with one another if they are to act in concert to secure their common future. The end of the Cold War destroyed the old basis of regional security. The Asia-Pacific region is in flux, and while Cold War-related conflicts have disappeared in other parts of the world, their remnants remain present in the region in the forms of the

Dr. Carolina G. Hernandez is currently the 1994 Visiting Chair in ASEAN and International Studies at the Centre for International Studies, University of Toronto. She is also a Professor of Political Science at the University of the Philippines and President of the Institute for Strategic and Development Studies (ISDS), Inc. She is associated with several international bodies, including the Asean-Institutes for Strategic and International Studies (ASEAN-ISIS), where she was Chairperson in 1993.

continuing divisions of Korea and of China. There is a need to design a new regional security architecture, but in the meantime, states in the region are prepositioning themselves for the form and shape that this new regional security architecture would take.

South East Asia is no exception. In particular, ASEAN has initiated ARF, a mechanism for discussing political and security issues in the Asia-Pacific which includes not only its dialogue partners in the region and the European Union, but also China and Russia. There is also the phenomenon of arms modernization in China as well as in ASEAN in part as a response to the new strategic environment, but also to retire aging military equipment and hardware in the case of many ASEAN countries.[2] Increased defense spending has raised alarm signals of an emerging "arms race"[3] in the region. By no means an arms race at present, this scale of defense spending could develop into a situation where a classic security dilemma could arise if it comes to a level grossly disproportional to the kind of arms modernization required by a nonoffensive defense posture. ARF was in part a response to the need to avert this possibility by providing a forum that includes all the major regional powers for the discussion of political and security issues affecting the region as well as to adopt measures to avert conflict.[4]   Thus, ARF stressed the importance of confidence and security building measures during its first meeting in Bangkok in 1994.

ASEAN has also moved to strengthen and expand security cooperation among its members. Its political amd defense officials now gather in a special senior officials meeting to consider political and security issues. This will make for a more comprehensive and coordinated approach to political and security policy among the ASEAN governments as it also serves the purpose of confidence building among them.

The Philippines is part of these dynamic developments that are taking place in the region. Even in the economic field, 1994 was a year that saw the Philippine economy perform well, with its GNP at slightly over 5 percent and other macroeconomic indicators posting positive results.[5]   There is optimism amid the recognition of remaining difficult challenges both on the political and economic fronts,[6] but there are also a number of political, economic and security issues in the regional environment about which the Philippines is concerned. This paper seeks to articulate these and provide perspectives on how the regional environment is seen in the Philippines by culling from the views of Philippine opinion leaders and decisionmakers.

THE REGIONAL ENVIRONMENT IN THE 1990s

Like most countries in the region, the Philippines sees the Asia-Pacific as a region in relative peace. The Presidential Security Adviser noted that the Philippines sees

> the security environment in East Asia as essentially benign . . . giving us the breathing spell to deal with our internal problems. As the new world order becomes established, we expect relations between the regional states to lose their ideological edge and be driven primarily by pragmatism and compromise. We see these good-neighborly virtues are being helped along by the recession of authoritarianism, the spread of democratic political systems—and most of all, by the increasing linkages of the regional economy[7]

The progress of the peace process in Cambodia, the accession to the ASEAN Treaty of Amity and Cooperation (TAC) by Vietnam and Laos, Vietnam's impending entry into ASEAN, and ASEAN's constructive engagement of Myanmar are seen as positive developments towards the evolution of one South East Asia in the medium to long term. The Philippines joined its ASEAN partners in the 27th ASEAN Ministerial Meeting (AMM) in Bangkok (July 1994) in a significant Joint Communique:

> It was the first time that the Foreign Ministers of all ten South East Asian countries were present . . . [The Foreign Ministers] hoped that relations with the four other South East Asian states would further intensify, and reiterated their commitment to building a South East Asian community through common membership in ASEAN . . . [and] affirmed their readiness to accept Vietnam as a member of ASEAN.[8]

The preoccupation of regional states in economic development means that they would seek regional stability as a context for this process. The priority China puts on its four modernization programs and its participation in multilateral fora such as the ARF and APEC are seen in this light, although there is concern over the direction toward the power projection Chinese military modernization is taking. Russia is not seen as a threat to regional peace for much the same reasons. Moreover, the deterioration of its political and economic conditions engendering reactionary developments could have negative implications for the region. Presidential Security Adviser Almonte once remarked that Russia's failure to transform itself to a free market economy "will present the world with a wounded, militarist and aggressive Russia."[9]

Despite an overall benign security environment, the Philippines is aware that remnants of the Cold War remain in the region that could threaten stability. The continuing division of the Korean peninsula and the nuclear weapons development program of North Korea, as well as the continuing problem of a divided China and the rise of a pro-independence movement in Taiwan are viewed in the Philippines as potential flashpoints.[10] Moreover, the uncertainties arising from the South China Sea dispute directly impact on Philippine perspectives about the regional environment.[11] As one of the six claimants to several islands in the area, any alteration of the status quo is viewed with concern, particularly because the largest East Asian state, China, is a principal claimant as well.

In addition, the Philippines is concerned about the fragility of Cambodian peace threatened by the Khmer Rouge and the problems associated with its reconstruction. The importance the Philippines attaches to Cambodia is indicated by the opening of a full diplomatic mission in Phom Penh in 1994. Finally, the Philippines also recognizes that even internal political, economic and social change among its other neighbors in East Asia can have implications for regional security and stability. Hence, the internal debate on the path of economic reform in Vietnam, internal developments in Myanmar between the State Law and Order Council (SLORC) and the opposition led by Aung San Suu Kyi[12] and the course of China's economic development and political succession after Deng Xiaoping are all of significant interest to the Philippines.

POLITICAL AND MILITARY ISSUES

South China Sea dispute constitutes the single most important political-security issue for the Philippines.[13] As a country claimant to the dispute, it would like to see it peacefully settled by all the claimants and pending settlement, to have a moratorium on military and oil drilling activities in the area unilaterally undertaken by any of the six claimants. Toward this end, it participates actively in the Indonesian-initiated workshops on the South China Sea and leads the Task Force on Marine Scientific Research created after the third workshop in Yogyakarta.

Philippine interests over the area it claims are both strategic and economic. Japan's invasion of the Philippines in 1941 was launched from one of the islands in the South China Sea. The area is also believed to be rich in oil and other natural resource deposits. To secure its interests, the Philippines supports the ASEAN Declaration on the South China Sea (1992), which calls for peaceful settlement of the dispute; for all parties to exercise restraint, explore possible cooperation in promoting safety of maritime navigation and communication, environmental protection, search and rescue operations, combatting piracy and illegal traffic in drugs; and to apply the principles of conduct contained in the ASEAN Treaty of Amity and Cooperation to their behavior with respect to the South China Sea.[14] But while it adheres to a peaceful approach, the Philippines is also committed to defend its territorial integrity.[15]

While bilateral and multilateral approaches to the solution of the dispute had been suggested by some officials,[16] the bilateral negotiations between China and Vietnam in 1994 was unsettling for the Philippine Government. Foreign Secretary Roberto Romulo expressed the country's concern over the negotiations by these two claimants on their overlapping claims in the Spratlys as well as their agreement to begin joint oil exploration of the area in November 1994.[17] Such bilateral action could be inimical to the just and fair resolution of the dispute particularly if the area in question has multiple claimants.

It must be pointed out that the most recent skirmishes in the South China Sea involving claimants were between China and Vietnam, two countries that have had a history of using force in international relations as late as the 1980s. They also happen to have two of the largest military forces in East Asia. The

Philippines, on the other hand, has one of the region's most outmoded and poorly equipped armies. It is, therefore, not in the Philippines' interest to have two of the most powerful rivals in the South China Sea forge a bilateral agreement of the sort achieved between China and Vietnam.

Another political-military issue of concern to the Philippines is the increasing military spending among its neighbors. While it understands that they remain within the limits of modernizing old inventories, it still believes in the need for greater military transparency among regional states. Consequently, the Philippines has proposed enhancing the exchanges of military intelligence and personnel, the publication of defense White Papers,[18] and the creation of a regional arms register[19], among other military programs between and among countries in the region.

Tension and conflict on the Korean peninsula do not serve Philippine interests. Philippine soldiers fought in the Korean war. Its workers are now employed in increasing numbers in South Korea, and South Korea is a source of trade and investment. Any instability on the Korean peninsula could disrupt the benefits the Philippines derives from its relations with South Korea.

On the more traditional side of security is the nuclear weapons program of North Korea, seen as destabilizing not only for the actual potential damage it can do in the event of its use, but also for the likely impact on the strategic calculations of South Korea and Japan. Despite refutation of the likelihood that South Korea and Japan are also developing nuclear weapons capability in the event of the North's acquisition of such a capability, some in the Philippines remain unconvinced. Japan, it is believed, could be driven to rearm, including nuclear weapons, in that eventuality.[20] Thus, Philippine protest over the shipment of plutonium that passed through the South China Sea to Japan in 1994 could have been generated by concerns beyond the dangers of environmental damage in the event of an accident at sea.

The nuclear weapons issue is related to the commitment of the United States to its Asian allies. Such commitment is often doubted, particularly because of the drawdown of U.S. military forces in the region and the growing mood of isolation among its leaders in Congress. Moreover, the rationale for overseas military presence during the Cold War can no longer be used to justify expenditures of this kind to the American people. This sort of reasoning underlies the persistence of opinion that questions the credibility of U.S. commitment to the defense of its friends in the region and to boost the argument of the likelihood of South Korean and Japanese nuclear weapons development in the event that North Korea acquires a nuclear capability.

This issue is also relevant in the face of growing difficulties in Japan's relationship with the United States on the economic front, difficulties that could spill over into the defense realm. The fluidity of domestic politics in Japan does not provide assurance that the present balance in favor of a self-defense security policy would be sustained into the foreseeable future. Though highly unlikely, a future scenario of hostile actors across the Japan Sea with nuclear weapons capability and the United States not being engaged can be a serious threat to regional security about which the Philippines cannot be indifferent. After all, it is the ASEAN country closest to this area.

As already noted, the Philippines is also concerned about the implications of the emergence of a pro-independence movement in Taiwan for cross-straits relations and for regional stability. The Philippines has good political and diplomatic relations with China and increasingly significant economic relations with Taiwan. Disruptions in cross-straits relations can harm the benefits the Philippines derives from both relationships, particularly as its economy appears on its way to growth. The outcome of Hong Kong's return to China in 1997 is of interest to the Philippines as well. Although not directly affecting Philippine security, the manner in which China will deal with its commitments regarding Hong Kong could be a litmus test on how it will deal with its other international commitments in the future and a measure of its credibility as an international actor.

The other issue of interest to the Philippines is arms modernization among its neighbors. As noted above, while it does not see current regional arms modernization expenditures as indicative of an arms race, it would like to see greater transparency in military and defense matters, increased cooperation in the promotion of regional stability and security through sharing of intelligence information and other military programs. At the same time, it seeks to modernize its own defense capability, particularly naval, because it needs to protect its long coastline and other maritime areas as well as its exclusive economic zone under the Convention on the Law of the Sea.

The modernization of the Armed Forces of the Philippines (AFP) has become more urgent because of the end of U.S. military presence in the country, and the redefinition of the military mission following the separation of the police from the AFP. Beginning in 1995, the Philippine National Police (PNP) is tasked to maintain peace and order and defense from internal threats. The AFP's primary responsibility would now be external defense for which a restructuring of forces is being done. However, the modernization program, though supported by the Philippine Congress, will take about 10 years to achieve because of current resource constraints.

ECONOMIC ISSUES AS SOURCES OF COOPERATION AND CONFLICT

President Fidel V. Ramos views security as ultimately founded on the country's economic strength, political unity and social cohesion. In this regard, he has devoted the first 2 years of his term of office to lay the foundation for these goals. He has succeeded in achieving a national consensus for reform and unity, renewing confidence in the economy, resolving the power crisis and other infrastructure inadequacies, moving to protect the environment, and streamlining the bureaucracy for greater responsiveness.[21] In his view, the Philippines has reached the time for take-off; it is ready for competitive performance in the Asia-Pacific.[22]

The Philippines' most important concern in the economic realm is trade protectionism. While a participant in the AFTA, and in general supportive of regional groupings, the Philippines is opposed to the evolution of such groupings into exclusionary protectionist trading blocs. In the President's view,

> These groupings answer the current need for scale, specialization, the pooling of talents and skills, and the reduction of national anxieties in a new world without definitive centers.
>
> But such groupings would be bad for global growth if they only result in protectionism on a wider scale.[23]

During the visit of Malaysian Prime Minister Dr. Mahathir Mohamed, President Ramos spoke against protectionism, inviting his ASEAN partner to work together to consolidate the achievements of the Uruguay Round . . . to continue our common struggle against the forces of economic protectionism that remain strong in the world . . . in the cause of global trade liberalization which is of great benefit to us both, as well as in the promotion of the product groups in which we have a common interest.[24]

As a member of ASEAN, the Philippines is also opposed to the inclusion of a social clause in GATT regulations as well as in multilateral trade regulations as part of the responsibilities of the newly organized WTO. The European Parliament already passed on 9 February 1994 a resolution to include the social clause in the system of multilateral trading and the Generalized System of Preferences (GSP). The social clause is "designed to combat child and forced labor and to encourage trade union freedoms and the freedom to engage in collective bargaining on the basis of International Labor Organization conventions."[25]

On the other hand, ASEAN believes that the link between international trade, including the GSP, does not address the problem of improving labor conditions in the developing world. It argues that the proportion of goods traded in the international market that is produced by child, prisoner, or forced labor may not be very large, and in any case cannot be precisely determined. These issues should be addressed at the proper international fora such as the International Labor Organization (ILO) or the United Nations Children's Fund (UNICEF). Moreover, ASEAN sees the social clause as tending to distort international trade, and since trade is the pillar of economic growth, decline in trade would have adverse effects on the economic well-being of peoples.[26]

The debate on the social clause is part of the larger debate on the link Organization for Economic Cooperation and Development countries make between international economic relations on the one hand, and "good governance" on the other. The latter includes human rights and democratization.[27] This link and the related conditions of aid and trade are objected to by the developing countries, including ASEAN and the Philippines. They have created tensions between developed and developing countries and are potential sources of future conflict if not managed properly.

Many in ASEAN see it as basically an economic issue, one that in the view of Dr. Mahathir, for instance, could reduce ASEAN's comparative advantage.[28] International pressure to improve labor conditions and promote human rights when linked to economic measures sometimes works, but not always as the unfortunate linkage of the most-favored-nation (MFN) treatment and human rights in China made by the Clinton administration showed. In the case of Indonesia, it has somehow served to improve labor's collective bargaining ability and minimum wage, and as one former official is said to have remarked, "Indonesia needs these pressures,"[29] presumably for social and political change.

An economic issue that has great potential for cooperation in South East Asia is the emergence of regional economic zones or growth areas. Spurred by natural complementaries and the autonomous movement of factors of production, it has arisen in the form of the Singapore-Johore-Riau (SIJORI) growth triangle and the planned Northern Growth Triangle between Indonesia, Malaysia and Thailand, as well as the East ASEAN Growth Area including Brunei, Indonesia, Malaysia and the Philippines. The potential benefits of this project for Philippine economic development is viewed to be significant and has been used by Indonesia to gain leverage on the Philippines over the holding by nongovernmental organizations of an international conference on East Timor in Manila in the spring of 1994. Expectation of gain has promoted cooperation instead of conflict, in spite of the initial period of tension and the dilemma it posed to the Philippine Government at the outset.

THE PHILIPPINES AND THE MAJOR POWERS

Among the major powers in the Asia-Pacific, the United States continues to be seen as an important factor for stability by the Philippine leadership. The centerpiece of the bilateral relationship is no longer the defense alliance, but economic partnership in the Asia-Pacific era. This is the theme of the messages sent to various U.S. publics during the visit of President Ramos in November 1993 around the time of the first APEC leaders' summit.[30]

At the same time, the continued post-Cold War engagement of the U.S. in Asia is seen as necessary in spite of the presence of multilateral systems of consultation and cooperation on economic matters in the region. According to President Ramos,

To complete this system of mutual reassurance, we must have America's continued engagement in Asia. We need America to help us build the new framework necessary to ensure that no power dominates the region . . . a different kind of security arrangement is needed—one that does not require extensive U.S. military presence in the region, but certainly requires U.S. leadership. The Philippines regards itself as an integral component of the network of security.[31] arrangements the United States maintains in the region.

To this end, the Philippines as a treaty ally of the United States supports the development of interoperability of the forces under the U.S.-led alliance network.

Japan is viewed very positively by the Philippines. Next to the United States, Japan is its most important trading partner and its largest Official Development Assistance donor. Japan is seen as "a force for regional peace,"[32] and even as it seeks a political role, it would play this role on the side of peace. This is because Japan needs peace more than any other great power; it is also vulnerable to nuclear conflict.[33] Moreover, the Philippines is likely to support Japan's bid to join the permanent members of the UN Security Council. In combination with the U.S.-Japan security alliance, Japan's exercise of its political role in multilateral arrangements like the United Nations and ARF are mechanisms of reassurance for those in the region who may have lingering doubts about Japan's intentions.

While political relations have been very positive with China since normalization in 1975, the South China Sea dispute makes the Philippines uneasy about its future relations with this country. This is exacerbated by the lack of consistency and coherence in China's actions affecting the dispute. The adoption of its maritime law, which claims the South China Sea as part of its territory including all the islands there at the same time that it was participating in the informal Indonesian-initiated workshops that endorsed shelving the sovereignty issue among the claimants is perplexing for the Philippines. From an official's vantage point, China is seen as not yet a status quo power to many South East Asians; these same peoples were objects of Chinese southern expansion in the past. It also has outstanding territorial disputes with many of its neighbors, including Russia, India, Japan, and the South East Asian claimants to the South China Sea islands.[34]

China's force restructuring suggests a striving for external power projection capability, which led the *Economist* to note, "China seems to be preparing to fight limited wars along its 'strategic borders,' which may lie beyond its 'territorial borders.' "[35]

Unease about China is also related to the presence of a large Chinese Filipino business sector in the country whose investments as of mid-1993 made the Philippines the fifth largest investor in China.[36] The latter's greater comparative advantage is feared to divert more investments away from the Philippines.

Finally, Russia is seen as a benign power preoccupied with internal reforms and unlikely to disturb regional peace while this process is underway. For the longer term, however, Russia's failure to reform could make it a more intractable and volatile actor in the region.

MULTILATERALISM IN THE ASIA-PACIFIC REGION

Despite its continuing bilateral alliance with the United States, the Philippines is also committed to multilateralism. Aware of its small power status and many limitations that stem from that status, it places high value on its membership in ASEAN. The end of the "special relationship" with the United States has made ASEAN even more valuable to the Philippines. This is indicated by the fact that the first official visits of its two presidents after Marcos were to ASEAN countries and not to the United States.

Its involvement in multilateral institutions may be viewed in terms of concentric circles with ASEAN as the core, an evolving South East Asian community as the next circle, followed by the ARF and APEC, and the UN system on the global level. In this regard, President Ramos sees the Philippines on the side of open regionalism in the Asia-Pacific. He explains:

> Filipinos regard our membership in ASEAN as our primary foreign commitment—and the larger Asia-Pacific region as the cornerstone of our foreign relations. . . . We in the Philippines see APEC and AFTA not as our countervailing forces in a post-Cold War economic balance of power but as building blocks of the global market.
>
> Closed trading blocs will not work, because no bloc can have, within its boundaries, all the markets, raw materials, energy and

technology, much less all the intelligence and talent, that human societies need for self-sustaining growth.[37]

An advocate of a South East Asian community, he initiated the call for Vietnam's early membership in ASEAN. In December 1993 he said,

> We can no longer be in doubt that with Vietnam in ASEAN both Vietnam and ASEAN will reap dividends in greater regional stability and growth. This is why this dialogue will reach its valued destination of bringing Vietnam into the ASEAN community—sooner or later, but it is certainly best that we do this soon.[38]

The emergence of a South East Asian community is seen as enhancing its collective competitiveness in the global market[39] and giving 450 million South East Asians enough economic weight to count in the future world.[40]

Toward this end, the Philippine Government supported an informal meeting of South East Asian scholars, analysts, officials and opinion leaders in May 1994 in Manila, which produced "South East Asia Beyond the Year 2000: Statement of Vision." The belief of the drafters is, "South East Asia should be a community [which] should be a major political, economic, cultural and moral entity on the world stage in the twenty-first century."[41]

The Philippines is also committed to APEC as a building block to the world market. In particular, it is interested in the establishment of an APEC Center for Technology and Training for Small and Medium Enterprises in the Philippines. With the rest of ASEAN, it also supports the creation of an East Asian Economic Caucus within APEC.[42]

ARF might be viewed as an expansion of ASEAN's consultative mechanisms and includes major regional powers like China and Russia which were not part of the regional dialogue process. Because of the sensitivity of political and security issues, a cautious approach is necessary in the initial stage of the ARF. Rushing to convert it into a security organization, even for South East Asia alone, could abort its development into a meaningful forum for dealing with political and security issues in the broader region. This would not serve regional security because the ARF is the only multilateral mechanism outside of the UN at present that has the potential of playing this role in the post-Cold War Asia-Pacific region. Together with its ASEAN partners, the Philippines is committed to make the ARF succeed.

Nonetheless, there is a continuing need for bilateralism in the security realm in the Asia-Pacific due to its diversity and the complexity of extant security issues there. Some issues, such as cross-straits relations and territorial disputes involving two parties, can be better dealt with through this modality. In the case of the latter, good offices by third parties can only be facilitative. Security issues can be dealt with through multilateral mechanisms, particularly with the increasing interconnectedness of the various dimensions that define security for South East Asia and the increasing economic interdependence of the countries in the broader region. South East Asian security is ultimately defined by both the domestic and the regional environment. The latter consists of its neighbors many of which are already in the ARF. For now, this forum is indeed invaluable for the security needs of the region.

NOTES

1. The Joint Communique of the Twenty-Seventh ASEAN Ministerial Meeting held in Bangkok on 22-23 July 1994 affirmed ASEAN commitment to build a South East Asian community through common membership in ASEAN, among other decisions, 1.

2. China's military modernization, especially the development of a blue water navy is of concern to many of its neighbors. On China's naval modernization, see Tai Ming Cheung, *Growth of Chinese Naval Power*, Pacific Strategic Paper 1 (Singapore: Institute of South East Asian Studies, 1990).

3. On this issue, see Amitav Acharya, *An Arms Race in Post-Cold War South East Asia: Prospects for Control,* Pacific Strategic Paper 8 (Singapore: Institute of South East Asian Studies, 1994).

4. On the evolution of the ARF see Kusuma Snitwonge's presentation at the Kyoto Conference on Disarmament sponsored by the United Nations Office of Disarmament Affairs, Kyoto, Japan, April 1992, and Carolina G. Hernandez, "Complex Interdependence and Track Two Diplomacy in the Asia-Pacific in the Post-Cold War Era," in her *Track Two Diplomacy and Other Papers* (Quezon City: Center for Integrative and Development Studies, University of the Philippines, 1995).

5. For a brief summary of these indicators, see Philippines Country Development Policy Framework Working Paper, Canadian International Development Agency, 15 December 1994, 5-6.

6. See Jose T. Almonte, "Philippine Prospects for 1995: Social and Political Developments," Philippine Policy Briefings for Heads of Diplomatic Missions, Manila, 6 January 1995.

7. Jose T. Almonte, "East Asian Security: A Philippine Perspective," a speech delivered before the Royal Institute of International Affairs, Chatham House, London, 19 December 1994, 1.

8. Joint Communique of the Twenty-Seventh ASEAN Ministerial Meeting, 1.

9. Jose T. Almonte, "National Security in the Philippines," a paper prepared for the Solidarity/Asia Foundation Study Group on Philippine-U.S. Relations after the Bases, 10 July 1993, 6.

10. Almonte, "East Asian Security," 5-6.

11. Ibid., 4.

12. Ibid., 3.

13. On Philippine perspectives about the dispute, see Aileen S.P. Baviera, editor, *The South China Sea Disputes: Philippine Perspectives* (Quezon City: Philippine-China Development Center and Philippine Association of Chinese Studies, 1992).

14. ASEAN Declaration on the South China Sea, Manila, 22 July 1992.

15. *The Philippines and the South China Sea Islands: Overview and Documents,* CIRSS Papers No. 1 (Manila: Center for International Relations and Strategic Studies, Foreign Service Institute, Department of Foreign Affairs, December 1993), 1.

16. Senate Resolution 415, Resolution on the formulation of a national policy on Spratly islands territorial dispute, introduced by Senator Leticia R. Shahani, May 1993.

17. As reported in various Philippine newspapers in November 1994.

18. Almonte, "East Asian Security," 5.

19. This was proposed by the Philippines during the 27th AMM in Bangkok in July 1994.

20. Almonte, in "National Security in the Philippines" argued that "Japan is the defining power of the twenty-first century— economically influential but militarily weak. (But will Japan continue to remain unarmed in the face of a North Korean [nuclear] bomb?" he asked; 6.

21. See Fidel V. Ramos, "Springboard for 1994," in *Time for Takeoff: The Philippines is Ready for Competitive Performance in the Asia-Pacific,* a third collection of speeches by the President of the Republic of the Philippines (Manila: Friends of Steady Eddie, 1994), 27-38.

22. Ibid.

23. "Vietnam and ASEAN—Reinforcing Cooperation," in ibid., 62.

24. "Neighbors, Relatives, Partners", in ibid., 56-57.

25. "ASEAN's Position on the Social Clause," *ASEAN Update*, March 1994, 4.

26. Ibid.

27. On divergencies in ASEAN and Western views about human rights and democracy in international relations and the similarities and divergencies within ASEAN on the same issues, see Carolina G. Hernandez, "ASEAN Perspectives on Human Rights and Democracy in International Relations: Problems and Prospects," Working Paper, Centre for International Studies, University of Toronto, November 1994.

28. "Nobody Elects the Press: Mahathir speaks out on media, culture and trade," *Far Eastern Economic Review,* 7 April 1994, 20.

29. Quoted in David I. Hitchcock, *CSIS Report, Asian Values and the United States: How Much Conflict?* (Washington, DC: CSIS, 1994), 7.

30. Ramos, *Time for Takeoff,* Chapters 12 - 18.

31. Ibid., 123.

32. Almonte, "East Asian Security," 9.

33. Ibid.

34. Ibid., 11.

35. Ibid.

36. Almonte, "National Security in the Philippines," 4.

37. Ramos, "The New Philippines in the Asia-Pacific Era," in *Time for Takeoff,* 71.

38. "Vietnam and ASEAN—Reinforcing Cooperation," in ibid., 62.

39. Ibid.

40. "The New Philippines in the Asia-Pacific Era," in ibid., 73.

41. South East Asia Beyond the Year 2000: A Statement of Vision, Manila, 31 May 1994, 1.

42. Joint Communique of the Twenty-Seventh ASEAN Ministerial Meeting, 6.

VIEW FROM INDONESIA

J. Soedjati Djiwandono

Multilateralism has never been an alien concept to Southeast Asia. Since the countries in the region gained independence in the postwar years, bilateral and multilateral activities have gained momentum. ASEAN is an initiative with multilateral underpinnings that has been ongoing for quite some time in the region. It is now a growing concern. The Association of Southeast Asia (ASA), which inlcuded Malaya, the Philippines, and Thailand, did not last, having been embroiled in a dispute between two its member states, Malaya and the Philippines. The dispute entailed the Philippine claim over Sabah, which was included in the formation of the Malaysian Federation. Alhough not officially disbanded, ASA was subsumed by the Maphilindo (a new regional grouping comprising Malaysia, the Philippines, and Indonesia), which was formed in 1963 in an attempt to resolve the dispute arising from the formation of the Malaysian Federation. Indonesia and the Philippones opposed the Malaysian claim to Sabah. The Malaysia Federation simply faded away since the adoption of Indonesia's confrontational policy.

What follows, therefore, will simply be a modest attempt to re-examine what factors have helped to make ASEAN a much more successful approach to regionalism than its predecessors. Additionally, we will assess why the ASEAN regional, or more accurately subregional, approach to multilateral cooperation

---

Dr. J. Soedjati Djiwandono is a Member, Supervisory Board, Centre for Strategic and International Studies (CSIS), Jakarta. He is also Vice President, Indonesian Political Science Association (AIPI), and a Member of the United Nations Secretary General's Advisory Board on Disarmament Matters. He is editor, co-editor, and contributor to books in international politics, articles in journals and mass media.

between states is even more appropriate now in the post-Cold War era than ever. The ASEAN experience may be a useful lesson for other regions or subregions of the world. And the principles underlying ASEAN regionalism, at least some of them, may be applicable as well.

POLITICO-SECURITY BACKGROUND

To my mind, the real significance of ASEAN regional cooperation can be understood considering the politico-security background of its establishment. One of the most decisive political developments that made the establishment of ASEAN possible was the abrupt and drastic change in the orientation of both domestic and foreign policies in Indonesia. After the abortive communist coup attempt at the end of September 1965. The failure of the coup finally led to the overthrow of the old regime under President Soekarno, and the ascendency of the new regime under General, now President Soeharto. The new regime calls itself the New Order, which has its own priorities and style of domestic and foreign policy.

The first major action in the field of foreign policy by the new regime was its new approach to Indonesia's neighbours. It began by terminating the policy of confrontation against the Federation of Malaysia. But of greater significance was Indonesia's readiness to associate itself with its neighbours in the regional cooperation of ASEAN, which was a concrete manifestation and affirmation of its commitment to a good neighbour policy.

Previously, Indonesia had been reluctant to take part in various forms of regional cooperation, particularly wiith anti-Communist states allied with the West. ASEAN was thus established against the background of regional intra-state disputes among its current member states: between Malaysia and Singapore, culminating in the expulsion of the latter from the Federation of Malaysia in 1965; between Malaysia and the Philippines over Sabah, aggravated by the formation of the Malaysian federation; between Malaysia and Thailand over incidents along their common land border; and the most serious of all, Indonesia's confrontation against Malaysia, to the point, if limited, of armed conflict. Motivated essentially by their respective politico-security considerations, these countries joined ASEAN in 1967. All shared the same interest in promoting good neighbour relations with one another and to ensure their respective national security as well as peace and stability of the region.

For the remainder of the member states of the association, Indonesia's commitment to a good neighbour policy has a special politico-security significance, especially for Malaysia, Singapore, and later Brunei, the newest member. All had been targets of Indonesia's aggressive policy of confrontation. They viewed the policy as an expression of Indonesia's expansionist ambition. Indonesia's membership in ASEAN is likely to help reassure its neighbors that there is no expansionist threat from Indonesia.

TOWARD MULTILATERALISM

In Southeast Asia, especially after the withdrawal of the American military bases from the Philippines, pressures were mounting for the promotion of a multilateral defense and security cooperation within the framework of ASEAN. At the initiative of the Philippines, two conferences were convened to discuss the issue. The first was held in Manila and the second in Bangkok. In Indonesia, meanwhile, former Foreign Minister Mochtar Kusumaatmaja has broached the idea of a trilateral security cooperation between Malaysia, Singapore, and Indonesia as a core for such a cooperation within the ASEAN framework in the future.

All of those ideas seemed to point to a recognition, an awareness, or a premonition that the end of the Cold War did not automatically create peace and stability in Southeast Asia. On the contrary, the demise of the Cold War seems to have created more complex problems of defense and security. In any event, the end of the Cold War has created considerable uncertainty in the region, though it is also true with the rest of the world it is not yet clear what kind of power constellation or world order is likely to take shape in the aftermath of the Cold War.

The main problem for the countries of Southeast Asia is not whether security cooperation is still necessary. The problem is whether the form of security cooperation that has been undertaken so far among the ASEAN member states should be continued on a bilateral basis. Eventually what may develop is what former Foreign Minister Tan Sri Gazhali Syaffie of Malaysia has aptly termed a "web of interlocking bilateral relationships"— with Indonesia remaining a key hub as it is currently—or whether such cooperation should be promoted to the multilateral level, within the framework of ASEAN. If so, how should ASEANrelate to the great powers? Should such security cooperation, bilateral or multilateral, be expanded to involve the other Southeast Asian countries that have remained outside ASEAN regional cooperation until now?

Whether the security cooperation among the member states of ASEAN will continue to be on bilateral basis or proceed towards a multilateral arrangement, it does not seem likely that it will involve all the countries of Southeast Asia before the end of the present century. The domestic political situation in Myanmar seems to remain uncertain for the years ahead. The conflict in Cambodia, in spite of the general elections sponsored and supervised by the United Nations, which have resulted in the formation of a coalition government minus the Khmer Rouge, has not been completely settled. The country has continued to be torn by civil war.

It therefore seems most realistic to expect security cooperation in Southeast Asia to be limited to the ASEAN member states, perhaps through the next decade. The need for the present is to strengthen security cooperation on a bilateral basis. Even this bilateral framework is yet to be expanded to involve all the member states of the association. The web is still incomplete.

This by no means suggests that the possibility of promoting security cooperation on a multilateral basis is to be ruled out altogether. But present circumstances would not favor such an undertaking even for the member states of ASEAN, let alone Southeast Asia. This is likely to be a long term process. We should move slowly, step by step, in that direction with caution.

Indeed, while strengthening and expanding the network of bilateral security cooperation, certain factors may nevertheless be considered and certain steps taken to pave the way for future security cooperation on a multilateral basis. The question of a common perception, particularly of external threats, as a glue that may serve to bind the parties to a multilateral security coopera-tion, may be open to debate. The key to the solution to this problem is the aim of such a multilateral cooperation. A common perception will be necessary, if such cooperation should be directed against a common external threat or enemy.

However, one may consider the possibility of multilateral security cooperation within the framework of ASEAN that is not directed against any common external threat or enemy, so that there is no need for such a common perception. It does not mean, nonetheless, that security cooperation, be it on bilateral or multilateral basis, needs a common perception of an internal threat. Although in the Declaration of ASEAN Concord mentions an internal threat in the form of subversion faced by the members states of ASEAN, the source or nature of such a threat of subversion may vary from one member state to another. Furthermore, the source or nature of such a threat may be the same for all ASEAN member states, the problem of domestic security should basically be the sole responsibility of the individual member state or states concerned. Any cooperation in this instance would perhaps be limited to an exchange of information and ideas, by which the member states may learn from one another's experience.

If not directed against any common external threat or enemy, ASEAN multilateral security cooperation should then serve as an extension or expansion of regional cooperation to reduce mutual suspicion and to build mutual confidence. In other words, it will be a confidence-building measure (CBM). Therefore, such cooperation will have no need for a formal structure of its own, but it may become an integral part of ASEAN regional activities as a whole. What is most important will be its common program of action. These actions may involve coordination in the procurement or manufacturing of weapons and other military equipment that may lead to a balance of power among the member states. This balance will enhance transparency and confidence-building measures; coordination in training, education, and exchange of military cadets and their teachers; military exercises; exchange of information and coordination in the formulation of strategic concepts and planning as well as military operations; search and rescue operations (SAR); exchange of intelligence, etc. Cooperation in these fields will also result in greater efficiency in human and financial resources for the development of skills and the advancement of weapons and military technology.

Of greater importance, however, is that multilateral security cooperation will not be a military pact in the traditional or conventional sense. This cooperation will not be directed against any nation. Nor will it involve or need the backing of any external great power.

Apart from confidence building, this cooperation will help prevent and contain possible differences or conflicts among member states. In this sense it will help prevent any possible threat of external interference, a preoccupation that motivated the establishment of ASEAN in the first place.

Cooperation in security has continued to be developed. Although the creation of an interlocking web or network of bilateral security cooperations among the member states is yet to be complete, shortly before ASEAN's 27th anniversary, the ASEAN Regional Forum was convened in Bangkok following the 27th Annual Ministerial Meeting last July. Attended by the six foreign ministers of ASEAN, seven of its dialogue partners (Australia, Canada, EEC, Japan, South Korea, New Zealand, and the United States), two consultation partners (China and Russia), and three observers (Laos, Vietnam, and the PNG), ARF was established to discuss regional disputes. It is premature and presumptuous to assert that ASEAN has established itself as a security community in the real sense of "one in which there is real assurance that the members of that community will not fight each other physically, but will settle their disputes in some other way." Yet while real assurance may still be lacking, the intent does exist on the part of ASEAN to develop a security community.

VIEW FROM MALAYSIA

Rajmah Hussain

THE GROWTH OF ASEAN

In our review of the multilateral developments that have taken root in South East Asia, an important starting point would be the formation of ASEAN in 1967. ASEAN today comprises the six South East nations of Brunei Darussalam, Indonesia, Malaysia, the Philippines, Singapore and Thailand. ASEAN covers a total land area of more than 3 million square kilometers, with a population of more than 360 million people. It is a region of racial, cultural, and religious diversity. From its humble beginning ASEAN charted a course in regional cooperation that has since become the shining example for other regional groupings to emulate. Through the challenges it has overcome, ASEAN has matured into an organization to be reckoned with on the international front. It has succeeded in spinning off other aspects of regional cooperation that are not only wider in their reach but incorporating new dimensions in cooperation such as in regional security. In many ways, ASEAN has contributed to the maintenance of regional peace and security, while group solidarity has enhanced the bargaining powers of its member states in many international negotiations. Economically, ASEAN has become one of the fastest growing regions in the world. When the global economy was stagnant or growing at a modest rate of 1 to 2 percent GNP, ASEAN's economy was growing at an average rate

Dr. Rajmah Hussain is Minister-Counsellor and Deputy Chief of Mission, Embassy of Malaysia, Washington. She has also served as Principal Assistant Secretary, Commonwealth Desk, and as Special Assistant to the Secretary General, Ministry of Foreign Affairs.

of 4 to 6 percent. In essence, ASEAN as an organization has provided the institutional setting within which the national and regional interests of individual member states can flourish.

POST-COLD WAR ASEAN REGIONAL FORUM

In South East Asia, the post-Cold War period resulted in a growing assertiveness by countries in the region to pursue their own national interests free from the encumbrances of big-power rivalries. Coupled with this development was a realization by these countries that their future security lies in their own hands and not in the hands of outside powers. The fact that ASEAN countries are confronted with a number of problems in the region that could potentially disrupt the security of the region, has made ASEAN more determined to respond to the changes and challenges of the post-Cold War period and build upon its achievements to strengthen peace and stability in the region. One way in which ASEAN countries thought they could encourage patterns of behaviour that would reduce the risks to security was through dialogue with outside powers. In the post-Cold War period, multilateral dialogue has replaced defense and military alliances as a credible mechanism to contain and avert hostilities.

The Fourth ASEAN Summit of Heads of State in Singapore in 1992 formally declared ASEAN's intention to intensify external dialogues in political and security matters using the ASEAN-PMC (Post Ministerial Conferences) mechanisms. The decision to institutionalize formal multilateral dialogue within ASEAN to consider and discuss both traditional and nontraditional security issues led to a number of preparatory meetings at senior officials level to prepare the way for the launching of an appropriate mechanism for this dialogue to take place. During the first senior officials meeting (PMC SOM) in May 1993, ASEAN and its Dialogue Partners agreed that consultation on security and political matters would be more meaningful if major regional actors were also included. This led to the decision to invite China and Russia, termed as ASEAN's Consultative Partners, to join the ASEAN Regional Forum (ARF).

The First Meeting of the ASEAN Regional Forum, held in Bangkok in July 1994, was attended by the six ASEAN countries, the seven ASEAN Dialogue Partners (United States, Canada, Australia, New Zealand, Japan, South Korea, and the European Union), the two Consultative Partners of ASEAN (China and Russia), and the ASEAN Observers (Papua New Guinea, Vietnam and Laos). The ARF Chairman's statement pointed out that the ASEAN Regional Forum, as a high consultative forum meeting annually , would enable countries in the Asia-Pacific region to foster the habit of constructive dialogue and consultation on political and security issues of common concern and thus contribute to efforts towards confidence building and preventive diplomacy in the region. The first ARF had endorsed the purposes and principles of the ASEAN Treaty of Amity and Cooperation in South East Asia as a code of conduct governing relations between states and a unique instrument for regional confidence-building, preventive diplomacy and political and security cooperation. Brunei, as the next chairman of the ARF, was tasked with the collation and study of various proposals recommended during the Bangkok meeting; studies on confidence and security building, nuclear nonproliferation, peacekeeping, maritime security issues, preventive diplomacy, comprehensive security, arms register, and so on. The ASEAN Regional Forum is still in its infancy and has a long way to go before it can reap its rewards as a security forum, but an important start has been made and a foundation laid that, if nurtured with care and sensitivity by ARF's diverse members, will allow the forum to reach full bloom in good time.

Malaysia is determined to build upon the ARF process, for the track record of ASEAN since 1967 is ample evidence that the home-grown and indigenous approach to security and confidence-building is the most suited for the South East Asian region. The Conference for Security and Cooperation in Europe (CSCE) as a foreign security concept cannot be transposed onto the South East Asian scene for it had been formed as a result of different security considerations. ASEAN, and ASEAN alone, will remain central to any security framework for the region. The ASEAN Treaty of Amity and Cooperation, the Zone of Peace Freedom and Neutrality and the proposed South East Asia Nuclear Weapons Free Zone are regionally endorsed concepts which can form good building blocks for the ARF to develop on.

Malaysia believes that the ARF will have room for expansion in the future at a pace that is comfortable for its members. Besides its present 18 members, there are other countries in and around the region that are equally interested in joining the dialogue on peace and security in South East Asia. In principle, Malaysia is not opposed to the expansion of the ARF; but, for the moment, the participation in the ARF follows a definite formula and the present participants have agreed on a moratorium on the admission of new members.

The United States has shown a greater readiness to endorse a multilateral security forum in South East Asia which would provide the security framework within which its strategic and economic interests will thrive. In a reversal of earlier policy, the United States has embraced with enthusiasm the development of the ASEAN Regional Forum and is a keen participant in the current security dialogue.

ASIA-PACIFIC ECONOMIC COOPERATION

The changing political-security landscape, coupled with the economic dynamism of the Asia-Pacific region have made the Asia-Pacific the centre of attention of the big powers. The US in particular, believes that there is no region more important than the Asia-Pacific as the centre of growth for the future, and has moved to reaffirm its engagement and leadership in the region in view of its vital security and economic interests. None other than President Clinton himself has outlined the U.S. concept of a "New Pacific Community," which would encompass a shared community based on a "shared strength, shared prosperity, and a shared commitment of democratic values." The Asia-Pacific represents the world's largest consumer market and the biggest export market for the United States.

The Asia-Pacific Economic Cooperation (APEC) was established in 1989 as a loose and informal consultative forum to promote cooperation in trade and investment among member economies on a programme and project orientated basis. Eighteen countries around the Pacific Rim, including Malaysia, are members of APEC. The Annual Ministerial Meeting determines the overall direction and nature of APEC activities while the Senior Officials Meeting is responsible for the overall APEC organisation and work programme and for ensuring that its operations are in accordance with the decisions of the Ministerial Meeting.

In November 1993, APEC Economic Leaders, with the exception of Malaysian Prime Minister Dr. Mahathir Mohamad, met for the first time in an informal summit on Blake Island at the invitation of President Clinton of the United States and agreed to a joint vision statement and proposed initiatives for implementation by APEC. On 15th November last year, the APEC Economic Leaders met again in Bogor and agreed to achieve free and open trade and investment in the Asia-Pacific Region by the year 2020 with industrialized economies reaching the goal by 2010.

Contrary to the belief in some quarters, Malaysia is actively engaged in the APEC process. It is for this reason that Malaysia has offered to host the APEC Ministerial Meeting in 1998. Because APEC members constitute diverse economies at differing stages of development, APEC members cannot develop at a standard pace. Taking this into consideration, Malaysia will continue to ensure that APEC remains a loose and non-exclusive consultative forum (not structured) promoting "open regionalism" with its members free to trade with any country they choose. Malaysia is adverse to initiatives to turn APEC into a negotiating forum and to create an Asia-Pacific Economic Community that may lead to the formation of a trade bloc. Malaysia is concerned that these efforts would be detrimental to free trade and would run counter to GATT. APEC should also develop at a pace that is comfortable for its members, with summit meetings among its leaders held only when necessary. The bottom line is that APEC should serve the interests of all members and not only those of the larger and more powerful few. In regard to APEC's membership, Malaysia is of the view that APEC, as a geographical grouping that is not ideological or political, and having the Pacific Ocean as the common factor, should offer membership to all countries whose shores border the Pacific Ocean.

With these concerns in mind, Malaysian Prime Minister Dr. Mahathir Mohamad, while attending the Bogor Meeting of Economic Leaders of APEC in Indonesia last November, found it necessary to register Malaysia's reservations on some aspects of the Leaders' Declaration of Common Resolve. While Malaysia accepts 2020 as a nonbinding target date to achieve a free trade area in the Asia-Pacific in line with its support for the principle of free trade, Malaysia nevertheless feels that APEC should give developing countries some flexibility to protect their economies so that they are not totally dominated by more advanced countries. Malaysia's reservations included the following:

- Malaysia will commit to undertaking further liberalization only on a unilateral basis at a pace and capacity commensurate with its level of development.
- The liberalization process to achieve the goal of free and open trade and investment in Asia-Pacific will not create an exclusive free trade area in the Asia-Pacific.
- The liberalization process will be consistent with GATT/WTO and on an unconditional MFN basis.
- The target dates of 2020 and 2010 are indicative dates and nonbinding on member economies.

EAST ASIA ECONOMIC CAUCUS

Reservations notwithstanding, Malaysia's commitment to the APEC process cannot be questioned. However, there are those who will advocate that Malaysia's lukewarm support for APEC is linked to its own proposal to form the East Asia Economic Caucus (EAEC). The EAEC, they claim, is a cog in the APEC wheel and represents an initiative which will undermine APEC. Nothing is further from the truth.

The EAEC, first mooted by Dr. Mahathir Mohamad in 1990 (then referred to as East Asia Economic Group), is envisaged to be a gathering of East Asian economies that will come together in a consultative process so as to provide opportunities for expanded regional cooperation. EAEC will not be a trade bloc, as feared by some quarters; it will only endeavour to promote open regionalism and the multilateral trading system. EAEC became an ASEAN initiative when the Fourth ASEAN Summit in Singapore in 1992 recognized the merit of having consultations among East Asian economies and endorsed the initiative. At the 26th ASEAN Ministerial Meeting in Singapore in 1993, the ASEAN Foreign Ministers agreed that EAEC should be operationalized as a caucus within APEC.

The larger APEC economies continue to harbour suspicion of EAEC stemming from their fear that EAEC will undermine the APEC process. Seen from Malaysia's perspective, this fear is unwarranted and there remains much to be done to allay the fears of the United States and others regarding EAEC. The decision by ASEAN Foreign Ministers to make EAEC as a caucus within

APEC should be evidence enough that ASEAN does not intend to supplant APEC with EAEC, rather to complement it.

FUTURE MULTILATERAL COOPERATION IN SOUTH EAST

Malaysia has established a national target of becoming an industrialized nation by the year 2020; it is a prerequisite that we advance toward this objective in peace and in harmony with our neighbours and with the world in general. Wars, friction and tension only undermine and destroy the capacity of nations to grow. On the other hand, good governance, visionary leadership, a productive work force, an innovative private sector and adequate resources, nurtured amidst a backdrop of peace and stability, are key ingredients toward creating dynamic and vibrant nations.

Malaysia's concern in pursuing bilateral and multilateral cooperation in the region is that any adverse developments may result in undesirable implications on regional security, trade, investment, and the economy. Thus it is essential that countries in the region manage their relations with each other and with external players as well. The region is littered with disputes involving overlapping claims of sovereignty both on land and in the sea. These disputes have their roots in the colonial history of the region where, with the exception of Thailand, all the other ASEAN countries have experienced colonial domination. Maritime disputes are over numerous islands and features in the South China Sea, as well as jurisdictions over the consequent maritime areas. The disputed area commonly known as the Spratlys is claimed partially or wholly by countries in the region, including Malaysia. There also exists maritime disputes of a more bilateral nature, with neighbouring countries claiming sovereignty over islands. Malaysia believes that the best way to resolve the issue of conflicting maritime claims in the South China Sea is through bilateral negotiations among the claimants and within the framework of the ASEAN Declaration on the South China Sea, agreed to in Manila in 1992, which had emphasised the necessity of resolving these disputes through peaceful means. Malaysia had engaged in bilateral negotiations with Singapore over the island of Pulau Batu Puteh, and with Indonesia over the two islands of Sipadan and Ligitan. Besides ASEAN, Vietnam has associated itself with the ASEAN Declaration on the South China Sea.

China, while opposing internationalizing the issue of Nansha Islands, has stated that the principles contained in the Declaration are similar to their position.

The strategic location of South East Asia—sandwiched between the traditional giants of Japan, China and the two Koreas in the north, the populous Indian subcontinent to the north east, the industrialised nations of Australia and New Zealand to the south, and the powerful nations the United States, Russia and the European Union on the outer periphery— have necessitated that the South East Asian nations juggle their relationships in order to safeguard their political, strategic, and economic interests. Instability in another region, whether resulting from a security problem or a trade dispute, could easily transport its effects into the ASEAN region, and vice versa. Trade disputes between the United States and Japan, and the United States and China, for instance, could have adverse effects on developing countries like Malaysia, if these disputes develop into nasty trade wars. A nuclear war in the Korean peninsula could also make its disastrous effects felt in South East Asia. Indeed, the world is so enmeshed in its interlocking relationships that, to employ the proverbial analogy, when America sneezes, the rest of the world catches cold.

In moving forward, Malaysia would want to be guided by the basic principle of seeking friends, not enemies. We want to be guided by the United Nations dictum of turning swords into plowshares. China, once-slumbering but now on the road to economic modernization, is one such country that Malaysia would like to look upon as a friend and not as a threat. Malaysia hopes to continue to forge good relations with China. We believe that as China embarks on economic modernization, it is in China's own interest to maintain a peaceful and stable external environment. However, China's increasing economic and military might has raised fears among other countries that it is developing hegemonic tendencies in the mid- and long term. These countries are watching developments in China very closely to determine which way the wind will blow, especially in the period after Deng Xiaoping.

CONCLUSION

In conclusion, I would like to maintain that multilateral activities and dialogue in South East Asia are important means of safeguarding both the national and regional interests of countries in the region. In this respect, I would like to stress the following desires of Malaysia in regard to multilateral security in South East Asia:

- Underscore the importance of security to the growth of any nation, big and small. For there can be no growth without stability, and no development without security.
- Underscore the multidimensional nature of security so that the economic and social aspects of security are also afforded adequate treatment within the context of "comprehensive security". In our view, to give priority to the military dimension of security only is to emphasise a lop-sided dimension. Security to us goes beyond the question of defence or military.
- Maintain the principle of mutual respect and non-interference in the internal affairs of nations. Western standards on human rights, labour, the environment, democracy and press freedom, held dear in some countries, may not necessarily be applicable to the same degree in nations of the East without destroying the delicate social fabric of these nations.
- Upholding the policy of noninterference, reject the policy of containment by larger and more powerful nations with interests in the region and support instead a policy of engagement. Major powers can lead, but without dominance and without double standards. In the post Cold War era, U.S. engagement in South East Asia should focus on providing sophisticated military hardware, transfer of technology and training, rather than on physical presence of its forward forces.
- Given the delicate nature of racial and religious issues within South East Asian societies, tread softly on the issue of racial integration.
- Build upon the APEC process to further liberalise trade and encourage investment in the region, taking into account the limitations of developing countries within APEC which must develop at their own pace. In this context, we will complement APEC's activities with EAEC, a consultative

forum of East Asian countries to discuss issues of common interest.

● Build upon the ARF process as a basis for political and security dialogue among countries in the region. The nature of the ARF would make it a significant forum to contribute to the confidence building and preventive diplomacy in the Asia-Pacific region.

● Advocate an indigenous framework as the best way to move forward in multilateral dialogue, within which the concerns of the regional states and the legitimate interests of the major players can be safeguarded.

● Maintain the centrality of ASEAN and build upon existing regional mechanisms (such as the Treaty of Amity and Cooperation in South East Asia; the Zone of Peace, Freedom and Neutrality in South East Asia; the proposed Nuclear Weapons Free Zone in South East Asia; the ASEAN Free Trade Area, etc.) as the foundation for laying other building blocks for security and economic cooperation in the wider Asia-Pacific. Malaysia is prepared to consider other forms of confidence-building measures and preventive diplomacy provided these meet with the requirements of the region.

In 27 years, ASEAN has proven through its track record that it has become a viable regional organization that remains as valid today, as it did in 1967, to the needs of the member states. While there is no denying the occasional dissension, ASEAN countries remain united in facing the difficult challenges of the post Cold War period. ASEAN's many diversities have not become a barrier to achieving regional unity. Rather, ASEAN is an example of unity in diversity. As a founder member of ASEAN, Malaysia would want to continue to reap the benefits from and to build upon ASEAN's success.

Part II

THE SOUTH EAST ASIA ENVIRONMENT: View From the Peripheral Nations

AUSTRALIA'S RELATIONSHIP WITH SOUTH EAST ASIA

Rory Steele

As the 20th century draws to a close, the strategic environment in South East Asia is at once benign and uncertain. On the one hand critical factors for peace and stability are currently in place. Countries with long cultural traditions and strong leadership are currently enjoying unprecedented economic growth and are thus well postured to meet the aspirations of their people. They can plan for this reassured by the continuing commitment to the region of the United States, the world's leading economy and military power, whose forward military presence underpins the tranquillity of the wider region and whose market remains open for its expanding exports.

On the other hand, powerful forces for change are in play. The sudden collapse of the Communist system and the accelerating prosperity of East Asian economies have combined to shake up the decades-long pattern of Cold War relationships in Asia and the Pacific. Pressure on political systems is coming from a whole host of new issues, ranging from demographics to revolutions in technology, from concern for the environment to a heightened focus on human rights issues. Australia views these developments not from a distance, nor from the periphery: it is caught up in the process of change, it is a factor in the hoped-for permanence of a

Mr. Steele is Assistant Secretary, Strategic Assessments Branch, Department of Foreign Affairs and Trade, Canberra. Prior to assuming his current position in 1991, he was the POLMIL Adviser in Canberra, and has also served as Ambassador, Baghdad, Iraq (1986-1988).

benign security environment, and its destiny is more than ever linked with that of South East Asia.

Australia has never lost sight of the importance of its near neighborhood, largely because of the pressing threat to its national security from that direction during the Second World War. In the immediately succeeding period it played a significant role in support of Indonesia's independence and through the establishment of the Colombo Plan as a vehicle for development assistance to the region. In 1971 Australia was a founding member of the Five Power Defense Arrangement, with Malaysia, Singapore, New Zealand, and the United Kingdom. In the immediately succeeding period it was accepted as ASEAN's first dialogue partner. Over the next 20 years bilateral relations with individual ASEAN members strengthened, as illustrated by trade statistics—6 percent of Australia 's exports went to ASEAN in 1974, but by 1994 ASEAN accounted for 14 percent of the total, becoming Australia's second-largest regional market, ahead of both Europe and North America.

The end of the Vietnam War in 1975 and the subsequent human tragedy in Cambodia under Pol Pot brought home the realities of the region to Australia in a different way. Mass movements of people into countries close to Australia placed a considerable burden on those countries and posed the question of what role Australia might play. It responded quickly and generously, accepting more refugees per capita than any other country in the world. These refugees, accepted as immigrants, amply tested the nondiscriminatory immigration policy introduced by a then predominantly monocultural Australia only 10 years before. Significantly, because of the ready acceptance by the local community, people of Asian origin will encompass fully 10 percent of the Australian population within the next generation.

Australia looks at South East Asia, then, from very close up. It sees a subregion, which in terms of economic effort demonstrates extraordinary dynamism, impressive recent achievement, and great potential for the future. A commitment by countries in South East Asia to more liberal economic policies, together with structural change, has encouraged strong export performances based on large capital inflows and led to sustained growth rates of around 7 per cent. World Bank forecasts put both Indonesia and Thailand among the world's 15 largest economies by 2020. Under these circumstances, and with ASEAN in any case likely to expand to embrace all 10 states of South East Asia, there will be on Australia's doorstep a potentially significant trading partner, a key market, and an important economic force in its own right. The economies of Australia and ASEAN are certain to become even more closely enmeshed, reflecting increased complementarity. Changes already under way indicate that manufactures and services will dominate Australia-ASEAN trade, in place of agriculture and minerals, although these will remain important. This partnership is likely to prosper in the context of a greatly liberalized regional trading regime.

Rapid economic growth in the wider region has prompted countries to consider new forms of economic cooperation and new institutions. In 1989 Australia launched the APEC initiative in Canberra, which was quickly supported by ASEAN countries in particular, with APEC ministers meeting in Singapore in 1990 and Bangkok in 1992. Heads of government, who met for the first time in Seattle in 1993, came together again in Bogor, Indonesia, in November 1994. There are evident opportunities for economic cooperation to develop momentum toward trade facilitation in areas such as technical standards, mutual recognition of qualifications, customs harmonization and investment guidelines, and perhaps to go beyond toward actual trade liberalization in the traditional tariff reduction sense. At Bogor, APEC members committed themselves to achieve free and open trade and investment in the region by 2020. Within South East Asia, ASEAN countries have taken a major step toward creation of a unified market by establishing the ASEAN Free Trade Area (AFTA). Prospects appear good for eventually combining AFTA with the closer economic relations arrangement between Australia and New Zealand to establish a larger free-trade area.

Cooperation among members of the region on noneconomic issues has been slower to develop, but an important beginning has been made, deriving from a recognition that the strategic environment was radically changing. Articulation of this change was made in December 1989 in a statement to Parliament by Australian Foreign Minister Senator Gareth Evans in which he noted that security in the Asia-Pacific region was now multi-dimension and that Australia would participate actively "in the gradual development of a regional security community based on a sense of shared security interests." In 1990 Australia proposed at the ASEAN PMC in Jakarta that systematic efforts be made to develop a security dialogue between states in the region, and that if this was to happen then at some stage there might evolve a more formal structure, perhaps an Asian version of the Conference on Security and Cooperation in Europe—i.e., a "CSCA."

This sort of thinking, being enunciated also by Canada, was not immediately accepted. Nevertheless, it was soon clear that others in the region also saw the strategic environment changing rapidly before them and were concerned to find appropriate ways to respond to the situation. Many heard the voices within the United States proclaiming it no longer faced a global strategic threat. They concluded from the calls for a "peace dividend" (which could only mean pressure for cuts in the defense budget) that there was a question mark over U.S. continued maintenance of a substantial forward military presence in the Pacific.

At the same time it became apparent within the region that the security environment was changing from within, in two important ways. One was that the countries of South East Asia were shifting their security focus from internal preoccupations such as Communist subversion to a broader definition of national interests, recognizing in particular the importance of protecting exploitable resources in expanded areas of maritime jurisdiction. The other was that economic prosperity was giving countries of the region unprecedented opportunities to modernize their defense forces—most ASEAN countries, with Thailand and Indonesia prominent, began to upgrade their naval capabilities, and some, notably Malaysia, to enhance their air forces. The advantage of a buyer's market in international arms post-Cold War was not lost on South East Asian countries. They were, however, conscious that this was a process that, if not carried out within some sort of framework, might ultimately promote an arms race. With a number of other security-related uncertainties beginning to emerge, it was clearly time to respond. The vehicle selected was that of dialogue; thus a process of multilateral regional security dialogue was launched.

During the Cold War, countries in Asia almost never discussed security matters among themselves. Those who felt the need for support for their national security position invariably looked for it beyond the region. Even within ASEAN, members did not talk about security questions. Nevertheless, at the ASEAN Post Ministerial Conference (the meeting between ASEAN and its dialogue partners) in mid-1991 and the ASEAN summit in early

1992 it was agreed that security issues should for the first time be put formally on the agenda of the PMC. The 1992 PMC thus saw the first security dialogue among the ASEAN countries and their dialogue partners. The 1993 ASEAN Ministerial Meeting and the PMC saw agreement to launch the ASEAN Regional Forum (ARF). It met in Bangkok in 1994, in a major step towards the realization of the vision of an Asia-Pacific regional security community. Gathered together for the first time at foreign minister level were the ASEAN members and the seven dialogue partners, together with China, Russia, Vietnam, Laos, and Papua New Guinea.

Australia has strongly supported ASEAN's initiative, recognizing as others have that it is the only available forum for multilateral dialogue on security issues in the region. Senator Evans congratulated ASEAN in Bangkok last year after the first meeting of ARF for showing the way to the rest of the region. In his view, ARF had certainly achieved the purpose of providing confidence and comfort to all members about the fledgling institution doing this without ducking the hard issues. He referred to the growing amount of dialogue activity, both at the official level as well as in semiofficial meetings involving in addition academics and think tanks. He hoped that this process would be rounded out by greater participation by military and defense planners. An early opportunity to advance in this direction was taken at the first intercessional ARF activity, a seminar in Canberra in November 1994, which considered trust and confidence-building measures and brought together not only foreign ministry officials but also defense practitioners, together with a number of academics.

Given the disparities within the region and the fact that there has been a minimum of exchanges among regional members on security issues to date, the building of trust is evidently one of the first tasks before ARF. A number of relevant aspects were identified in an Australian paper commissioned by the 1993 ASEAN PMC Senior Officials Meeting on confidence-building measures applicable to the region and submitted to the first ARF Senior Officials Meeting the following year. These measures included observers at military exercises, dialogue on strategic perceptions and defense planning, exchanges between military academics, training cooperation, and participation in a regional arms register. The Canberra seminar provided the first opportunity for ARF members to discuss measures such as these in detail, albeit in an informal way. That seminar will be followed by a second ARF intercession seminar on peacekeeping in Brunei in March, and a third on preventive diplomacy, in Seoul in May. The seminars will provide important material for the current ARF chair, Brunei, to collate and draw from in preparing for the ARF meeting later in the year.

At this stage ARF is not in a position to take on the major security issues of the region, including the particularly difficult problems on the Korean peninsula or the still precarious situation in Cambodia. Overlapping claims in the South China Sea and disputes that might follow from them are also for the time beyond the ARF's abilities to resolve, despite the excellent work done by Indonesia in organizing a series of workshops to promote an informal exchange of views among claimants. It is Australia's expectation, however, that ARF will quickly strengthen as a forum not only for discussing actual and potential problems in the region but also come to be accepted as being the institution to turn to for the resolution of problems. The region will need to acquire, as soon as possible and through the good offices of ARF, the habit of seeking multilateral ways to overcome what otherwise might be serious threats to security. In addition to those mentioned, the sorts of obvious issues include questions relating to the possible proliferation in the region of sophisticated weapons, including weapons of mass destruction and their means of delivery.

Australia approaches the question of regional security from three complementary directions. It has its traditional alliance with the United States and is in no doubt that the continuing military presence of the United States in the Asia-Pacific is an asset to be promoted, for the greater good of all in the region. Australia has also been developing its security links with its neighbors on a bilateral basis, in some cases over a period of decades and in other cases with a particular effort being made in recent years, to good effect; security ties with Indonesia, for example, are now closer than they have ever been. These bilateral efforts have explicitly been directed toward the evolution of a strategic partnership between Australia and South East Asia, including the concept of a common strategic identity. Finally, Australia has been energetically working on a multilateral approach to regional security. Australia's long-term goal here, as noted, is for a regional security community, which might complement the sort of economic community that could emerge through APEC.

There is something of a sense within the region that a window of opportunity is currently open, and that it might close as a result of developments that cannot now be precisely outlined. Some issues can be discerned amongst the uncertainties:

- The potential for further substantial population movements, including refugees.
- Environmental issues are likely to be of increasing concern, to governments and to their constituents.
- Greater economic progress, the march of technology, particularly information technology, and the globalization of economic and political factors will operate in the direction of greater transparency, openness and liberalization of societies, some of whom may be ill prepared to meet these challenges.

These are all issues that, together with others such as the problems of AIDS, piracy and narcotics, can cross national frontiers, could test harmonious relations in the region, and will require greater efforts to be made by its members to find new mechanisms and habits of consulting. These efforts should be directed into preventive diplomacy and conflict resolution, consistent with ideas for international cooperation advanced by the United Nations Secretary General and by the Australian Foreign Minister in his 1993 book, *Cooperating for Peace.* If made on a multilateral basis and within a regional framework, such efforts should of themselves advance the idea of a regional security community.

Australia is keen to be part of this process, as a player increasingly drawn into the issues of central concern. It has been at the forefront of looking for ways to engage bilaterally and strengthen ties with individual countries of the region. It has also been a strong advocate of the multilateral dialogue process and of finding ways to advance this process in practical ways. It is particularly concerned to ensure that the region remain free of weapons of mass destruction and has supported the concept of the South East Asia Nuclear Weapons Free Zone. It has indicated a readiness to adhere to the Treaty of Amity and Cooperation, signed in Bali in 1976. Australians, common citizens as well as government officials, are conscious as never before that their destiny is enmeshed with that of South East Asia.

CHINA'S CONSTRUCTIVE ROLE IN SOUTH EAST ASIA

Peng Guangqian

SOUTH EAST ASIA'S STRATEGIC IMPORTANCE

The strategic importance of South East Asia dramatically increased after the Cold War, and South East Asia is increasingly in the international spotlight thanks to its political stability and rapid economic development. As an influential neighbor, China also has succeeded in modernization and reform. Because of its geographical proximity, China and the South East Asian countries historically have developed close economic, political, and cultural relations. This paper will examine future progress in the relationship between China and South East Asia and China's positive role in promoting regional peace and security.

Political Stability

Although South East Asia was influenced by the Cold War, it remained secondary in the East-West competition. Unlike Europe, where minority disputes combined with religious and territorial conflicts to create wars and instability, South East Asia was able to maintain considerable political stability.

Senior Colonel Peng Guangqian is a senior researcher and former vice-director from the First Institute of the Department for Strategic Studies, Academy of Military Science, PRC. He is currently a senior fellow at the Atlantic Council of the United States. Colonel Peng is a council member of the American History Research Association of China and a member of the Sino-American Relations Association of China.

The post-Cold War political map reflects the contrast between South East Asia's prosperity and stability and Europe's chaos and recession. Recently, to further promote long-term regional stability, ASEAN countries successfully began a dialogue on security. Important conferences such as the Foreign Ministers Conference (FMC), Post Ministers Conference (PMC), and ASEAN Regional Forum (ARF) have been held to promote a new regional order. They have contributed greatly to the Asia-Pacific region and the international community.

Growing economic strength has improved South East Asia's strategic position in the international community. While many countries in other parts of the world were in the midst of recession or even on the verge of economic collapse, ASEAN countries were generally prosperous. South East Asia has tremendous potential for further development with rich strategic resources. The level of oil and natural gas reserves in South East Asia, mainly in the South China Sea, is comparable to that of the Middle East. As oil and natural gas reserves in the rest of the world decrease, while world demand gradually increases, the prospect of developing South East Asia's natural gas and oil reserves is crucial to the global political economy and security.

Strategic Position

South East Asia serves as the bridge between the Pacific Ocean and the Indian Ocean, dominating the major sea route from Northeast Asia to the Middle East via the Indian Ocean. This explains why world powers have historically competed for dominance in the region. The Strait of Malacca, which is situated between Indonesia, Malaysia, and Singapore, and the Sunda Strait near Indonesia are regarded by the United States as one of the 16 major sea routes of the world. During the Cold War, the United States and the Soviet Union established their respective Subic Bay and Cam Ranh Bay military bases. Although the East-West military confrontation in the region has cooled down since the end of the Cold War, South East Asia has become even more strategically important for the expansion of maritime trade.

Possible Challenges to Regional Security

At present, South East Asia as a whole is relatively stable, although it is by no means an utopia. Factors that have caused chaos in Eastern Europe since the end of the Cold War are also present in South East Asia but in varying degrees.

- Competition for regional leadership during the Cold War gave way to the bipolar East-West global conflict. Contention for regional dominance in South East Asia and other parts of the world might arise during the process of political and economic reconstruction.

- The increase in economic activities can bring closer economic interdependence or economic conflict and competition, or elements of both. Access to domestic markets and trade barriers, balance of payments deficits or surpluses, intellectual property rights, technological transfers and blockades, economic sanctions and resulting retaliation and other kinds of disputes will inevitably increase as a result of the expansion of regional economic activities that affect regional stability.

- Contrary to most Western countries which are trying to reduce military expenditures, South East Asia is undergoing military expansion and development. Emphasis was on naval construction, high-tech fighters, missiles, and warship modernization. Such military expansion involves normal improvement of military equipment and strengthening of defense capacity. In addition to mere military enhancement, some countries intend to build a strong military capability in order to improve the exploitation of ocean resources and influence major trade routes, strategic islands, and competition for regional leadership. If these concerns ever become the main motivation for military buildup, the limited amount of resources in the region will soon become further exhausted. Not only will regional economic development be hindered, but regional peace and security also will be deeply affected.

- There have always been unresolved conflicts among South East Asian countries and their neighbors due to historical or practical factors. Most of these disputes are the legacy of history and difficult to resolve, especially when the concept of sovereignty is involved. Regional security will be endangered if these disputes are not dealt with properly and cautiously.

- Ethnic and religious concerns must not be overlooked as they may influence the future of South East Asia. In addition to factional competition within certain countries that can lead to political instability, ethnic conflict and religious contentiousnous also threaten stability as they have in other parts of the world.

THE BASIS FOR SINO-SOUTH EAST ASIA COOPERATION

To maintain South East Asia's prosperity and stability and to overcome future challenges to regional security, the efforts of South East Asia countries themselves and a favorable external environment are essential. This includes friendly relations and cooperation between China and South East Asia. As South East Asia's neighbor, China has a natural relationship with the region so that further development of friendly relations between the two is highly likely and important.

Sino-South East Asia's political, economic, and cultural relations can be traced back more than 2,000 years. Historical cooperation between China and Indonesia in the southern region of South East Asia dates back to the seventh century. In the 15th century, Zheng He, the great Chinese explorer, accomplished seven voyages between Africa and Karimantan of Indonesia. He travelled to the south portion of South East Asia, establishing relations with South East Asian countries.

Contemporary history shows that the efforts of the Chinese people in defense against external aggression and in the struggle for national liberation have been welcomed enthusiastically in South East Asia. Contact, mutual trust and understanding have long been consolidated. Although there have been times that China and some South East Asian countries have tread on rough ground, these were brief moments in the long history of friendly relations between China and South East Asia.

Since China adopted the open-door policy, trade between China and South East Asia has soared and economic relations have become closer. In addition, investment by ASEAN countries in China is growing. Closer economic relations can strengthen the foundation for mutual cooperation and economic development.

China and South East Asian countries are developing countries with similar histories and the common goal of nation-building and economic development. All nations desire both regional and international long-term peace and stability. In a 1955 Asian-African conference in Indonesia, Chinese Premier Zhou En-lai talked about the famous "Five Principles of Mutual Co-Existence." Together with Asian and African friends, including the countries of South East Asia, Premier Zhou put forward the resolution known as the "Spirit of Bandung," which has since served as the foundation for friendly relations between China and South East Asia.

Asian culture calls for harmony between man and nature, between self and object, and harmony among people. Personal relations, respect, collectivity, and society are all highly valued. This spirit of harmony is pursued by Asians in their call for international cooperation and negotiation among the world community.

CHINA'S ROLE IN PROMOTING PEACE AND DEVELOPMENT IN SOUTH EAST ASIA

Actively developing solidarity and cooperation between China and South East Asia is the foundation of China's foreign policy. China's effort to promote peace and development in South East Asia is in accordance with the interests not only of all the countries of South East Asia, but also of the Asia-Pacific region and the international community.

Maintain Regional Peace

Even with the end of the Cold War, power politics still exists as the major influence on peace and development in the world. With South East Asia's growing strategic importance in particular, various political and economic powers have entered the region to gain regional influence. Regional issues, as a consequence, will be relatively prominent. China has consistently opposed power politics in promoting peace and economic development in South East Asia. This position has two components:

- *China guarantees that it will never pursue a hegemonist policy in South East Asia.* There are no special interests for

China in the region. China never seeks gains beyond the legitimate rights and interests that are vested in sovereign states by international law to be enjoyed by all sovereign states. China does not aim to be a super power and will not align itself with any power or bloc. With the collapse of the bipolar system, China has no intentions of filling the so-called strategic vacuum emerging in post-Cold War South East Asia. Furthermore, China has no intentions of taking the place of any political or economic power to act as an overlord in South East Asia. China will make every effort to seek fair and equitable settlement of issues between China and South East Asian countries on the basis of equal consultation and mutual benefit. China will never under any circumstances resort to force or threats of force nor will it ever force her unilateral views on others.

● *China will firmly oppose any effort to carry out power politics in South East Asia.* All kinds of power politics—whether from some internal power of the region or from some external power of the region—should be challenged. Regional affairs in South East Asia should be conducted according to the principles of international law and unanimity through consultation, in keeping with the aspirations of the peoples of South East Asia, conforming to the fundamental interests of the people of South East Asia and the South East Asia-Pacific region and even the whole world. Power politics in any form emerging in South East Asia is not only a disaster for regional peace and development, but also represents a serious threat to neighboring countries, the neighboring region, and international peace and development.

China has opposed power politics so firmly not only because power politics is contrary to contemporary trends and the principle of international law, but also due to China's bitter historical experiences. Although China is a great nation with a civilization that is thousands of years old, in the last 200 years, Beijing has been occupied three times by armed foreign invaders. Under the threat of foreign powers' guns, the imperial Chinese government had to sign a series of unequal treaties to cede territory and pay indemnities that tremendously hindered Chinese development. Even since the establishment of the People's Republic, China has still suffered bitterly from political containment, military threats, and economic blockades. China has suffered greatly as a result of power politics and consequently will never forget history's wounds, will never let power politics go unchecked, and will never implement a policy of hegemony in return.

It is clear China would never carry out power politics at present or in the future, as a developed and much stronger nation. Limited natural resources spent pursuing power politics would adversely affect the people's welfare and delay the nation's prosperity. This would be against the interests of the state and against the willingness of the Chinese people. No doubt, China's military modernization has to be under the guidance of this fundamental principle.

The most urgent tasks for China are to fully develop social productive forces, to concentrate on economic modernization, to dramatically raise comprehensive national strength, to eradicate backwardness and poverty and to improve the living conditions of the people. These are of prime importance to a nation's rise and fall and to general national strategy. National defense construction and military force construction have to submit to and serve the overall interests of economic construction. Thus, it is unnecessary and impossible for China to spend a large amount of money on military expenditures, thereby obstructing and interfering with the overall interests of economic construction.

In recent years China's economic situation has improved greatly. Nevertheless, compared with developed countries, China still has a long way to go. Limited by national financial resources and material resources, no matter how much defense expenditures increase, its absolute value will still be relatively small vis-a-vis other countries. China is among the countries with the lowest defense expenditures in either absolute terms or relative value. The total amount of China's defense spending equalled 43.2 billion yuan in 1993. If converted according to the exchange rate at the time, it was only 2.5 percent of the U.S. military budget which was $291 billion. China's per capita military spending was 43 yuan (U.S. $5) in 1994, compared with $1,000 per capita in the United States, $600 in Britain and France, $360 in Japan, and $8 in India. Since 1949, the People's Republic of China's total defense spending over 45 years is nearly equal to a current annual military expenditure in the United States. Such a low level of defense spending is seldom seen in the world.

China's strategic defense policy, armed forces structure, and military deployment are defensive, rather than offensive. China's overriding military strategy is still one of territorial defense. China has no military bases overseas, and not a single PLA soldier is deployed in foreign territory. China's military forces are concentrated in land forces. It is totally groundless to say that China is developing an oceangoing navy. In terms of naval and air combat equipment, China does not have a warship with tonnage exceeding 5,000 tons in its existing ranks or projects under construction. The main purpose of China's armed forces is for the defense of its territory and coastal areas. China is among those countries with minimal defense capabilities. It can in no way constitute a military threat to other countries.

Finally, although in recent years China's defense spending has increased to some extent, this was partly to offset earlier years of unduly low defense expenditures. The increase also has compensated for the loss of buying power caused by high inflation. For example, while military expenditures increased by 16.7 percent in 1993 over 1992, the inflation rate was also 16.7 percent in the same period. Last year, China's defense budget increased 20 percent, which is lower than 21 percent inflation rate of that year. The actual increase of China's military spending, therefore, is very limited. In fact, military spending is declining in proportion to the gross national product (GNP). China's expenditures on defense is generally declining, as other areas get higher priority.

Maintain a Mutually Beneficial Economic Order

Since the end of the Cold War, countries have focused on economic development. This is the inevitable result of the progression of time and historical development. Economic development is of vital importance not only to the people's livelihood and a nation's permanent stability but also to world peace and security. In international relations, each country increasingly attaches importance to its own economic interests. Economic factors have had a growing impact on international relations, even playing a decisive role in some instances. With the further development of world economic integration, regionalization, and concentration, two trends have emerged that merit attention:

- Increasing economic interdependence, international competition, and intensified trade friction make South East

Asia one of the most economically dynamic regions in the world. Consequently, under the principle of equality and mutual benefit, building and maintaining fair and reasonable economic order in South East Asia is essential.

• Reducing trade friction, normalizing economic activities, strengthening regional economic cooperation and harmony as well as helping supply each other's needs and making up each other's deficiencies in much greater scale, are the only ways to promote regional economic development and common prosperity, as well as the important basis of world peace.

There are close economic ties between China and South East Asia. Since the 1980s, bilateral economic activities have increased rapidly in terms of commercial interaction, market development, circulation of funds, industrial transfer, science and technological exchange, and information flow. With the deepening and widening of China's economic reform, economic interdependence and mutual cooperation with South East Asia have increased day by day. To promote the establishment of equality and mutually beneficial economic order is not only the fundamental need for South East Asia's long term development, but also China's and the world's common interests.

Because of the reality of diversity and interdependence in the Asia-Pacific region which includes South East Asia, in the APEC meeting in Indonesia in November 1994, Chinese leader Jiang Zemin proposed five principles for Asia-Pacific economic cooperation:

• Mutual respect and reaching unanimity through consultation
• Proceeding in an orderly fashion step by step and developing steadily
• Opening up to each other instead of exclusionism
• Wide cooperation and mutual benefit
• Reducing disparity and promoting common prosperity.

These principles are universal and suitable for establishing new economic order in South East Asia.

In this sense, we can say the five principles are a new contribution toward the establishment of new economic order in South East Asia. Two points deserve special attention: recognizing the reality of diversity, and gradually reducing disparity between rich and poor countries to realize common prosperity. The first means that each country has different political positions, different development emphasis and strategy. Every country has its strong and weak points, therefore, all the countries should be treated equally and with respect. Developed countries should do their best to help developing ones overcome difficulties and become prosperous. Without the economic progress of developing countries, regional economic cooperation and economic development will have no reserve strength, and the developed countries' economic growth will not be sustainable. Through reform, a thriving and prospering China is the reliable friend of South East Asia countries. China would firmly develop economic cooperation with South East countries, promote equal interchange and mutually beneficial cooperation, and commonly greet a new era of stability and prosperity.

Establish a Security Mechanism in the Region

The turn of the century presents a vital opportunity for the development of South East Asia and the establishment of a common security mechanism based on mutual trust, equal benefit, and mutual exchange. There is no doubt that China, which has been trying very hard to maintain a lasting peace in the Asia-Pacific and the whole world, will enthusiastically greet every new step in realizing regional peace and stability, will actively support all efforts to establish a security mechanism in this region.

The most important factors in creating a security mechanism are to consider the regional reality, each country's characteristics and diversity, and every side's legal interests. South East Asia is different from Europe in that South East Asia was not a focal point as Europe was during the Cold War. There was no acute military confrontation between the two military blocs as there was in Europe. Instead, disputes and conflict in this area were localized. South East Asia's development cannot compete with that of Europe, and therefore continuing the region's development is more necessary than in Europe. Consequently, South East Asian nations cannot simply imitate European countries' mechanisms; it certainly is not necessary or possible to apply the European model on South East Asia. It is also not necessary to establish a single security system, when a multilevel, multichannel security mechanism suited to diversity would better serve the purpose.

In addition to establishing a reliable security mechanism, there is also the need to eradicate outdated Cold War concepts such as "group politics," "camp politics," "big family," and "spheres of influence." In the new era, South East Asia's security mechanisms should possess new characteristics and should:

- Be open, based on mutual trust, rather than being closed and exclusive. It should not treat any country in or out of the region as a potential or present threat.
- Concentrate on actively preventing crisis, not on military confrontation. It should strive to overcome disputes and to terminate potentially unsafe factors. In the event of a crisis the crisis could be effectively controlled and prevented from escalating. In short, these mechanisms must be positive, not negative, assertive rather than submissive. They should be characterized by initiative, not apathy.
- Be a consultative mechanism instead of a compulsory interventionist mechanism.
- Have as their motivating power a variety of the strategic powers based on mutual trust and strategic harmony and not rely on containment and preservation of a balance of power.
- Focus on safeguarding regional security.

In short, establishing new security mechanisms requires new strategic thinking. If we continue to use Cold War thinking for guidance it will be impossible to achieve real security, and the South East Asian security mechanisms would become disruptive.

For South East Asian security mechanisms to be established, China would like to see a multilevel, multichannel, or multilateral security dialogue to promote understanding and security cooperation among South East Asian nations. China will coordinate with South East Asian countries to establish Asia-Pacific security. At the right time China might consider to publish a National Defense White Paper outlining National Defense Policy, views on military strength, and modernization policy, the National Defense Budget plan, and increased transparency of national defense activities. China will insist that the military be used only for defense and firmly opposes any type of military competition. China and South East Asia should strengthen visits by ranking military officers and military academic exchanges, and they must create a crisis prevention system and procedures, and crack down on the activities of smugglers and pirates. They must also work together to manage marine affairs, ocean environmental protection, and marine research and rescue. Finally, they should support joint UN-peacekeeping activities.

Promote Peaceful and Fair Resolution of International Disputes

Compared with other regions, South East Asia is currently enjoying economic growth and a political stability. However, among the countries of South East Asia there are still many unresolved disputes over territories, particulary on the issues of territorial boundaries, jurisdiction of islands, the demarkation of ocean territory and resource development. These issues are complicated and therefore may have a great impact on peace and stability in South East Asia. China's consistent policy has been to use peaceful means to solve such international disputes. Each side involved in disputes not only thinks about their own interests but also those of their opponents', seeking common ground while preserving difference, mutual understanding and mutual concession to reach solutions acceptable by every country. Since 1980 Chinese leaders have devised such creative proposals as "shelve disputes," "joint exploitation," and "consultative dialogue." These proposals have offered new thinking for the international community in solving disputes. These proposals would be useful if applied to present South East Asian issues to reach a peaceful solution.

In the overall interests of keeping Asia-Pacific including South East Asia stable and promoting the traditional friendship among China and South East Asia, China still magnanimously looks forward to making a creative proposal to "shelve disputes, jointly exploit." The core of the proposal is to change hostility into friendship and to use common economic interests to link all sides of the dispute. Through joint exploitation, improved mutual trust and understanding, promotion of friendship among all countries, and creation of favorable circumstances for solving disputes reasonably results in "win-win" conditions.

In order to realize the above proposal, China has been making unrelenting efforts for a long time. The most recent progress came with the Chinese leader's visit to Vietnam in November 1994. Leaders of both countries reached common ground on peacefully solving boundary disputes and both sides agreeing to the following principles:

- Resolve the disputes through negotiation
- Refrain from further complicating and enlarging disputes before the solution of the issues
- Refrain from the threat of force or the use of force
- Respect each other
- Respect international law
- Resolve those issues that are resolvable and to continue to exchange views on those issues that are still unresolved so as to find a way to resolve them without having them affect the promotion of relations between the two countries.

After establishing two groups of experts from the two countries to deal with border issues and the Dong Jing (Tonkin) Gulf issue, the two sides agreed to set up an additional group of experts to consult on issues relating to territorial waters. The above shows that the peaceful resolution of the Nansha issue was another important step forward. It is believed that through joint efforts, the common aspiration of building the South China Sea into a peaceful and developed area, and of building the Pacific into a real pacific ocean would come true soon.

CONCLUSION

China is South East Asia's reliable and trustworthy neighbor, as well as an important source for world peace and stability. Chinese development cannot be separated from that of the world, and the world's development benefits from China. At this vital moment of tremendous change, China is facing the great historical mission to deepen reform and develop economically as soon as possible. China urgently needs a long-term peaceful and stable international and domestic environment. It is a fundamental national policy to preserve honest and friendly cooperation with China's neighbors, including South East Asia, and promote the peace and development of the whole Asia-Pacific region. China does not have any political or territorial ambitions in South East Asia and its interests in the region are legitimate and according to the principles of international law. The greatest interest for Chinese is to never pursue power politics; even as China grows stronger in the future, China will never act as a hegemonist. In the future, China will stand shoulder to shoulder with South East Asian countries to play a constructive role and make an active contribution to keeping stability, maintain reasonable economic order, promote the establishment of regional security mechanisms and resolve regional disputes via peaceful means.

INDIA'S ROLE IN
SOUTH EAST ASIA

C. Raja Mohan

INTRODUCTION

The re-emergence of India on the South East Asian scene has been one of the more interesting developments in the region over the last few years. Despite strong historical and cultural links and some early warmth for each other in the postcolonial era, India and the nations of ASEAN steadily drifted apart during the Cold War. In the 1980s, ASEAN became highly suspicious of the expansion of Indian defense capabilities and its strategic intentions. The cleavage between ASEAN and Indo-China, and the Indian tilt toward the latter, further clouded India's relations with the region.

The end of the Cold War has liberated India from the restrictive confines of bipolarity in Asia. The strategic nexus between New Delhi and Moscow and the American alignment with Pakistan and China had severely restricted India's room for maneuver in Asia in the last two decades of the Cold War. The collapse of the Soviet Union, the end of the Cold War, and the altered regional context has opened up unprecedented opportunities for Indian strategic interaction with the United States, China, Japan, Taiwan, South Korea, Australia, ASEAN countries, and Indo-China.

Dr. C. Raja Mohan is the Washington correspondent of The Hindu, *a leading English language daily published from Madras and six other centers in India. Prior to his current position, he was a Jennings Randolph Peace Fellow at the United States Institute of Peace, Washington, DC. Dr. Mohan specializes in issues of arms control, nonproliferation, and regional and international security.*

After years of marginalization from the East, India has been engaged in an ostpolitik aimed at deepening and broadening India's relationships in the region. Nevertheless the determination of the Indian government's thrust to the East has begun to pay dividends, if only modest at this point. The broad public support to the policy "looking East" ensures that India's Ostpolitik will be a sustained and intensive process.

Although initially reluctant, the region has begun to respond to the Indian overtures with some enthusiasm. Both New Delhi and ASEAN are beginning to recognize the mutuality of interests in opening up a broad-based interaction including economic, political and security cooperation.

Despite the steady improvement of India's bilateral relations with the key great powers as well as the South East Asian nations, and the significant potential the current Indian interaction with the East may hold for the future, there is no consensus in Asia on the kind of role India could play in the current multilateral initiatives in the region to promote economic integration, reduce political tensions and stabilize the security situation.

This paper briefly delineates the Indian perception of the security environment in South East Asia, and presents an analysis of Indian interests in the region. The paper will examine the recent Indian strategic interaction with the great powers as well as the South East Asian nations and ends with a brief discussion of the prospects for Indian contribution to multilateralism in South East Asia.

THE CHANGING SECURITY ENVIRONMENT

The region has seen unprecedented economic growth, and ASEAN has emerged as an economic powerhouse. Once-poor ASEAN states have transformed themselves into rich and prosperous nations. The laggards of the region, Vietnam and Burma, appear to be on the verge of sustained economic growth. Yet despite the prosperity and long economic and political cooperation with the West, the leaders of ASEAN are now caught in an ideological debate with the West on the question of values. The relationship between democracy and development and the role of human rights are issues that have driven apart long-standing allies, the United

States and ASEAN. The South East Asian leaders, who have gained enormous self-confidence over the decades of economic growth are dismayed to discover that the United States is leading an ideological assault against them in the name of promoting human rights and democracy. They are concerned that the rhetoric on human rights has also become a cover for rising protectionism in the United States and the West. Their anger often veers towards the perception that the United States is not only facing economic but also cultural decline and the United States can cope with its own crisis of values by looking East.[1]

At the heart of the new East-West ideological divide is the dispute over sovereignty. The post-Cold War foreign policy thought in the United States has emphasized the decline of the relevance of notion of sovereignty in the post-Cold War world. The impulses of rapid economic integration, instantaneous global flows of capital and information, the imperatives of spreading democracy and the new power of human rights internationalism have made the traditional notions of sovereignty meaningless, many in the West have argued. In the East, sovereignty remains a valued political concept critical for preserving autonomous social development, and choosing one's own political system. The South East Asian nations are unwilling to submit to what they see as attempts by the West to homogenize the international system in name of universal human values. This "civilizational clash" has unified the leaders in the region who represent different political systems in China, India, Indo-China, and ASEAN.

The reordering of the great power relations has generated fears among the South East Asian states about a "power vacuum" in the region. The fears are largely based on the sense of a possible declining commitment of the United States towards South East Asia. American leaders have repeatedly sought to reassure the region that the United States will stay engaged—militarily and politically, but the question keeps coming up.[2] In its first 2 years the Clinton administration's policies towards the region saw pointless fights over trade and human rights with almost all the key nations of the ASEAN—Singapore, Indonesia and Malaysia. Concerns among the South East Asian nations about declining American engagement now have turned into challenges against the kind of attention they are getting from Washington. Despairing over American policy towards the region, the Assistant Secretary of State for East Asia and the Pacific wrote in a memo to Secretary Warren Christopher, "They now are beginning to resist the nature of [the U.S.] engagement.[3]

The apprehensions about American disengagement and the consequent "power vacuum" in the region have now been overtaken by the fears that China is emerging as the "hegemon on the horizon."[4] The hopes that China will steadily move towards greater economic integration with the rest of the world by further economic reform and would essentially be a benign power in the region are being replaced by concerns that China might use its new found capabilities—economic and military—to further its political and territorial ambitions in the region. The South East Asian nations are apprehensive about the growing military capability of China and sense that it will not be averse to using it for political purposes. Even in the normally taciturn South East Asia there is open expression of fears about China. If the South East Asians had been troubled by the assertion of Chinese sovereignty over much of the South China Sea under the 1992 Chinese Law on Territorial Waters and Contiguous Zones, they have been alarmed by the recent Chinese actions in the Spratlys, including the takeover of Mischief Reef just 135 miles from the Philippines. Over the last few years the South East Asian states believed that sustained engagement of China is necessary, even as they worried about the expanding Chinese power. There are growing thoughts now about containment of China in the region, but few in the region would want to make it open and invite hostility from Beijing. Finding a right balance between engagement and containment of China will be the biggest challenge for the other Asian great powers as well as the nations of South East Asia.

The drift toward balance of power arrangements, even as multilateral approaches are being widely discussed in the region, are likely to aggravate mutual suspicions among the Asian great powers. This complicates the traditional alliance systems in the region and exacerbates insecurities in South East Asia. A major reflection of the new insecurities and the determination to expand one's own leverages in the new balance of power game is the emerging arms buildup among a number of Asian states. While it might be premature to call it an arms race[5] as some have done, the reality of the expanding military capabilities in the region is difficult to ignore. It must be noted, however, that the South East Asian nations are partly propelled by the need to modernize their military forces and beef up their rudimentary naval forces as they shift focus from domestic counter-insurgency threats of the earlier decades to external maritime threats envisaged in the 1990s. Besides, there are supply side pressures from the arms manufacturers who have come to see exports as important to preserve jobs as well as the defense industrial base at home.

Besides the potential for conflict from the persistent territorial and border disputes among the states of the region, there is also growing concern about the consequences of intra-state tensions. The South East Asian nations have enjoyed a prolonged period of domestic stability and have successfully coped with the internal threats to security. But the prospects for ethnic tension and religious conflict cannot be considered remote. Most states of the region are multiethnic and the threats to internal stability are never too far from the surface. Uneven development, insufficient internal democratization, the lack of federal tradition and inadequate protection of minority rights have the potential to create trouble anywhere and South East Asia is not immune, notwithstanding the claims for the "Asian Way."[6] As it gains influence across a large part of the Afro-Asian world, Islamic fundamentalism will remain a major challenge to some of the South East Asian nations. Although Indonesia, the world's largest Islamic nation, has managed to contain the threat of fundamentalism at home, the possibility for a surge of Islamic militancy cannot perhaps be totally discounted. Besides Islamic fundamentalism there are a host of other nonconventional security threats in the region, including piracy, narcotics trade, refugee flows, and environmental degradation.

Among these, piracy comes closest to the traditional security concerns about protecting sea lanes of communication. According to the Malaysian based International Maritime Bureau, during 1991-93 incidents of piracy in the South And East China Sea accounted for half the total such acts worldwide.[7] The South East Asian nations are concerned that the line between Chinese antismuggling operations and piracy by rogue elements of the Chinese armed forces are beginning to blur. There is also apprehension that the Chinese navy is deliberately staging the incidents of piracy to buttress its claims of sovereignty in the South China Sea.

As the new security situation unfolds in Asia, two broad views of the prospects for peace and stability in the region have emerged. The pessimistic view suggests the inevitability of conflict and tension in the region and argues that the ongoing processes of economic integration and multilateral discussions on security are unlikely to prevent a dangerous drift to war.[8] The pessimists also argue that power politics will triumph over the imperatives of interdependence and collective approaches to security. The optimists, however, suggest that the Western impatience with the slow evolution of institutional development in Asia may be off the mark. They argue that the Asians prefer a low-key diplomacy and promotion of cooperation through informal understandings, and not the formal institution building favored by the Western diplomatic approach.[9] Some Asians have reacted strongly to the predictions of inevitable conflict in the region. Mahbubani of Singapore has written that Western projections of doom in Asia "are not merely analytical predictions, but indicate the wish of status quo powers that East Asia not surpass them. This tendency to extrapolate the future of East Asia and the Pacific from the past of Europe reveals an intellectual blindness: the inability to see that non-Europeans may have reached a stage of development where they can progress without having to repeat Europe's mistakes.[10]

INTERESTS IN SOUTH EAST ASIA

Since the end of the Cold War, India has been grappling with two daunting tasks, reorienting its foreign policy after the demise of the Soviet Union, and embarking on fundamental structural reform of its economy that had drifted toward state-led socialism since the late 1960s. The simultaneity of these two challenges was compounded by the end of the Nehru-Gandhi dynasty at home and the enormous weakening of the 100-year-old Congress Party. Yet the Indian government under the leadership of Prime Minister Narasimha Rao has succeeded in reworking its relations with almost all the major powers, setting in motion a process of economic reform that has won international recognition.

As India coped with the twin challenges of economic and foreign policy reorientation, Asia-Pacific in general, and South East Asia in particular, have become a region of prime importance for India.[11] The India that traditionally looked toward the West and North in addressing its security dilemmas has now recognized the great importance of the East in its urgent drive to transform itself. Since the early 1990s India has reached out systematically to all the nations in the region seeking to rebuild political relations and expand commercial links. There have been a surfeit of exchanges at the highest political and economic level between India and South East Asia in the recent years, that has laid the basis for strong potential partnerships at the bilateral level with all the major players of the South East Asian region. India hopes this will eventually lead to fruitful interaction with the new institutional structures under consideration in the region.

Economics

Commerce and trade are the driving forces behind India's current eastern orientation, but security and political factors are not too far behind in the Indian overtures to South East Asia. Given India's openly expressed desire to participate in many of the multilateral institutions in the region including the ASEAN Regional Forum designed to address security issues, it will be difficult to separate India's economic and security strategies in South East Asia.   India is looking for a comprehensive engagement of the region, seeking progress, however limited, in every possible direction.

India had long turned its back on international trade, by adopting the inward-looking import substitution strategy, but New Delhi is now seeking to become a major trading nation. As India seeks to carve out international markets for its goods, it cannot rely just on its traditional destinations in Western Europe, Russia and the United States for the very high growth rate in trade it needs. It recognizes that getting a piece of the action in Asia, where the economies continue to grow at phenomenal rates, is crucial. Besides the importance of tapping the Asian markets, India has been concerned at the emergence of regional trading blocs, just when it has embarked on a strategy of trade led growth. Fears about being isolated from the new trends have pushed India into seeking integration into the Asian trading arrangements. Starting as it does from a very low trading base, India needs reliable partnerships and hopes Asia will provide them. As Prime Minister Rao said in his Singapore lecture in September 94, Asia will be "our springboard to the global market place.[12]

In terms of complemental aspirations, Singapore offers the best foil to India's capabilities, and has been the most enthusiastic in its response to Indian commercial overtures to the region. The Prime Minister of Singapore has sought to promote a "mild India fever" in the city state to balance the ongoing China fever. Singapore believes the prospects for economic growth in South Asia could offer it a second wing to maintain its soaring economic prosperity. Singapore has surplus funds to invest, skills in tourism, industrial planning, and urban development. Singapore can act as a gateway to business with and from India. The Prime Ministers of Singapore and India have met three times in less than 12 months during the last year, and the relationship is deepening. Singapore's support will be important for India's integration into the multilateral structures in South East Asia.

Even as it seeks to join APEC and ASEAN in the east, India is also looking for cooperation among the states of the Indian Ocean rim. South Africa is keen on promoting such a mechanism, and India has enthusiastically backed it.[13]   India, South Africa, Mauritius, Australia, Kenya, Oman, Sri Lanka, and Singapore, are other nations that have reportedly expressed interest in such a grouping. India and South Africa do not see such a grouping as a rival to ASEAN and APEC, but as another inclusive grouping that would draw together the booming South East Asia nations as well as other Indian Ocean rim states. Supporting the proposal, and calling for a conference of the Indian Ocean rim states in June 1995, Australian foreign minister Gareth Evans said, "We're not talking about exclusive trade blocs, we're talking about regional economic cooperation arrangements which together and individually work to advance the larger objective of international trade liberalization.[14]

India sees its participation in larger trading arrangements as critical in its current efforts to break out of the inability of the South Asian nations to promote trade liberalization among themselves, thanks to the opposition from Pakistan.   It could indeed be argued that given India's size and economic potential, it need not rush into free trade arrangements with other nations. Supporting the thrust under GATT/WTO toward liberalization of the global trading regime may be seen as adequate to meet India's requirements. But given the current instability of its trade structure, India is keen to become part of a larger regional trading arrangements. The proposal for a trading bloc among the rim states of the Indian Ocean, long seen in New Delhi as its natural region for external engagement, has been received warmly in

India, but New Delhi recognizes that free trade in the Indian Ocean region is only for the long term and that it can be achieved only in cooperation with the trading nations to the east of the Indian Ocean.

South East Asia also offers a large potential for joint ventures for the Indian companies. About 148 Indian companies already have a presence in the APEC region mostly in South East Asia. [15] Many large Indian companies have ambitious plans to turn themselves into multinational entities, as they restructure themselves at home to become globally competitive.[16] Many of them, including the Birlas, Essar Gujarat, Ranbaxy, and Thapars, have experience of operations in South East Asia and are likely to look forward to major manufacturing activity in the region. India has long standing economic links with the countries of Indo-China, although much of it has been focused around intergovernmental cooperation. As Vietnam steps out as the next Asian tiger, New Delhi has some economic oppportunities to offer.

Export of labor is likely to be another major Indian economic interest in the region. Since the 1970s, India has gained significant foreign remittances from its expatriate labor in the Middle East. Now, South East Asia appears to offer a similar potential. India exports labor at both ends of the spectrum—semi-skilled labor as well as medical and computer professionals. South East Asia is now importing labor, and India can be expected to meet some of the demand [17]

Political and Strategic Interests

India has a range of political and strategic interests in South East Asia. The pursuit of some of these interests in the past, most notably forays into Indo-China,[18] contributed to cooling of Indian relations with ASEAN and the United States. India's support to the Indo-Chinese states and its recognition of the Heng Samrin regime in Cambodia in the early 1980s ran headlong into the position the ASEAN states had adopted.[19] Although satisfied that phase of mutual suspicion between the two sides is now over, and India could contribute toward stabilizing the balance of power in the region and open up important opportunities for political and strategic cooperation between India and the South East Asian nations, neither side is prepared to make this explicit at this stage of evolution of Asian relations. The developments in the region, however, may be nudging the two sides toward greater cooperation in the realm of security. For example, India is naturally sympathetic to the South East Asian concerns about Chinese intentions in South China Sea. India and South East Asia do also share the objective of limiting the emerging Chinese influence in Burma.

Burma, naturally, is of immediate concern to India, which has been worried about the growing Chinese economic, political, and military presence in Burma. For decades, any expansion of Chinese influence among Indian neighbors has been a source of great discomfort to India. Three major Indian concerns stand out in relation to Burma:

- India prefers Burma remains a peaceful, stable and neutral buffer state between India and China. Excessive tilt towards China by the Burmese leadership is seen as inimical to India's interests.

- India has always been concerned about the instability in its North Eastern provinces that have seen prolonged insurgencies and the region continues to be restive.[20] In the 1960s, India was concerned about Chinese aid to insurgencies in the region through Burma. With the overt penetration of China into Burma, New Delhi is apprehensive that China will acquire additional leverages against India. Burma has a long land border with these North Eastern provinces, and India is concerned about rampant smuggling operations and the flow of narcotics from Burma through these provinces.

- India is worried about the growing Chinese arms sales to Burma, the increasing profile of the Chinese navy in the Bay of Bengal, and the reports about Chinese military facilities in the Cocos Islands, just north of the Indian Andaman.[21] A member of a recent Indian delegation from the Institute of Defence Studies and Analyses that visited Burma wrote, "In the great game that will unfold in the next century, transborder 'presence' will become a major tool in the inventory of nations and China seems to have a clear perception of where it will establish such presence and how it will use it."

These fears about rising Chinese presence in Burma have forced India to adopt a more moderate policy toward the military regime in Rangoon. After initially treating the regime as a pariah state and putting public pressure to release the jailed leader Aung

San Su Kyi, New Delhi has taken a more pragmatic approach of engaging the Burmese regime, with the hope that it can be wooed away from total dependence on China.[22] India's new approach toward Burma is in line with the tone of the ASEAN policy, which has opposed the punitive diplomacy of the United States and called instead for constructive engagement of the regime. India would prefer the integration of Burma into a web of interdependence with the ASEAN rather than push it deeper into a Chinese embrace.

As one of the major naval powers of the region, India has a strong interest in protecting the sea lanes of communication in the Indian Ocean, including its eastern part. The growth of the Indian Navy in the 1980s and its strengthening of operations off the Andaman islands, its actions in Maldives and Sri Lanka, and its acquisition of a nuclear powered submarine from the Soviet Union triggered intense speculation in South East Asia about India's intentions. Part of the blame must be laid at the door of New Delhi, which failed to explain the reasons for its naval expansion and its legitimate maritime interest.[23] The reaction from South East Asia was also partly driven by Cold War considerations and the fact that India was close to the Soviet Union and Vietnam. For some of the ASEAN states, the criticism of the Indian Naval expansion was an indirect way of expressing concern about the expansion of Chinese naval capabilities, but in the changed international context there is much greater appreciation of India's maritime interests in the region.

The sea lanes of communication in the region will acquire greater importance in the future not just because of the current tensions over the Spratly Islands. Oil and energy politics could emerge as paramount concerns in the future as China becomes a net importer of oil. If the present economic growth rates are sustained in Asia in general, and India and China in particular, there may be enormous pressure on the oil market resulting in the upward movement of oil prices and bringing the protection of sea lanes of communication to the center-stage of geopolitics in the Indian Ocean and South East Asi.[24] India, which straddles the sea lanes between the Western and Eastern parts of Asia, believes it has an important role in the protection of SLOCs.

As it transforms its economy,   India has a fundamental interest in the stability and prosperity of the South East Asian region. Having hinged its own success to the dynamism of the

South East Asian economies, New Delhi would like to see the sustained growth in the region that could help lift India's own economic condition. At the political level, India, unlike China, has always been a status quo power with no territorial or hegemonic ambitions over Asia. And, unlike Japan, India's historic interaction with South East Asia has been a happy one. India believes that, as a nation with significant military capabilities and enormous potential for economic growth, it could contribute towards broadening of the power structure in Asia-Pacific and thus help the stabilization of the Asia and the Pacific in the difficult times ahead.

Despite being a long-standing democracy, India does not believe in exporting its values to the rest of the world. On the other hand, India has joined hands with the other Asian powers in resisting attempts by the West to impose its cultural values on the East. India also hopes the South East Asian nations will be able to contain the spread of Islamic fundamentalism in the region. As the home to one of the largest Islamic populations, India will do its best to prevent the emergence of a paradigm of "Islam versus the rest." Such an outcome would not be in the Indian interest, and it prefers that tolerance and moderation—the ancient virtues of the East—would prevail in Asia and provide a boost its own dramatic experiment in pluralism.

BALANCE OF POWER

Two major objectives of New Delhi stand out in relation to South East Asia—the economic integration into the region and participation in an expanded structure of balance of power in Asia. The past few years have seen intensive Indian engagement of the four great powers that have had the greatest influence in shaping the destiny of South East Asia in the recent years—United States, Russia, China, and Japan. There has been significant movement in Indian relations with all these countries since the end of the Cold War. The nature of the Indian interaction with these great powers is likely to have significant impact on the kind of role India could play in South East Asia.

Among the four powers, there is a big question mark over the changing role of Russia in the South East Asian region. There are good reasons to argue that the significance and influence of Moscow in Asia is on the decline.[25] Preoccupied as it is with "near abroad," Russia is unlikely to contribute directly to the shaping of the security environment in the region for the foreseeable future. But in an indirect manner, Russia could still contribute to the dynamic of changing balance of power among the great powers. By acting as a source of a number of key strategic and military technologies, Russia may be facilitating the rapid military modernization of Chinese nuclear weapons, missiles and conventional arms. The latest in the series of Chinese military purchases from Russia, and of particular concern for South East Asia, are said to be four diesel submarines.[26] Of long term consequence for the region is the extraordinary fit between a cash-poor but technology-rich Russia and cash-rich and technology-poor China in the arena of arms production.

The collapse of the Soviet Union had sharply brought into relief the excessive Indian defense dependence, particularly of the Indian Air Force, on Moscow. The chaos in the former Soviet Union had also adversely affected India's large trade and energy cooperation with Moscow. Previous arrangements, such as the transfer of cryogenic rocket technology, came under pressure from the United States, which has been concerned about the growing Indian missile and space programs. After more than 3 years of confusion, New Delhi and Moscow appear to have sorted some of the problems relating to cooperation in defense supplies and have made a political decision, during Prime Minister Rao's visit to Russia in mid 1994, to revive their sagging cooperatio.[27]

The revival of defense cooperation between Washington and Moscow has acquired an interesting dimension in relation to South East Asia. Faced with a declining international sales of its weapons, Russia has made a determined bid to sell arms to South East Asian nations and succeeded in selling MiG 29 aircraft to Malaysi.[28] India and Russia have now signed an agreement to set up an aviation company to produce spares and provide services to MiG range fighter aircraft in India and elsewhere.[29] If successful, such a venture could help acquire self-sufficiency in a key sector as well as give it opportunities to export defense items. Meanwhile, Malaysia has an agreement with India to train its air force pilots and technicians in the use of MiG 29.[30] The defence cooperation between India and Malaysia, although small, symbolizes the prospect for larger security cooperation between India and South East Asia.

India's relations with China entered a complex and dynamic phase in the 1990s. The Sino-Indian hostility of the 1960s and 1970s yielded to a limited dialogue on resolving intractable border disputes in the early 1980s. After a brief tension on the border in the mid 1980s, the relations have seen substantial expansion. Once the two sides decided in the late 1980s not to hold improvement of relations hostage to the resolution of the border dispute, bilateral cooperation has blossomed in a number of fields. On the border question itself, India and China have moved towards making the line of actual control on their border into a line of "peace and tranquility." The two sides have instituted a number of confidence building measures on the border, such as "hot-lines" and regular meetings between field commanders; during Prime Minister Rao's visit to China in September 1993, New Delhi and Beijing agreed to reduce troop concentrations on the border and expand the CBM regime to include nonviolation of air space.[31] The relaxation of tensions on the Sino-Indian border has given rise to a new sense of confidence within the Indian military that the "short-term Chinese threat is all but over.[32]

But the longer term view in India is different. Many Indians believe China remains a long-term military threat to India. The primary justification for the Indian nuclear and missile programs remains the perceived threat from China. Other Indian concerns provide a limit to the ongoing Sino-Indian rapprochement, including apprehensions about expanding Chinese influence in South Asia, and now in Burma, the continuing strategic nexus between Islamabad and Beijing, and the Chinese naval expansion into the Indian Ocean. The Chinese, too, are worried about Tibet and the potential for mischief there by India, and they have expressed misgivings about Indian military capabilities, particularly in the naval sector. At the same time, the two sides see significant benefits in expanding bilateral cooperation. For India the new relationship with China has been an important tool in preventing Beijing from actively siding with Pakistan in the Kashmir dispute. Given its concerns on Islamic fundamentalism and its impact on Western China, Beijing has come out against independence for Kashmir and has occasionally restrained Pakistan from internationalizing the dispute.[33] As it struggles to resist American pressure on human rights, trade, and other global multilateral issues, China has found Indian support convenient.

Despite the intense ambivalence about each other, China and India have found themselves cooperating in some key strategic areas. China and India have ongoing cooperation in space technology and interesting complementary capabilities—China is strong in launchers and India has advanced in the building of various types of satellites. This cooperation has extended even to the sensitive nuclear field. When India was thoroughly isolated on the question of getting enriched uranium fuel supplies for its Tarapur Atomic Power Plant, China stepped in to supply the fuel without insisting on full-scope nuclear safeguards. There has been talk about Sino-Indian cooperation in the development of a civilian airliner, and China has reportedly expressed interest in collaborating with India in the production of a Light Combat Aircraft.[34]

India 's approach to China clearly reflects the very same ambiguity that most Asian nations face in dealing with China. There are strong concerns about the emerging Chinese power, and at the same time there are strong incentives for expanded cooperation. Like other nations, India, too, faces the difficulty of engaging and containing China at the same time.

In contrast to the tension and dynamism in Sino-Indian relations, Indo-Japanese relations remain tentative and inhibited. If the Indian government expected that Japan would rush in with investments at the launch of Indian reforms, it was disappointed. Among all the major economic powers, Japan has been slowest to respond to the emerging economic opportunity in India. The wait-and-watch attitude of Tokyo appears to have been a result of a number of factors including wariness about the commitment of the Indian government for sustained reform, the ongoing economic recession in Japan, and a preference for investments in China and South East Asia. There are signs of change in 1995, as Japan has identified India along with China and Vietnam as holding the most potential for economic investment. Strong Japanese interest in participating in Indian economic growth will be critical for New Delhi's aspirations to join the multilateral economic fora in Asia.

The Cold War, radically divergent foreign policy philosophies, and conflicting approaches India and Japan have taken toward America, Russia, and China throughout the last four decades had virtually precluded any serious Indo-Japanese conversation about security issues in the past. But in the changed international context, there is some prospect for a low-key political exchanges on Asian security between the two countries.

The initial foray of Japan into the field of nonproliferation, military expenditures, and human rights, as part of its new international activism, did not endear itself to New Delhi. Despite the fundamental differences between New Delhi and Tokyo on the nuclear issue, New Delhi is not unaware of Tokyo's reservations on the Nuclear Non-Proliferation Treaty (NPT). Making the Treaty permanent, India knows, will forever freeze the nuclear asymmetry between China and Japan. Interestingly, India and Japan found themselves on the same side at the United Nations in the fall of 1994, when the two countries initiated moves urging the abolition of nuclear weapons. However, under pressure from the United States, which wanted no moves that could complicate the indefinite extension of the NPT in May 1995, both New Delhi and Tokyo had to tone down their disarmament activism at the United Nations.

As concerns mount in both India and Japan about Chinese military capabilities, it is possible to conceive of a growing, if limited, convergence of interests between New Delhi and Tokyo. Both of them, however, will be constrained from such an open concert, given their own separate but complex relations with Beijing, but the two could initiate cooperation in such noncontroversial areas as international peacekeeping, and open up regular meetings between the two national security establishments.

The most important relationship, from the point of view of India's ambition to be part of Asian security structures, is the one with the United States. Chafing as it did at the emergence of a unipolar world at the end of the Cold War, achieving a *modus vivendi* with the United States has been one of the principal foreign policy objectives of India in the 1990s. Much of India's diplomatic energies in this period have been devoted to providing stability to Indo-U.S. relations, In the last 5 five years, Indo-U.S. ties have expanded significantly; although it needs to be remembered that the two countries had set in motion elements of this process during the mid 1980s. It is only with the end of the constricting Cold War·that the door for tapping the full potential of Indo-U.S. relations has opened.

The attempts to rework the relationship in the 1990s has seen many ups and downs. During 1993-94, the bilateral ties sank to their lowest point as the Clinton administration sought to promote human rights, push diplomatic solutions to the conflict in Kashmir, and curb India's nuclear and missile programs. As the American approach began to recoil, the Clinton administration shifted to a quieter diplomacy on controversial issues, searched for minimum possible accommodation on difficult issues, gave greater emphasis to India as one of the big emerging markets, and set in motion high-level political exchanges between the two countries. The new approach appears to be paying dividends to both sides.

From the security point of view, the most important development has been the recent visit to India by U.S. Secretary of Defense William Perry and the signing of an agreement that set forth broad parameters for defense interaction between the two countries.[35] The agreement was only codifying what was already in place for awhile: expanding cooperation between the military services of the two countries, that will include regular joint military exercises that will steadily expand in scope and sophistication; promoting cooperation in defense research and production; and further cooperation in international peacekeeping. The agreement added an apex body consisting of civilian officials from the Pentagon and the Ministry of Defense, who will direct and coordinate the defence cooperation between the two sides.

Cautioning against exaggerated expectations from the defense cooperation agreement, an American observer has written, "Concretely, it can contribute to Asian Security by ensuring open sea-lanes in the Indian Ocean and South East Asia through joint naval exercises. Closer U.S.-Indian security ties will thus add a new element to the evolving security architecture of the Asia-Pacific region.[36]

While there is potential significance to Asian security from the emerging Indo-U.S. security cooperation, most analysts keep their fingers crossed. There are important reservations on both sides, and it will be a long while before India and the United States can overcome their doubts. As Secretary Perry has stated, India remains an unknown commodity for the U.S. defense establishment. There is not enough confidence in the Pentagon that India can be a reliable partner, and many in the United States recall the Indian decision to withdraw refuelling facilities it had offered the United States during the Gulf War. The United States is also not certain whether the Indian political leadership can overcome the domestic political opposition to deepening Indo-U.S. defense interaction.

From the Indian side, there is unhappiness at the inability of the United States to firm up the prospects for defence technology transfer. New Delhi is also concerned at the failure of the United States to liberate the Indo-U.S. relationship from being hostage to the Pakistani factor.[37] Few American agencies are willing to look at India on its own merit; the only honorable exceptions to this appear to be the U.S. Commerce Department and the U.S. Pacific Command, whose "jurisdiction" touches India but not Pakistan.

Clearly India has come a long way from the days when it appeared to campaign for the withdrawal of U.S. forces and bases from the Indian Ocean. But today, there is growing understanding in India that continued American presence in Asia and the Indian Ocean region is not inimical to its interests. "Asia without America" could well imply a free for all jousting among the Asian powers, an outcome far worse than the present one in the region. The objectives of India, as a status quo power in the region, are widely seen in New Delhi as being compatible with the American strategy of preventing the domination of Asia by any one particular power.

One of the major developments in Indian foreign policy in the 1990s has been the end of its military isolationism. The policy of nonalignment insulated Indian armed forces from international interaction, despite a long tradition of external involvement. After its independence, India did retain military links with the British Commonwealth and participated in some of the joint military exercises (which included Pakistan as well). India also was active in U.N. peacekeeping operations, but the impact of the great power politics on the subcontinent, the radical reinterpretation of nonalignment under Mrs.Gandhi in the late 1960s, the formalist reading of the membership criteria of the nonaligned movement in relation to military links with great powers, and India's championing of the Indian Ocean as a Zone of Peace pushed India into military isolation. Although India and Soviet Union warmed up to military cooperation in the 1960s, Indian political leadership proscribed service-to-service interaction, joint military exercises, and other forms of strategic interaction with the Soviet armed forces.

Not only has India shed its military isolationism, it has also shown considerable interest in using its armed forces, though in a limited way so far, in an effort to develop security cooperation with many nations in South East Asia. Besides the United States with which India now has an agreement to conduct military exercises of steadily increasing sophistication, New Delhi has opened out for exercises with a large number of other countries in the region, including Australia, Singapore, Malaysia, Indonesia and Thailand. [38] Besides bilateral exercises, India has also sought to promote multilateral naval fleet concentrations involving India and its South East Asian neighbors. In February 1995 the first such rendezvous occurred at Port Blair, the capital of India's Andaman and Nicobar Islands. Among those agreed to participate were Thailand, Malaysia, Singapore, Indonesia and Vietnam.[39] India had also reportedly invited Bangladesh, Sri Lanka, and Burma to join these multilateral exercises in naval confidence building, but had declined for different reasons.

Clearly, suspicions of the Indian naval intentions in South East Asia are now a thing of the past and India's efforts at reaching appear to be paying off. "The naval environment in our security zone has improved substantially and there is better understanding of our security concerns by our littoral neighbors", according to the top official of the Indian Defence Ministry.[40] Pointing to the long-term significance of India's initiatives, he said, "Asia's security is best guaranteed by Asian nations themselves through self-reliance and co-operation. Improved political relations and increased transparency in military postures would be necessary and provide the basis for confidence-building.[41]

Besides joint exercises, India and South East Asia are also looking toward greater cooperation in military training and arms production. Singapore has been interested in using some of Indian military facilities. Singapore has already used the Indian missile testing facilities at Chandipur and is also interested in developing ASW capabilities in cooperation with India [42]

Defense cooperation between India and Malaysia appears to have considerable potential. Besides the MiG 29 agreement, Malaysia has reportedly expressed interest in the training of marine commando forces and servicing its naval boats in India. It is also looking at the possible purchase of defense equipment from India.[43] Indonesia, which had purchased a large number of East German ships, is looking toward New Delhi for arrangements to maintain and repair its naval ships at Indian dockyards. Such an arrangement could be mutually beneficial, with Indian shipyards looking for work and the Indonesians for a reliable partner. According to an official of the Indonesian embassy in New Delhi, "We are looking for a permanent or long-term place to maintain and repair our naval fleet. As Indonesian maritime boundaries are very near to the Indian coastal border, India suits our requirements."[44] Thailand is also considering expanded defense interaction with India that could expand cooperation in training and allow Indian suppliers of defense equipment to participate in the bidding for the requirements of the Thai armed force.[45] India also signed an agreement with Vietnam in September 1994 to provide training and other assistance to its armed forces that could include eventual upgrade of Vietnamese equipmen.[46]

As India opens its doors for extensive military interaction with its neighbors to the East as well as with the United States, New Delhi may be prepared to consider a wide range of other options, including institutionalization of cooperation in peacekeeping, opening commercial and military access to Indian naval facilities, protecting sea-lanes, joint efforts against piracy, sharing of intelligence, promoting maritime research, and environmental preservation.

CONCLUSIONS

As India seeks to join the economic and security multilateralism in Asia, it is not unaware of the uncertainty and ambiguity that surrounds the current efforts in the region. Like Europe, Asia has now acquired its own alphabet soup: ASEAN, AFTA, APEC, ARF, EAEC, FPDA and now South East Asia Community. Even as the South East Asian nations and ASEAN have acquired an international identity after three decades of patient diplomacy, there are profound apprehensions about the meaning, scope, direction and pace of the new multilateral initiatives. There is also the fear that ASEAN might have become the victim of its own success. Some fear an enlarged economic grouping such as APEC might reduce the identity and influence of ASEAN as a group.

On the security side, the creation of ARF is an important achievement for ASEAN, but it is nowhere near the problem-solving stage; ARF may be "threatening to eventually take on a life of its own and, perhaps, disown its parentage."[47] As ARF becomes the vehicle for conceiving the larger security architecture of Asia, some believe the great powers could end up calling the shots. Further, there is no consensus among the great powers or among the group as a whole on the basic principles that should guide the multilateral security efforts. For the United States, the security multilateralism is a means to cope with current uncertainty, before the faultlines of the Asian strategic scene become clear. Beijing rejects the current talk about the Chinese threat and is concerned about the current security multilateralism transforming itself into an overt alliance against it.[48] Australia has reportedly expressed the hope that the Five Power Defence Arrangement "could be made the basis of a wider regional alliance incorporating the other members of Association of South East Asian Nations (ASEAN).[49] Indonesia, against whom the FPDA was created, has natural reservations about continuing the FPDA in the changed circumstances.

The current focus on the security multilateralism regarding confidence-building measures such as transparency is useful, but it is easy to overstate their significance. The CBMs in Europe served a stabilizing purpose between two competing alliances that had reached a military stalemate, but the context is radically different in Asia, where the biggest uncertainties relate to the future evolution of the policies of the major powers and their interaction in the years to come. The CBMs currently under consideration are unlikely to achieve very much, given the larger strategic questions that remain unanswered in Asia. The current security multilateralism in Asia is clearly a holding operation, and India as a leading military power with a significant economic potential is waiting in the wings carefully observing the scene, expanding its engagement of the region and getting prepared to contribute its bit to the promotion of peace and stability in Asia.

NOTES

1. Kishore Mahbuani, "The United States: 'Go East, Young Man'," Washington Quarterly (Spring 1994): 5 - 23.

2. Richard C. Macke, "Rest assured, America's Asia-Pacific commitment is here to stay," *International Herald Tribune*, January 13, 1995.

3. For a report on the leaked memo of Mr. Lord, see Susumu Awanahara, "About Face: U.S. policy architect has a change of heart," *Far Eastern Economic Review*, May 19, 1994, 22-23.

4. There has been a large amount of discussion of the rise of China and its implications for international security and Asian relations. See Nicholas D. Kristoff, "Rise of China," *Foreign Affairs* (November-

December 1993): 59-74; Denny Roy, "Hegemon on the Horizon? China's Threat to East Asian Security," *International Security* (Summer 1994): 149-68; Michael G. Gallagher, "China's Illusorty Threat to the South China Sea," ibid., 169-194; Richard L. Grant, "China and its Asian Neighbors: Looking Toward the Twenty-First Century," *Washington Quarterly* (Winter 19914): 59-70.

5. Michael T. Klare, "The Next Great Arms Race," *Foreign Affairs* (Summer 1993).

6. For a discussion of the anti-Chinese violence in Sumatra in Indonesia, see "Days of Rage," *Far Eastern Economic Review*, April 28, 1994, 14-15.

7. "Gunboat Diplomacy," *Far Eastern Economic Review,* June 16, 1994, 22-28.

8. For a comprehensive articulation of the pessimistic view see Barry Buzan and Gerald Segal, "Rethinking East Asian Security," *Survival* (Summer 1994) 3-21; see also Robert A. Manning and Paula Stern, "The Myth of the Pacific Community," *Foreign Affairs* (November/December 1994): 79-93.

9. James L. Richardson, "Asia-Pacific: The Case for Geopolitical Optimism," *National Interest* (Winter 1994/95): 28-39.

10. "The Pacific Way," *Foreign Affairs* (January/February 1995): 102.

11. Sunanda K. Datta-Ray, "India Looks East, Belatedly Taking Nehru's Advice," *International Herald Tribune*, February 24, 1994.

12. Salil Tripathi, "Rediscovering the East," *India Today*, September 30, 1994, 36.

13. John F.Burns, "Mandela, Visiting India, Discusses Arms Exports and an Indian Ocean Trading Bloc," *New York Times*, January 30, 1995, A 6.

14. "Australia Calls Meet on Ocean Grouping," AFP report, *The Hindu*, February 9, 1995.

15. Indian Prime Minister Narasimha Rao in his public address in Singapore on September 8, 1994. For the text see, *Strategic Digest*, October 1994.

16. Daksesh Parikh, "Indian Multinationals: On the Wings of Hope," *India Today*, September 15, 1994, 86-90; see also S. Satyanarayan, "Birla Plans Big Thailand Expansion," *India Abroad*, December 2, 1994.

17. "Room at the Inn: Migrant Labor-the unsung hero of Asia's development," editorial in *Far Eastern Economic Review*, Dec.29/Jan.5, 1995, 5; see also "Family Ties: Indian Villagers take on unwanted Thai jobs," ibid., September 1, 1994.

18. John W. Garver, "Chinese-Indian Rivalry in Indo-China," *Asian Survey*, November 1987.

19. For a discussion of Indian compulsions on Cambodia in the early 1980s and its insensitivity and lack of timing see, G.V.C. Naidu, "Post Cold War Pacific Asian Security: Indian perceptions and Options," *Delhi*

Papers, no.1 (New Delhi: Institute for Defence Studies and Analyses, September 1994), 75-76.

20. Hamish McDonald, "Rebel Redoubt: New Delhi fights tribal insurgencies in the North East," *Far Eastern Economic Review,* June 9, 1994, 31-35.

21. For a review of Chinese military cooperation with Burma, see P.Stobdan, "China Forays into Burma: Implications for India," *Strategic Analyses,* April 1993; see also Bert Lintner, "Arms for Eyes," *Far Eastern Economic Review,* December 16, 1993, 26.

22. Hamish McDonald, "Mutual Benefits: A New pragmatism Drives India's Burma Policy," *Far Eastern Economic Review,* February 3, 1994.

23. G.V.C. Naidu, 77-79.

24. For a brief discussion of the impact of Chinese and Indian demands for energy on the oil market, see "Power to the People: A Survey of Energy," *The Economist,* June 18, 1994.

25. For a discussion of the changing role of Russia in Asia, see Charles E. Ziegler, "Russia in the Asia-Pacific: A Major Power or Minor Participant," *Asian Survey,* June 1994.

26. Kathy Chen, "China Buys Russian Submarines Raising Tension Level in Region," *Wall Street Journal,* February 9, 1995, A 10.

27. Arvind R. Deo, "India and Russia Back to Normal Relations," *India Abroad,* July 15, 1994; Hamish McDonald, "The Price is Right: India turns to Russia Once Again for Arms," *Far Eastern Economic Review,* June 23, 1994, 29.

28. Michael Vatikiotis, "Wins of Change: Malaysian jet deal gives Russian an Asean Foothold," *Far Eastern Economic Review,* June 16, 1994, 20.

29. Tarun Basu, "Russia Visit Termed a Success," *India Abroad,* July 8, 1994.

30. "India to Train Foreign Pilots," *India Abroad,* August 19, 94.

31. For a discussion of recent developments in Sino-Indian relations, see Zheng Ruixiang, "Shifting Obstacles in Sino-Indian Relations," *The Pacific Review* 6, no.1, 1993, 63-70; Sumit Ganguly, "Slouching Towards a Settlement: Sino-Indian Relations 1962-93," Occasional Paper no.60, Asia Program, Woodrow Wilson Center, Washington DC, May 1994.

32. Manoj Joshi, "Shy Hands Across the Himalayas," *Asia-Pacific Defence Reporter,* April-May 1993, 15.

33. Ahmed Rashid, "South Asia: The China Factor," *Far Eastern Economic Review,* January 13, 1994.

34. "China Asks to Develop LCA Fighter with India," *Defense News,* August 15-21, 1994; "China Eyes LCA Participation," *Defense News,* January 30-February 5, 1995.

35. K.K. Katyal, "India, U.S. to confer on defence issues," Hindu International Edition, January 21, 1994; John F. Burns, "U.S.-India Pact on Military Cooperation," *New York Times,* January 13, 1994.

36. Satu P. Limaye, "Indo-U.S. Security Ties," *The Hindu*, February 4, 1995.

37. "Since the Pentagon-Pakistani Army and CIA-ISI relations are strong, and India has no analogous links with the U.S. at present, Pakistan is able to wield undue influence on Indo-U.S. military relations." See K. Subrahmanyam, "Indo-U.S.Defence Cooperation," *Times of India*, January 3, 1995.

38. George Tanham, "India and ASEAN: Barriers Tumbling but Progress Slow," *Asia-Pacific Defence Reporter*, October-November 1994, 16.

39. "Passage to India," *Far Eastern Economic Review*, January 19, 1994, 2.

40. Indian Defence Secretary K.A. Nambiar quoted in *StraitsTimes*, August 17, 94; see FBIS-NES-94-160, August 18, 1994, 47-48.

41. Ibid.

42. George Tanham.

43. G.V.C. Naidu, 80.

44. "Indonesians Court India to Maintain Fleet of Ships," *Defense News*, August 22-28, 1994.

45. "Joint Naval Games Likely," *India Abroad*, January 28, 1994.

46. "India Signs Pacts with Vietnam, Singapore," *Defense News*, September 12-18, 1994.

47. Frank Ching, "Growing Asean Faces Strains," *Far Eastern Economic Review*, December 29, 1994, 23.

48. For a discussion of Chinese views, see Banning Garrett and Bonnie Glaser, "Multilateral Security in the Asia-Pacific Region and its impact on Chinese Interests: Views from Beijing," *Contemporary South East Asia*, June 1994, 14-33.

49. Michael O'Connor, "FPDA Helps Stabilize South East Asia," *Defense News,* January 24-30, 1994, 24.

SOUTH EAST ASIA AND JAPAN

Watanabe Akio

ECONOMICS

It is almost a cliche nowadays to speak of Asian dynamism. One author gave an attractive title to his recent book about the transformation of Southeast Asia: *From Dominoes to Dynamos.*[1] The dynamos are the robust economies of five ASEAN countries whose GDP multiplied on the whole nearly 15 times during the 25-year period between 1965 and 1990. Most experienced faster growth in the 1965-80 period than in the 1980-90 period. Their economies soared even during those years when dominoes rather than dynamos were a commonly perceived image of their future.

ASEAN economies continued to be vigorous into more recent years. The average annual growth rate of six ASEAN economies during 1988-1992 ranged from 2.8 to 11.7 percent. The fact that they recorded more than a 5 percent annual growth, except for Philippines, is impressive when compared with the corresponding records of the G-7 economies during the same period; only the three little dragons in East Asia (8.0 percent for Korea, 6.7 percent for Taiwan, and 4.7 percent for Hong Kong) can be compared to them.[2]

Some of the former Socialist countries have joined this growth, and despite the official slogan of "socialism," China is in fact

---

Professor Watanabe Akio is Professor, School of International Politics, Economics and Business, Aoyama Gakuin University. Prior to his present position, he was Professor, Department of International Relations, University of Tokyo (1978-1993). He has written numerous publications in English, including his most recent, The Global Trend Toward Regional Integration.

becoming part of the regionwide market economy, experiencing a remarkably rapid economic expansion, with an average annual growth rate of 6.8 percent from 1988 to 1991. The Vietnamese also have launched an economic restructuring policy as the government aimed at converting the socialist economy to a market-based one. The country's GDP growth was 7.2 percent in 1993 and is estimated to have surpassed 8.0 percent in 1994. They are now keenly interested in drawing overseas investments and investors. Taiwan, Hong Kong, France, and Japan have actively responded to their wooing. Japan pledged in November 1993 to offer Vietnam approximately ¥60 billion of Official Development Aid, almost half of the amount pledged by the donor countries. The United States decided in February 1994 to lift its long-standing embargo, and the international financial institutions (IMF, Asian Development Bank, etc.) have resumed lending to Vietnam.

If these Asian economies continue to be successful into the next century, according to one estimate their combined GDP will account for nearly 24 percent of the world total in 2001, narrowly surpassing the estimated GDP of the United States (23 percent).[3]

NATIONAL AND REGIONAL RESILIENCE

One outstanding feature of the Asia/Pacific region is the confident belief in statehood among the political and intellectual leaders. It is a belief absent from many parts of the globe nowadays, especially among developing countries, and indeed, the "failed states" have lately attracted much attention in today's media. With the U.N. Transitional Authority in Cambodia being the almost sole exception, the rest of the peacekeeping operations in the post-Cold War era have been directed at places other than the Asia/Pacific.[4] It seems unlikely, however, that the Asia/Pacific region will become a theater requiring major U.N.-type multilateral activities in the near future. "Peace building" in Cambodia, however, is yet an unfinished task and some other countries (like Papua New Guinea) are barely integrated, where tribal and communal cleavages might erupt into bloody clashes at any time.

The degree of resilience is remarkable, in view of the relative youth of many of the East Asian states. The Indonesian concept of national "resilience," now widely shared by other ASEAN members and applied in a regional context, developed from two apprehensions: fear of internal disturbance and fear of intraregional conflict. Leaders of the ASEAN countries have been successful in containing these two fears, common to many emerging states, with a thoughtful and creative approach to security issues. This approach may be described as that of "comprehensive security," resembling but somewhat different from the Japanese concept. While the Japanese version is strongly characterized by their fear of vulnerability to unpredictable changes in world economy, the ASEAN version puts more emphasis on social coherence and regional dimension.[5]

MAJOR SECURITY ISSUES IN THE REGION

If the above analysis is correct, the nature of security issues in Asia/Pacific in general and in South East Asia/South China Sea in particular are essentially state centric; there will be no Bosnias or Somalias in this region. Notwithstanding the unfinished task of national unification of Korea and the question of the ambiguous status of Taiwan, we do not see any signs of impending crises in this region comparable to Africa, the Caribbean, the former Yugoslavia, and some members of the CIS. Even the questions of Korea and Taiwan are different from ethnic conflicts in other regions, because they are part of an incomplete task of nation building. The question before us is therefore whether and how we can create and maintain stable international (i.e. state-to-state) relations. From that standpoint the following issues can be singled out for discussion: arms buildup/transfer, maritime freedom, and territorial disputes.

Arms Buildup/Transfer

The immediate impact of the end of the Cold War upon Asian countries was, in marked contrast to Europe, significant in that it generated greater efforts toward the buildup of armaments (table 1). The end of the Cold War meant a decline in the strategic importance of the region in the eyes of both contestants of the Cold War, thus the regional countries were forced into more self-reliance in security matters. Furthermore, proud of long-cherished statehood and confident of the newly acquired economic dynamos, many East Asian countries can afford to divert more energies and resources than before to the modernization of military capabilities. They now have the motivation and resources to achieve military modernization.

TABLE 1. *Recent Trends of Military Budgets:*
Comparison between East Asia and Major NATO Countries
(percentage of increase or decrease against the previous year)

	1989	1990	1991	1992	1993
China	14.0	18.0	12.2	13.8	14.9*
ROK	9.0	10.4	12.3	12.8	9.6
DPRK	5.4	26.8	0	-13.8	4.9
Taiwan	11.2	9.7	7.3	4.7	4.8
Thailand	0	13.6	15.2	13.6	15.7
Indonesia	--	--	12.8	19.3	12.3
Malaysia	-11.1	12.8	11.8	5.7	1.2
Singapore	11.5	5.5	19.5	--	--
Philippines	150.8	-12.9	13.9	7.3	2.7
Japan	5.9	6.1	5.5	3.8	2.0
USA	4.6	-1.7	-9.4	9.3	-2.9
UK	4.8	5.4	13.2	0.9	-3.4
Germany	3.7	1.8	-3.1	-0.9	-4.3
France	4.6	3.9	2.7	0.4	1.4

(Source: Military Balance, Japan's Defense White Paper, Korea's Defense White Paper, Finance Minister's Report at PRC' Peoples' Assembly).
*The increase of defense expenditure of China in 1994 was 22.4 percent. See Research Institute for Peace and Security (RIPS), *Asian Security 1994-95* (Brassey's, 1994), 95.

This is not peculiar to the East Asian region. While the overall trend within the economically advanced nations has been a gradual drawdown of military spending since 1989, the developing countries have begun to increase spending on military hardware. This is partly because of the recent trend that has been favoring the buyers in the weapons market. While the absolute volume of arms sales continued to decline since 1987, both in global terms and in East Asia, the share of East Asia in arms imports increased from 9.8 percent in 1981 to 14.4 percent in 1991, while that of Europe declined from 19.5 percent to 16.1 percent during the same period. (Noteworthy is that this apparent decline of Europe in the weapons market is due to the collapse of the military might of the Warsaw Pact countries. NATO Europe's world share in arms imports, in fact, rose from 8.4 percent to 14.6 percent during the 1981-91 period.)

One does not need to subscribe to warnings made by alarmists concerning the arms race among the Asian countries. Japanese defense analysts do not foresee any major moves that are likely to upset the existing military balance among the South East Asian countries, pointing to the basically inward-looking nature of their armed forces. Referring to the recent moves in Asia for military modernization, the Japanese Prime Minister's Advisory Group on Defense Issues said in its report issued in August 1994:

> Now that the Cold War is over and the influence of the two superpowers has relatively diminished, it is no wonder that Asian nations full of youthful vitality are beginning to pursue their own security policies. In the background of their efforts to deal more seriously with security problems is the fact that power relationships in Asia are becoming fluid as a a result of the end of the Cold War. Thus many nations of Asia, including China, now have political motives and economic foundations for improving their military power. This is the first characteristics of the security environment in this region.[6]

That said, however, we should be mindful of pitfalls in our way. First, people are still remembering vividly past hostilities. In addition, some of the difficult political issues stand in the way of achieving harmonious relationships. Secondly, being young in statehood, Asian nations have not yet amassed sufficient experiences of multilateral diplomacy on their own. What is important, therefore, is the joint efforts to alleviate mistrust among ourselves. To that extent we can be successful in those endeavors, and thus we would be assured of avoiding a fall into a pit of our own making, i.e., an uncontrollable arms race.

Maritime Freedom

Another area of common concern for the countries in the Asia/Pacific region is maritime freedom. The heavy dependence of Japan on overseas markets is well known. As much as 93 percent of its energy and about a third of its food depend on overseas supply. Approximately 20 percent of the seaborne trade all over the world is conducted by Japan. The three largest importers of Japanese goods are the Middle East (25.2 percent), Asia other than China (21.3 percent), and Australasia (21.1 percent). For Japan, the importance of sea lines of communications (SLOC) through the South East Asia/South China Sea subregion is obvious.

The problem of maritime freedom is not solely Japan's. The more interdependent Asia/Pacific economies become, the more important the SLOC will become for all the regional members, for military as well as commercial reasons. International ocean freight in the Asia-Pacific region has been dominated by the Trans-Pacific routes in the Northern Pacific and the North-South routes in the Western Pacific. The former, known also as the Far East-North American routes, are currently the biggest shipping routes in the world, but the North-South routes are growing fast because of the rapid expansion in recent years of the Western Pacific trade with other parts of the world, and intraregional trade. According to one expert's estimate, ocean freight traffic in the Western Pacific could triple by the year 2000.[7]

As one recent study of Asia Pacific arms buildups rightly pointed out, "the most conspicuous feature of most recent acqusition programs is the priority placed on the development of naval and maritime air capabilities in favor of increased sea-keeping and endurance".[8]

Most of the South East Asian countries have traditionally been preoccupied with coastal defense, reflecting the geographic composition of their countries (especially archipelagic countries like the Philippines and Indonesia). Recent efforts of the Royal Thai Navy to upgrade its capabilities from coastal defense to offshore operations can be, however, explained more plausibly by their changing threat perception vis-a-vis the Indian and Chinese naval strength.[9] Similar responses could be envisaged from other South East Asian countries so long as the recent activities of the Chinese navy in the South China Sea are perceived as a threat to their interests in the Spratly Islands.[10]

Territorial Disputes

Apart from the disputed islands in the South China Sea, there are some other long-standing problems, awaiting political settlement in one way or another. The Japanese are concerned with the potential rekindling of the dormant issue over the Senkaku Islands, which are regarded by the Japanese as part of the Ryukyu Islands but which have been claimed by the Chinese government from time to time.[11] Likewise a small uninhabited island in the Sea of Japan has been disputed between the Republic of Korea and Japan. (Incidentally, the name of the "Sea of Japan" itself has been questioned by the Koreans, who insist on their own name, the Eastern Sea. The Eastern Sea for the Japanese is the Pacific Ocean!). One cannot finish the list without mentioning the unsettled issue of the so-called Northern Islands (Kuril) between Japan and Russia.

While the above-mentioned problems are outstanding in Northeast Asia, ASEAN countries are not entirely free from border disputes. They have been dormant for sometime, attesting to the effectiveness of ASEAN as a mechanism for "pacific settlement of disputes" as provided in Chapter VI of the U.N. Charter.

The existence of these territorial disputes signifies the fact that politics are still very much border-dependent even in the days of borderless economies. Important characteristics of these border disputes in Asia/Pacific is that they are, unlike those in other parts of the world, propelled, at least for the moment, more by interstate struggle for economic resources than by struggle for political rights of ethnic or minority groups within a given state. In that sense they are, one hopes, more manageable than otherwise.

This sort of optimism would be shattered instantly if and when the existing framework of the states becomes in jeopardy. Such an eventuality cannot be ruled out entirely for some of the member states in Asia/Pacific. One recent study looked carefully at China (with regard to sub-states of Hong Kong, Inner Mongolia, Taiwan, Tibet and Xinjiang); Indonesia (with regard to sub-states of Aceh, East Timor and Irian Jaya); Papua New Guinea (with regard to a sub-state of Bougainville); and Philippines (with regard to a sub-state of Mindanao).[12] In order to prevent such eventualities, political leaders of the countries concerned should spare no pains in working out flexible and imaginative solutions to the problems. A device for absorbing shocks of political earthquakes with a greater ease is clearly in order. The Chinese concept of "one state, two regimes" is probably a step forward in that direction.

POSSIBILITIES OF COOPERATIVE SECURITY IN ASIA-PACIFIC

The countries in Asia and the Pacific are, it seems, getting increasingly interested in regional cooperation first, economic issues second, and security matters third. The ASEAN Regional Forum (ARF) has made a modest start. At a nongovernmental level, the Council for Security Cooperation in the Asia Pacific Region, also launched into experimental activities.

Some people are skeptical about the merit of multilateral activities for the purpose of enhancing security in Asia/Pacific. Such a skeptism is in part grounded on the fear about devaluation of American military presence and of the American-centered alliance networks. The strong reservations of the Bush administration about any ideas of multilateral forum for regional security in Asia/Pacific was an example. Because every country in the region is definitely in favor of the continued, if somewhat reduced, military presence of the United States, such fears are rather groundless.

A more important question is whether and how long the U.S. forces would be able to remain engaged if the American taxpayers begin to feel that their military presence in Asia is not worthwhile from the viewpoint of their own national interest. In this instance, any increase in individual and joint efforts on the part of the Asian countries for regional security should be valued positively. The more vigorous multilateral activities among regional members become, the more confident American soldiers and taxpayers will be regarding the value of their continued presence in Asia/Pacific.

It is for this reason that the Advisory Group for Japanese Prime Minister spoke in favor of multilateral cooperation:

> The cooperative security policy must be pursued not only at the United Nations but also at the regional level. Already at the ASEAN Regional Forum (ARF) security dialogue among the participating nations is under way. Japan, which has involved itself positively in the establishment of this forum from the beginning, should continue to make further efforts for its development. We believe this forum should take up such questions as creating a regional system for increasing transparency in the mutual disclosure of information pertaining to the transfer and acqustion of weapons, the deployment of military forces and military exercises, etc., as well as building a framework of cooperation concerning the prevention of maritime accidents, maritime traffic safety and peacekeeping operations. As a private-level body to complement regional dialogue at the governmental level the Conference on Security Cooperation in Asia and the Pacific (CSCAP) was established recently. If, through such forums, dialogue is promoted with nations from which it is difficult to obtain information on military policies, such as China, Russia, Indochinese states and the Democratic People's Republic of Korea, then transparency in the security environment in Asia and the Pacific will increase, and as a result the sense of security among nations of the region will also increase.[13]

This would be the surest way in which the countries in this region could hope to prevent the suffering that more unfortunate people in other parts of the globe have been experiencing.

NOTES

1.   John Bresnan, *From Dominoes to Dynamos: The Transformation of Southeast Asia* (A Council on Foreign Relations Book, 1994).

2.   Japan Institute for Social and Economic Affairs (comp.), *Japan 1994: An International Comparison*, 11 and 15.

3.   One caveat: Asia is defined here as constituting the following 12 economies, i.e. ROK, Taiwan, Hong Kong, Singapore, Thailand, Malaysia Philippines, Indonesia, China, India, Vietnam and Japan. Sakura Sogo Kenkyujo, Kan Taiheiyo Kenkyu Senta, *Shinseiki eno Ajia hatten no shinario* (Daiyamondsha,1994), 20-21.

4. For the list of these PKO operations, see Gareth Evans, *Cooperating for Peace: The Global Agenda for the 1990s and Beyond* (Allen & Unwin, 1993), 101-2; Urano Tatuso, *Gendai Funso Ron* (Nansosha, 1995), 330-1.

5. For a detailed account of Japanese concept of "comprehensive security," see Eto Shinkichi and Yamamoto Yoshinobu, *Sogo anpo to mirai no sentaku* (Kodansha,1992). See also Asia-Australia Institute, Australian-Asian Perceptions Project Working Paper Number 5, *Perceiving "National Security"* (Academy of the Social Sciences in Australia and the Asia-Australia Institute, April 1994). The latter makes a comparison between Japanese and Indonesian versions of comprehensive security (see page 24).

6. *The Modality of the Security and Defense Capability of Japan: The Outlook for the 21st Century, A report of the Prime Minister's Advisory Group on Defense Issues,* August 1994, 5.

7. PECC Triple T Task Force, "Trends in Asia/Pacific Ocean Freight," in PECC, 105-6.

8. Shannon Selin, *Asia Pacific Arms Buildups*, Part One: Scope, Causes and Problems, Institute of International Relations, The University of British Columbia, Working Paper No.6 (November 1994), 36.

9. RIPS, 1994, 174. More generally, see Ross Babbage and Sam Bateman, eds., *Maritime Change: Issues for Asia* (Allen & Unwin, 1993).

10. For the recent "discovery" by the Philippines navy of the fact that some constructions were made by the Chinese on the several islands off Palawan, see Yomiuri Shimbun, 10 February 1995, 5. The Chinese authorities described the fact as an act by "local fishermen."

11. Chinese fishing boats appeared in flocks, entering into territorial waters off the Senkaku Islands in April 1978. Japan lodged a protest and China pulled back the fishing boats abruptly. This happened when the two countries were approaching conclusion of Peace Treaty, that was signed in August 1978.

12. Morton Halperin & David Scheffer, *Self-Determination in the New World Order* (Carnegie Endowment for International Peace, 1992).

13. *The Modality of the Security and Defense Capability of Japan: The Outlook for the 21st Century,* A report of the Prime Minister's Advisory Group on Defense Issues, August 1994, 9.

Part III

AFTA, APEC, AND THE WTO:
How Do They Fit Together?

AFTA, APEC, AND WTO:
The Interlocking Pieces

Wisarn Pupphavesa

INTRODUCTION

A lthough AFTA, APEC, and WTO were all formed about the same time, they differ in level of formality, scope in terms of reference, number, homogeneity and degree of commitment of member countries, as well as the time frame of development. Their emergence and development have been intertwined and influence each another as member countries weigh their interests, objectives, influence, benefits, and burdens in their participation in and consideration for the modality of each organization. The South East Asian countries, particularly those members of ASEAN, have played different roles in the formation of the three organizations. While the ASEAN countries' contributions to the shaping of WTO were rather marginal, and their acceptance of WTO was a forgone conclusion, their reluctance about and concerns with modality have had a significant impact on the formation of APEC. On the other hand, the ASEAN countries have complete control over the modality and progress of AFTA, although with due consideration and in response to the development of WTO and APEC. The simultaneous development

---

Dr. Wisarn Pupphavesa is Director, International Economic Relations Program, Thailand Development Research Institute. From 1983 to 1991, he was Assistant Professor at the School of Development Economics, National Institute of Development Administration, Bangkok, Thailand. Dr. Pupphavesa is currently a Member of the Working Group on Establishment of Industrial Research and Development Center, Ministry of Industry.

of AFTA, APEC and WTO, therefore, reflects ASEAN countries' efforts to ensure that the three fit together and are favourable to their cause of social and economic development.

The following is an attempt to explain how AFTA, APEC, and WTO fit or may fit together and how they can further the common cause, if any, of the ASEAN countries; describe the economic setting of ASEAN countries and their relationship with the major players in the world as well as identifying the common cause of these countries; highlight the salient features of WTO, AFTA and APEC and how they fit together for the ASEAN countries; and provide a conclusion and policy prescriptions for the ASEAN countries to further their cause within the framework of AFTA, APEC, and WTO.

ECONOMIC SETTINGS OF ASEAN COUNTRIES

Today, ASEAN's importance as a major economic area within the world economy is widely recognized. Over the period 1980-1991, the compound annual GDP growth rate of the six ASEAN countries was estimated at 6 percent, their GDP having increased from US$ 182 billion to US $350 billion. However, with the exception of Singapore, ASEAN member countries are still classified as developing countries.

Over the past several decades, ASEAN's exports have risen substantially to about US$ 161.9 billion in 1990. ASEAN's rapid increase in its share of total world exports have been facilitated by the steadily decreasing trade barriers in the crucial markets of the United States and other industrial economies. Today, trade plays a vital role in the structural development of the six ASEAN economies, so much so that the ASEAN countries, much like the newly industrialized economies (NIEs), are ever increasing their share of total world trade. Indeeed, the prospects of the six countries are crucially linked to their openness to trade and investment.

One characteristic feature of the six ASEAN economies in recent years has been their highly successful outward-oriented development strategies, which have allowed these countries to upgrade their industrial structure to increasingly more advanced export products. Regional flows of technology and capital, coupled with the flexibility of markets, have been instrumental in the industrial shift.

PUTTING THE PUZZLE TOGETHER

● WTO is governing and dictating the global trade environment in which the ASEAN countries are aspired to benefit from improving market access, at the same time being inevitably committed to their obligations to open up their own domestic market to international competition. WTO will continue to push for a freer and more open competitive global trade environment. Toward this ever changing environment, the ASEAN countries must adjust themselves.

● AFTA is by design a useful instrument to facilitate transformation of the ASEAN countries to fit into the world of free trade in the long run. However, AFTA appears to fall short of expectations unless it is improved both in depth and coverage of issues for liberalization.

● APEC can usefully serve as a natural intermediate step of progression for the Asian countries from AFTA to the ultimate free trade world goal of WTO as it offers a larger and more diversified number of economies with adequately large market and wide variations of comparative advantages. APEC can also serve to lead and develop a prototype model of international agreement on various emerging issues based on common interests and benefits of APEC members. APEC is also a natural instrument bridging NAFTA and AFTA and can help nullify the trade diversion effect, if any, between NAFTA and AFTA. The problem remains, however, how to strike a balance in institutional design for APEC to be palatable for ASEAN while ensuring a satisfactory degree of progress and effectiveness.

AFTA

Looked at as an aggregate block, ASEAN's trade structure is characterized by several things:

● ASEAN's trade with the industrialized countries—the United States, the EU and Japan—outstrips all other trade with other countries. However, intra-ASEAN trade is increasing.

• ASEAN's proportion of manufactured items in terms of its total exports has grown significantly, especially in the last two decades. Nonetheless, the percentage share of chemicals and related products, crude and mineral fuels as part of total exports is still significant.

• In recent years there has been, and continues to be a concerted effort (both at national and regional levels) to liberalize trade and investment regimes especially since the ASEAN economies attract a higher proportion of foreign direct investment than most developing countries. The trade structure in the individual ASEAN countries varies widely in terms of sourcing, commodity composition, policy and so forth.

Prior to the adoption of the ASEAN Free-Trade Agreement (AFTA), ASEAN countries had not had much significant success in their economic cooperation. The Preferential Trading Arrangement (PTA), the ASEAN Industrial Project (AIP), the ASEAN Industrial Complementation (AIC), and the ASEAN Industrial Joint Ventures (AIJV) schemes all progressed slowly and produced insignificant results in terms of intra-ASEAN trade and investment. Until the Third ASEAN Summit in 1987, ASEAN leaders were not ready to accept the idea of an ASEAN Trade Area (a free trade area approach with a mute "free"). However, the changes in the economic environment since then made AFTA the right idea at the right time when Thailand proposed it in 1991.

• Among the right environment for AFTA was the emergence of NAFTA and the growth of the European Community. Although they did not raise trade barriers against nonmembers, they did increase trade preferences for members and attracted foreign direct investment (FDI) not only from member home countries, but also from major nonmember home countries such as Japan, Taiwan, and Hong Kong, which had been the major sources of FDI for the ASEAN countries.

• The emergence of transitional economies like China and Vietnam as well as economic reforms in India also offered a shift in comparative advantage and a more competitive labor-intensive export base. New large market opportunities that could lure away foreign direct investments arose.

• As a result of technological development in products, production processes, transportation, and telecommunication, parts and components, and different stages of production can be efficiently processed in different locations where the multinational corporations (MNCs) can enjoy a comparative advantage more effectively than before. Consequently, the MNCs have been locating production plants for various production processes, parts, and components where they see fit. The ASEAN countries could be a competitive regional production base if they could facilitate such production strategy through free trade.

• Lack of progress in the Uruguay Round of multilateral trade negotiation when the major economic powers could not compromise reflected the weaknesses in the collective bargaining power of small, though large in number, economies including the ASEAN countries whose interest in freer trade were overlooked. ASEAN countries had also been subject to pressure and unilateral action time and again by some major economic powers. The ASEAN countries had been quite successful earlier in cooperation with their dialogue partners based on political solidarity and security concerns. The bargaining power of the ASEAN countries, however, seemed to deteriorate with the end of Cold War. There was therefore a need to renew solidarity of the ASEAN countries through a major economic integration to increase their collective bargaining power.

• Regardless of the outcome of the Uruguay Round, the ASEAN countries would have to improve their competitiveness to overcome the increasing protectionism in the event of failure, or to meet the challenge of greater competition in the event of a successful conclusion of the Uruguay Round. This would mean reducing the disparity of comparative advantage, then restructuring according to comparative advantage, and improving technology and productivity.

• The ASEAN countries had already gone some distance in trade and industrial liberalization and gained confidence in more systemic liberalization. Their import structure had also turned around to consist more of capital goods, intermediate inputs and raw materials, rather than consumer goods. Tariff reductions would mean cost reduction and improving the competitiveness of domestic producers against imports or other countries's exports.

Within this environment, the ASEAN countries agreed to implement AFTA within a 15-year time frame, with the goal "to increase ASEAN's competitive edge as a production base geared for the rest of the world"[1] AFTA was meant to attract and facilitate production integration of FDI as well as to serve as a transitional stage toward broader and stronger challenges from MFN liberalization.[2]

In contrast to NAFTA, which contains thousands of pages of detailed provisions as a result of thorough negotiations, the Common Effective Preferential Tariff (CEPT) Scheme for the ASEAN Free Trade Area (AFTA) contains only 10 Articles in 12 pages. It is a simple agreement on principle, leaving all the details to be worked later.

The CEPT covers all manufactured products including capital goods and some processed agricultural products. Unprocessed agricultural goods and services are not covered by the agreement. The CEPT stipulates tariff reductions on the covered products to no more than 5 percent and removal of non-tariff barriers over the 15-year period from 1993 to 2008.

Fifteen product groups are separated into a fast track where the tariff on those items with a current rate at 20 percent and below will be reduced to 5 percent or less the year 2000. Those with a current rate above 20 percent will be reduced to 5 percent or less by the year 2003. Included in the fast track group are vegetable oils, cement, chemicals, pharmaceuticals, fertilizer, plastics, rubber products, leather products, pulp and paper, textiles, wooden and rattan furniture, ceramics and glass products, gems and jewelry products, copper cathodes, and electronics.

The remaining products are grouped into a normal track where the tariff for those items with an existing rate above 20 percent will be reduced to 20 percent in 5 to 8 years and further reduced to between 0 and 5 percent by the year 2008. For those items already at 20 percent or below, the tariff rate will be reduced to between 0 and 5 percent by the year 2003. The CEPT provides for temporary exclusion of "sensitive" products from a tariff reduction schedule with a review of the list in 8 years, after which schedules are to be devised to reduce tariffs to between 0 and 5 percent by 2008.

The Common Effective Preferential tariff means that a member will not be eligible to enjoy the preference granted by the other members on any item until its own tariff on such item is reduced to 20 percent. This will require further "talk" on harmonization of tariff lines or matching of different national definition of products by tariff lines. In order to qualify for the tariff preference, the import items must pass the rule of origin criteria of 40 percent gross ASEAN content. It is still, however, under negotiation for an alternative criteria of lower ASEAN content or substantive transformation criteria for textiles.

As the tariff reduction schedules are prepared according to each member country's existing tariff structure and its officials' idea of tariff liberalization, which tended to emphasize cautiousness, gradualism, and concerns for adversely affected domestic import competing producers, it is observed that the reduction schedules have very few items in common preferences in a broad ASEAN context, but mostly bilaterally "common" preference until the year 2001. This will hinder ASEAN's ability to provide a cost effective regional production platform and to exploit the diversity of the the ASEAN countries to the fullest extent. Moreover, electrical machinery, vehicles, parts, accessories, and petrochemicals constitute a major portion of the temporary exclusion list. These are items which are relevant to MNC's globalization strategy. By placing these items on the temporary exclusion list, the ASEAN countries have reduced their attractiveness as a production base for these industries.[3]

Following the conclusion of the Uruguay Round and the Seattle APEC Meeting, the ASEAN officials felt the pressure of competition and more urgent need to accelerate actualization of AFTA and realization of its anticipated impact, the ASEAN Economic Ministers (AEM) at its 26th Meeting in September 1994 agreed to shorten the time frame for the normal track and the fast-track tariff reductions to within year 2003 and 2000, respectively, and to include unprocessed agricultural products in the CEPT scheme. The temporary exclusion list will be reduce by 20 percent annually and totally removed in 5 years. This will significantly improve the effectiveness of AFTA.

APEC

The first intellectual initiation for Pacific cooperation came from Professors Kyoshi Kojima and Kurimoto Hiroshi, who proposed a Pacific Free-Trade Area (PAFTA) modeled on the European Economic Community (EEC) and the European Free- Trade Area (EFTA) in 1965. Later in 1973, Professors Hugh Patrick and Peter Drysdale proposed an Organization for Pacific Trade and

Development (OPTAD) to take a form similar to the Organization for Economic Cooperation and Development (OECD). Both proposals appeared to be too ambitious, inappropriate, impractical, and poorly timed for an intergovernmental arrangement, given the political and economic diversity of the region.

Kojima's initiative, however, led to formation of two nongovernmental institutions—the Pacific Basin Economic Council (PBEC) and the Pacific Trade and Development Conference (PAFTAD). The PBEC was formed in 1967 as a private sector institution devoted to the study and discussion of issues concerning the interests of businesses in the Asia-Pacific region. The PAFTAD Conferences—the first of which was held in Tokyo in 1968—provide a forum for regional academics to discuss trade, investment, structural adjustment, and environmental issues pertaining to the economies in Asia and the Pacific. OPTAD was proposed as a means to promote a "revitalization of United States' economic leadership in the Asia-Pacific Region"[4] following a drawdown period of American presence in the region. However, as a governmental institution it was considered premature. In 1980, a tripartite structure bringing bureaucrats, industrialists, and academics together in a nongovernmental forum was suggested that gave birth to the Pacific Economic Cooperation Conference (PECC).[5]

The first meeting of PECC in Conference in 1980 was attended by delegates from 11 countries: the five ASEAN countries plus Australia, Canada, Japan, New Zealand, South Korea, the U.S., and a joint delegation of Papua New Guinea, Fiji, and Tonga. The delegates consisted of representatives from the academic and business communities and government officials acting in their own unofficial capacity. The memership later expanded to include Brunei, as a new member of ASEAN, Chile, China, Hong Kong, Mexico, Peru, Taiwan, and the Pacific Island Nations. PECC has provided a foundation for the establishment of the Asia Pacific Economic Cooperation (APEC) conference by way of identifying issues for cooperation, fostering a consensus in the region on the benefits derived from an open, multilateral trading system. PECC is encouraging more positive, outward-looking attitudes toward cooperation, and providing a forum in which China, Taiwan, and Hong Kong are politically willing to sit at the same table to conduct policy oriented discussions. Because of its tripartite structure and because government participants acted in their own capacities, PECC provided relatively open debates for sound and practical analyses and conclusions. However, there remains the problem of translating PECC's output into constructive regional policy making.[6]

To this problem of intergovernmental policy making, it was the ASEAN Post-Ministerial Conference (PMC) where the foreign ministers from ASEAN held annual dialogues with those from Australia, Canada, Japan, New Zealand, and the United States and representatives from the EC—immediately following the ASEAN Foreign Ministers' meeting—that provided a framework for high level meetings on economic cooperation and thus contributed to building the foundation for APEC.

APEC was convened by former Australian Prime Minister Bob Hawke's speech in Seoul in January 1989 in which he urged ministerial-level regional consultations be convened in order to (a) defend and strengthen the multilateral trading system as it is embodied in GATT, (b) determine the common economic interests of the Asia-Pacific nations, and (c) discuss the barriers to trade in the region. This led to the first meeting of APEC in Canberra on November 6-7, 1989. It is interesting to note that initially North America was not included in Australia's vision of the inter-governmental Asia Pacific Forum. However, Deputy Minister of International Trade and Industry (MITI) Shigeru Muraoka successfully stirred up support for inclusion of the United States and Canada.

A question of special concerns to ASEAN has been what form APEC's relationship with ASEAN will take? ASEAN was skeptical about the possibility of APEC undermining ASEAN's solidarity and collective-bargaining strength. Thus, the Australians first held consultations with the ASEAN nations to ease their reservations by making assurances that APEC was designed to build constructively on, rather than compete with, existing institutions. In recognition of the fact that without ASEAN concordance APEC could not have moved beyond the initial stages, U.S. Secretary of State James Baker III stressed at the ASEAN-PMC meeting in Brunei in July 1989 that any Asia-Pacific institution must "respect, preserve and perhaps even enhance the uniquely beneficial ASEAN contribution to the region and to the world."[7] Further recognition of the primary role of ASEAN is evident in the consensus reached among all the participants in

APEC that every other general meeting shall be held in an ASEAN country. More importantly, a number of suggestions made by ASEAN were adopted by consensus at the November Canberra meeting as the guiding principles of the APEC process. Among the nine principles, those that serve the ASEAN's interests well include decision by consensus, non-formal consultative exchanges, strengthening the open multilateral trading system without formation of a trading bloc, and complementing and drawing upon rather than detracting from existing organizations in the region such as ASEAN and PECC.

The first APEC ministerial meeting thus took place in Canberra in 1989, attended by 26 ministers from 12 regional economies : five developed Pacific countries, six ASEAN countries and South Korea. That particular meeting agreed on among other things, that APEC's objectives should be to sustain growth and development in the region and to improve living standards; strengthen an open multilateral trading system (although not under the auspices of a new trade bloc); and to focus on economic (including fostering of constructive interdependence by encouraging the flow of goods, service, capital and technology) rather than on political or security issues.

At the second ministerial meeting held in Singapore, seven work projects aimed at "developing the habit of cooperation" were established. These included cooperation in technology transfer, human resource development, energy, marine resources, telecommunications, transportation, tourism, fisheries and the improvement of data on the flow of goods services and investment. It was at this meeting that it was agreed that APEC's main theme should be that of promoting a more open trading system, coupled with the exploration of the scope for nondiscriminatory regional trade liberalization.

At the third APEC ministerial meeting in Seoul in 1991, China, Hong Kong, and Taiwan were admitted as members. In addition, the meeting adopted the Seoul Declaration, which set out the scope of activities, principles, and mode of operation for participation in APEC. The declaration was mostly the re-affirmation of what had been agreed upon in the previous two meetings.

The fourth meeting, held in Bangkok in 1992, was mostly devoted to setting up a permanent secretariat in Singapore that would act as a support mechanism and a fund for APEC activities.

The ministers also agreed to establish an Eminent Persons Group (EPG) to enunciate a vision for trade in the Asia Pacific to the year 2000 and identify constraints and issues that APEC should consider in advancing regional trade liberalization over the next 10 years. In order to provide concrete benefits in the shorter term, it was agreed to prepare detailed guides on the region's investment regulatory procedures; harmonize and facilitate customs procedures and practices; examine the administrative aspect of market access and recommend ways of reducing their cost on trade; and to establish an electronic tariff data base for APEC members to facilitate regional trade through better information flows.

Mexico and Papua New Guinea were admitted to APEC at the fifth ministerial meeting, in Seattle in 1993.[8] In addition to formally establishing a Committee on Trade and Investment (CTI), the members adopted the "Declaration of an APEC Trade and Investment Framework" and called for an early and successful completion of the Uruguay Round. A notable addition to this particular summit was the unprecedented APEC informal leaders meeting, proposed and hosted by U.S. President Clinton and attended by all leaders from all APEC member economies except Malaysia. This meeting is believed to have contributed substantially to the successful completion of the Uruguay Round. The leaders welcomed the challenge to achieve free trade in the region and endorsed some of the initial EPG recommendations, including a voluntary APEC investment Code. The leaders also agreed to meet again in Indonesia in 1994.

The last leaders meeting to date was held in Indonesia in November 1994, during which a Declaration of Common Resolve was adopted. In addition to reaffirming past goals of APEC, this document agreed to, among other things:

- To see to it that APEC not only builds on the momentum generated by the Uruguay Round, but takes the lead in strengthening an open multilateral trading system through active participation in, and support of the WTO by all APEC economies
- Refrain from using measures which would increase levels of protection
- Adopt a long-term goal of free trade and open investment in Asia/Pacific by the year 2020[9]

- Continue to oppose turning APEC into an inward-looking trading bloc
- Complement and support the process of liberalization by expanding and accelerating APEC's trade and investment facilitation programs
- Recognize the role of the business sector in economic development by integrating the business sector in APEC's programs
- Recognize the developmental differences of the various APEC economies by allowing the developing economies to defer participation in some areas until later dates
- Demonstrate APEC's leadership in fostering further global trade and investment liberalization.

APEC is still an evolving organization and is seen as a major experiment in regional institution building. Its future direction is far from clear and as such, debate is still ongoing as to whether it should keep its original informal status or whether it should evolve into a closer regional structure. The ASEAN countries are genuinely concerned about how the vast disparities in income, technology, and skill-level among the APEC economies could lead to asymmetrical benefits, dependence, heightened tension, and even rich-poor polarization within APEC. Most importantly, the ASEAN countries prefer a voluntary and nonbinding approach and are not ready (or willing) to negotiate with the advanced countries on liberalization in various sectors including services. In the multilateral framework, ASEAN countries could enjoy to a relatively large extent a free-riding market access. However, in the APEC framework, they would become a more focused target of market access while their gain in market access is obviously smaller than in the multilateral negotiation. Furthermore, ASEAN would not like to be subsumed and dominated by a wider regional organization.

WTO

The 1986-1993 Uruguay Round of multilateral trade negotiations aimed to improve market access for goods and services by reducing tariffs, reducing nontariff support in agriculture, eliminating bilateral quantitative restrictions, reducing barriers to trade in services. It also sought to increase the legal security of the new levels of market access by strengthening and expanding rules, procedures, and institution. One major success of the Uruguay Round was the establishment of the World Trade Organization (WTO). Five specific tasks have been assigned to WTO:

- To facilitate the implementation of the results of the Uruguay Round
- To provide a forum for multilateral trade negotiations and a framework for the implementation of their results
- To administer the dispute settlement procedures
- To administer the Trade Policy Review Mechanism
- To cooperate with the IMF and the World Bank group of agencies.

The WTO will be headed by a Ministerial Conference meeting at least once every 2 years. A General Council will be established to oversee the operation of the WTO between meetings of the Ministerial Conference, including acting as a Dispute Settlement Body and administering the Trade Policy Review Mechanism. A Council for Trade in Goods, a Council for Trade in Services and a Trips Council will aspirate under the general guidance of the General Council. In this manner, the WTO will oversee the operation of all the agreements that form part of each WTO Member's commitments.

Any contracting party to the GATT 1947 that has submitted schedules of commitments on goods and services can automatically become members by accepting the WTO agreement within 2 years of its entry into the organization. Other states and autonomous customs territories may accede to the WTO Agreement on terms approved by a two-thirds majority of the WTO Members.

Besides the WTO, the Uruguay Round has successfully reached several important agreements such as Multilateral Agreements on Trade in Goods, Agreement on Agriculture, Agreement on Textiles and Clothing, Agreement on Trade Related Investment Measures, Agreement on Trade Related Aspects of Intellectual Property Rights, and General Agreement on Trade in Services, Agreement on the Application of Sanitary and Phytosanitary Measures, Agreement on Technical Barriers to Trade, Agreement on Subsidies and Countervailing Measures, etc., which will significantly improve market access and security and reduce trade distortions.[10]

The Uruguay Round results in a 40 percent overall reduction of the developed countries' tariff on industrial products (excluding petroleum), from a trade weighted average rate of 6.3 to 3.8

percent with some reduction in tariff escalation and improved market access security by increasing tariff binding coverage by 76 percent of tariff lines or 67 percent of imports value on the part of developed economies, and 70 percent of tariff line or 58 percent of import value on the part of developing economies. Agricultural products will be 100 percent under bound rates while export subsidy is to be reduced and market access opportunities increased.[11]

One of the Uruguay Round's principal aims was to reduce tariffs, and non-tariff barriers, as well as to eliminate bilateral quantitative restrictions, and reductions in barriers to trade in services.

According to GATT figures, for developing economies the percentage of tariff lines for industrial products over 35 percent would be reduced from 42 percent to 20 percent after the Uruguay Round agreement was implemented. However, the percentage of tariff lines in the 15.1-35.0 percent range would increase from 30 percent to 55 percent after implementation of the Agreement. The other ranges are virtually unchanged. This may be interpreted to mean that the number of products falling in the top range would be reduced, but would then fall into the 15.1-35.0 percent range. The trade-weighted tariff average for developing economies (other than least developed economies) pre-Uruguay Round is 6.8 percent and post-Uruguay Round is 4.4 percent, a percentage reduction of 37 percent.

NOTES

1. ASEAN Secretariat, *AFTA Reader* 1, November 1993.
2. The ASEAN Free Trade Area: A Proposal.
3. Wisarn Pupphavesa, "AFTA: The State of Play," presented at conference on The Deepening and Widening of ASEAN in the Post-Cold War Era (Singapore: Institute of Southeast Asian Studies, 1994).
4. Miles Kahler, "Organizing the Pacific," in *Regional Dynamics: Security, Politial and Economic Issues in the Asia-Pacific Region,* Robert Scalapino, Seizaburo Sato, Jusuf Wanandi, and Sung Jao Han, eds. (Jakartya: Centre for strategic and International Studies, 1990),400.
5. Saburo Okita, "Pacific Cooperation: Past, Present and Future," remarks made at the Seventh Pacific Economic Cooperation Conference (Auckland, November 12).
6. Andrew Elek, "Asia Pacific Economic Cooperation (APEC)," in *South East Asian Affairs 1991,* Sharon Siddique and Ng Chee Yuen, eds. (Singapore: Institute of South East Asian Studies, 1991).

7. *Bangkok Post*, July 7, 1989; cited in Donald E. Weatherbee, "ASEAN and Pacific Regionalism," ISIS Paper no. 4. (Bangkok: Institute of Security and International Studies, Chulalongkorn University,1989).

8. It was also agreed that Chile would be admitted the following year, after which the consideration of additional members would be deferred for 3 years.

9. 2010 for the developed APEC economies.

10. GATT, *Final Act* (Geneva: The GATT Secretariat, 1994).

11. General Agreement on Tariffs and Trade, "The Results of the Uruguay Round of Multilateral Trade Negotiations" (Geneva, 1994).

NAFTA, AFTA, AND APEC

Pearl Imada-Iboshi

INTRODUCTION

Regional solutions to trade issues have become popular in recent years. While several integration groupings have existed across the Atlantic, new groupings have been formed in Asia and the Pacific only in the past 10 years. Beginning with a free-trade area with Israel in manufactures in 1982, the United States began to move in the direction of bilateral trading arrangements, a movement which gathered momentum in the second half of the 1980s and the 1990s with the Caribbean Basin Initiative (1983), the U.S.–Canada Free Trade Area (1989), and the North American Free Trade Area (1994).[1] With the exception of Israel, all comprehensive regional accords negotiated by the United States have been with its Western hemisphere partners. In fact, recent discussions regarding the next round of bilateral negotiations continue to be focused in this area, with the Western Hemisphere Free-Trade Area (WHFTA) being considered.

Across the Pacific, Australia and New Zealand formed their free trade area, Closer Economic Relations (CER) Trade Agreement in 1983. Additionally, the leaders of the Association of Southeast Asian Nations (ASEAN) agreed to form the ASEAN Free Trade Area (AFTA) in 1992. This move for ASEAN came after more than 20 years of flirting with minor preferential arrangements and is to a large degree in response to the increasing trend toward regional arrangements in other countries.

Dr. Pearl Imada-Iboshi is a Fellow with the East-West Center Program on International Economics and Politics. She is an authority on free trade in Southeast Asia and on impacts of NAFTA on member-nations and in Asia.

Most recently, the members of the Asia Pacific Economic Cooperation (APEC) agreed to "free trade in the area."[2] Originally proposed in 1989 by Australian Prime Minister Robert Hawke, APEC has served as an official forum for discussion of trade-related and other economic issues and has grown to include eighteen Asia-Pacific member states.[3] Despite the fact that several Asian countries have reiterated their desire that APEC remain a consultative body, the agreement for "free trade in the area" is likely to move this group toward a more formal framework.

The recent interest in creating or expanding trading blocs in the world economy has generated a great deal of debate regarding the costs and benefits of such a trend. Because the movement includes many of the world's richest and largest traders, nonmembers have become apprehensive, fearing negative impacts of such trading blocs on their economies. Since the seminal article written by Viner,[4] economists have been wary about the negative impacts of preferential trading agreements on members and nonmembers because of trade diversion, i.e., the shifting of production from an efficient nonmember country to a less-efficient member country. There is also concern of possible "investment diversion" away from nonmember economies to those of member countries. As developing countries have been placing more emphasis on international markets in their economic development strategies, trade and investment diversion are particularly problematic. Furthermore, the political energy spent on creating these blocs is considerable, leading to concern that liberalization in the world trading system will be neglected.

Clearly, however, it is not necessary to create a free trade area or customs union to expand economic integration among a group of countries. The East Asian countries have increased trade between themselves from 30 percent in 1985 to more than 40 percent presently without a formal institutional framework (appendix 2). Rapid economic growth in Asia and the increasing openness of regional economies to trade and investment were the major factors behind this rise in interdependence.[5] This phenomenon reflects what Tinbergen called "negative" integration, or integration caused by the removal of discriminatory and restrictive institutions in favor of more liberal economic transactions.[6] Other examples of policies promoting cross-border integration without resorting to the discriminatory policies inherent in formal trading blocs often relate to the removal of nonborder restrictions and include such measures as the setting up of common technical standards, harmonization of investment codes and fiscal practices, microeconomic coordination, and development of a regionwide customs classification system and data collection. Furthermore, this paper argues that the creation of a formal preferential arrangement is not necessary to enhance intra-regional trade and investment. Measures including increasing openness on a multilateral basis and acceding to international standards can do much to encourage intra-regional trade. Such an "evolutionary approach" would allow the different groupings—AFTA, NAFTA, and APEC—to co-exist with minimal negative impact or conflicts.

Yet, Tinbergen's terminology, though useful, is somewhat deceptive. "Negative" liberalization seems to imply deleterious effects, whereas in fact the term simply draws a distinction from a "positive" action to create institutions to promote integration. Applied to Asia-Pacific economic cooperation in light of the complicated nature of international economic relationships in the 1990s, it would instead be more accurate to adopt the term *evolutionary integration* to highlight the more natural process through which integration occurs and expands over time. Evolutionary integration relates to a comprehensive assessment of bilateral, plurilateral, and multilateral initiatives, including both bottom-up, private sector–led economic cooperation as well as policy-driven processes. In many ways, evolutionary integration is more difficult to promote, as it involves changes in domestic policies, but its predominant nondiscriminatory features make it more likely to be purely welfare-enhancing. The objectives behind the creation of the Asia Pacific Economic Cooperation (APEC) organization derive from the recognized need to facilitate this evolutionary integration pattern in the region.

Given the success of the evolutionary integration to promote growth and interdependence in the Asia-Pacific, and the region's tremendous economic, social, political, and cultural diversity, it is argued in this paper that there is little reason for APEC to go the route of creating an integration area along the lines of a discriminatory arrangement in the short and medium term. The disparities among the countries in the region in terms of economic development, openness to trade, and investment and the differences in their approach to trading agreements argues against the formation of a formal integration grouping. Instead, APEC should work to foster economic cooperation through a step-by-step approach, which might be called "building blocks" of cooperation. These building blocks will work to enhance economic cooperation from the bottom up, i.e., strengthening and expanding private-sector links. As countries work toward building such blocks, the important economic features of a free-trade area will naturally develop, without having to deal with the economic and political fallout of a top-down, formal free trade area. The blocks are free standing and sufficiently additive to be developed as a whole, a group, or a subgroup without a general loss of effectiveness. Hence, this approach allows for maximum flexibility while still providing direction.

This paper briefly describes the major trading groups in the region, NAFTA and AFTA, and examines the roles of these groupings within the APEC framework. A review of trade measures in most of the APEC countries compiled in appendix 2.[7]

TRADING GROUPS IN THE REGION

There exist three major regional trading groupings (NAFTA, CER, and AFTA) and one group in its initial stages of cooperation (APEC).

NAFTA

The recent moves by the United States to form various trade groupings represents a shift from the exclusively multilateral (GATT) approach of the past. The rationale for the change in U.S. trade policy is complicated and subject to controversy, but a number of elements did play a part.[8] First, the role of the United States in the world economy has been changing rapidly. In the decades immediately following World War II, the United States was the dominant economy in the world and, as such, it shouldered the responsibility for keeping an open international marketplace based on the principles of most-favored-nation treatment. While the United States allowed or even encouraged regionalism in Europe on political grounds, it also emphasized that European integration was an exception to the multilateral rule. Yet, as Europe and Japan rebuilt their economies, and as other economies in the world—particularly those in Asia—emerged as rapidly growing areas, the relative dominance of the United States fell, and its ability and will to be the lone leader, sacrificing domestic for international policy goals, fell with it. Multilateralism ceased to be the United States' limited commercial policy option.

Second, the United States became increasingly disenchanted with the GATT process in the 1980s. Although GATT was able to successfully reduce tariff barriers to trade in manufactures in the past, nontariff and "structural" impediments to trade were becoming increasingly important. At the same time, foreign barriers to trade took on greater importance as the U.S. trade deficit ballooned. Facing these problems, the United States moved toward regional preferential agreements that were easier to negotiate and could address nontariff and structural issues that became exponentially more complicated at the bilateral level. Nevertheless, further economic integration efforts in the Americas will have only marginal effects on world trade and investment. Canada and Mexico constitute upwards of 90 percent of U.S. trade with the region and the lion's share of U.S. direct foregn investment; in 1992, 14 percent of U.S. DFI went to Canada alone, while 18 percent went to all of Latin America.[9] Hence, WHFTA would be in effect more of a political rather than an economic accord.

Third, more aggressive regionalism in Europe began to be met with suspicion in the United States, where it was seen as a movement toward a potentially inward-looking trade bloc. Also, the perceived success of European economic integration suggested to U.S. policymakers that regionalism could yield benefits beyond what the multilateral liberalization process could offer.

The NAFTA Agreement is a highly legalistic document that spells out in great detail how and when the agreement will be implemented. It also clearly specifies steps to be taken in case of disputes. NAFTA is in many ways a pioneering agreement covering areas only now beginning to be addressed in the multilateral trading framework, e.g., agriculture, services, transportation, intellectual property rights, government procurement, direct foreign investment as well as the environment and labor issues. NAFTA made a major step forward by committing (for the most part) to national treatment in services. NAFTA also included commitments regarding the rollback of intraregional National Tariff Barriers duty drawbacks were eliminated for trade within the area, and export processing zones were phased out for intramember trade. Further, NAFTA has taken the bold move of banning all performance requirements for investors. Regarding standards, each party is allowed to maintain its own standards as long as there is a scientific basis for the standard and it is not a disguised restriction on trade. NAFTA countries essentially agreed to give national treatment to suppliers from other member countries.

Significantly, NAFTA is the first agreement between a large developing country and industrialized countries negotiated without a large number of special arrangements made for the developing country. Agreements between unequal partners tend to be very difficult to conclude because of questions of sovereignty and distribution of gains.

Recent discussions regarding the next round of U.S. bilateral negotiations continue to be focused in the Americas with the WHFTA being considered. Nevertheless, further economic integration efforts in the Americas will only have marginal effects on world trade and investment. Canada and Mexico constitute upward of 90 percent of U.S. trade with the region and the lion's share of U.S. DFI; in 1992, 14 percent of U.S. DFI went to Canada alone, while 18 percent went to all of Latin America. A WHFTAwould be in effect more of a political rather than an economic accord.

On the other hand, there have also been some ideas tabled regarding possible regional arrangements with the United States' Asian partners, either through a "hub-and-spoke" approach—such as U.S. or NAFTA arrangements with individual countries—or a comprehensive agreement—such as a Pacific Asian Free-Trade Area. Singapore, for example, has expressed its interest in acceding to NAFTA, and the reports by the Group of Eminent Persons (1993), commissioned by the Asia-Pacific Economic Cooperation (APEC) forum, mentioned that a free-trade area should be the ultimate goal of APEC.[10]

AFTA

When the AFTA concept was first endorsed at the Fourth ASEAN Summit in Janaury 1992, the plan was to lower import tariffs on most manufactured goods within 15 years. Unlike NAFTA, the AFTA agreement briefly describes the goals while leaving the details to be worked out later. While this allowed ASEAN leaders to make the announcement sooner, there remained a great deal of uncertainty as to how and when the agreement would be implemented. The original agreement allowed the member countries the option of up to 3 years to start implementing their tariff reduction program. AFTA also allowed countries to exempt certain "sensitive" items from being included in the agreement with no clear definition of what "sensitive" means.

Filling out the details was not a simple task, and thus progress was slower than initially envisioned. For example, while the ASEAN countries have adopted the highly sensitive system, many of the member-states further disaggregate the standard six-digit HS code in preparing their tariff schedules. Brunei, Indonesia, Malaysia, and Singapore report trade and/or tariff data at the nine-digit level, while the Philippines uses a HS eight-digit classification, and Thailand a six-digit system. At these more disaggregated levels, tariff lines are not necessarily comparable across countries, and these differences are difficult to reconcile. For example, Indonesia disaggregates other vegetable oils (HS150790) into "neutralized and bleached and other," while Malaysia employs the same HS code to designate "solid fractions not chemically modified and other." Most of the details have now been spelled out, and work on harmonization of tariff nomenclature, customs procedures, and customs valuation should be completed by the end of 1995. A decision to speed up AFTA by 5 years (to January 2003) and to extend the tariff cuts to cover unprocessed agriculture was endorsed by the ASEAN Economic Ministers in September 1994. All member countries have also agreed to implement tariff reductions all at the same time and the temporary exclusion list will be systematically ended within 5 years.

It should be noted that AFTA members are extremely outward looking; intra-ASEAN trade accounts for less than 20 percent of their total trade. The major expected benefit of AFTA is to enhance the competitiveness of the region for production geared towards the global market through tariff reductions and elimination of nontariff barriers. In other words, the goal of AFTA is to generate greater efficiency and effectiveness of business transactions in the region rather than to create an inward-looking trading bloc.

ASEAN members have begun to seriously consider allowing other Southeast Asian countries such as Viet Nam, Cambodia, and

Burma into the group. Exactly what form this widening will take is still not determined. Political differences, uncertainty, and different market structures are likely to make substantive integration efforts difficult.

APEC

APEC began as a forum for discussion and some members have reiterated their desire that it remain only that. The odd name, which does not contain the word group, organization, or any other indication of a formal body (sometimes described as adjectives in search of a noun), exemplifies the problem.

Nevertheless, APEC has increasingly acquired the trappings of a formal organization. It now has a Secretariat, standing committtes, and annual Ministerial and leaders' meetings. The most significant push for formalization came from the APEC leaders' meeting in Bogor, Indonesia, November 1994. There the leaders announced that they were committed to "achievement of our goal of free and open trade in Asia Pacific no later than the year 2020. The pace of implementation will take into account the differing levels of economic development among APEC economies, with the industrialized economies achieving the goal of free and open trade and investment no later than the year 2010 and developing economies no later than the year 2020."[11] The long time frame and loose wording are major factors why the agreement was reached. It remains to be seen exactly what form this agreement will take but the "agree first and negotiate later" approach taken is much closer to that of AFTA than NAFTA.

A FRAMEWORK FOR COOPERATION

All Asia-Pacific countries rely on international markets for trade and investment, and it is not in the interest of any individual country to inhibit the process of global economic integration. This fact was borne out during the Uruguay Round negotiations; the United States and its Asia-Pacific partners worked hard to ensure the successful completion of an effective, comprehensive trade agreement to meet the needs of the modern international economy. Hence, any regional cooperative arrangement must not only be consistent with GATT but should guard against the negative consequences of discriminatory trading arrangements by committing to the concept of "open regionalism," whereby any regional cooperative arrangement would lower barriers to trade of nonpartner exports at the same time that regional cooperative arrangements were implemented.

East Asia is by far the most important overseas market for the United States; it is also the fastest-growing region in the world and is forecasted to grow at an impressive rate in the future, suggesting continuing opportunities for lucrative trade and investment. The United States remains the most vital export market for a majority of Asia-Pacific countries and a key source of and host-country to regional investments. Yet, as was noted above, the U.S. relationship with many of its economic partners appears to be more focused on the negative aspects (e.g., trade disputes, copyright infringement) than on the larger picture of a positive and thriving economic partnership. Hence, it would behoove the United States and its Asian partners to develop a framework for cooperation that would ensure rapid and just resolutions to economic disputes, formulate innovative joint initiatives and resolutions designed to maximize mutually beneficial gains from economic interaction, and develop a vision of economic cooperation in the future toward which Asia-Pacific member-states could work.

It is a mistake to believe that the United States can plunge headlong into a free trade area with Asian countries. Rates of protection vary widely among the APEC countries. For the developed countries in the region, the simple average most-favored-nation (MFN) rates are relatively low, ranging from 2 percent for Japan to about 7 percent for Australia. With the exception of Singapore, the average MFN rates of the developing countries in the region are higher, ranging from nearly 8 percent for Korea to 24 percent for the Philippines in 1993. The range in tariff levels within each country's tariff structure is also much wider in the developing countries, with some tariff "spikes" as high as 300 percent. The economic systems of these potential member-states are far too diverse at present; a premature "ramming through" of the free-trade area process would hold political and economic perils for all parties. In this sense, it would be imprudent to think that the best way to promulgate economic integration in the region would be for Asian countries eventually to accede to NAFTA in the short run.

The case of ASEAN economic cooperation provides a useful view of institutions in the region. Formal trade and investment cooperation in ASEAN began at a very modest level, but was allowed to progress at its own pace, finally culminating in the decision to form an ASEAN Free- Trade Area in 1992. Hence, while the push for economic integration in the Asia-Pacific at a rapid pace is laudable, it will be important to keep the agreement flexible and simple, rather than insisting on a formal legalistic structure. This is particularly important in light of the fact that the Asia-Pacific countries have highly diverse legal structures, and the presumption that a "Western" approach should be taken would not be accepted. An emphasis on "building blocks" will be an important means of pushing integration forward without the rigidity of a preferential trade bloc.

Using the framework developed in a previous paper,[12] a possible framework of cooperation that can be considered to strengthen the process of evolutionary integration is outlined below. Such a nondiscriminatory approach could be taken by APEC as a whole, bilaterally, or between groups such as ASEAN and the United States or NAFTA. The discussion is separated into both short- and long-run policies. Short-run policies are defined in a period of implementation parallel with the Uruguay Round schedule; long-run arrangements will be implemented in post–Uruguay Round negotiations.

Short-Run Commitments

Dispute Settlement. An important impediment to intraregional trade and investment has been the failure to rectify disputes expeditiously and amicably, often disrupting mutually-beneficial trade and investment. The new WTO dispute settlement mechanism helps to ensure the rapid resolution of complaints; the APEC or ASEAN–U.S. dispute settlement mechanism would complement this process by setting up, in response to complaints: (a) a consultative forum to discuss the merits of disputes and possible compromises; (b) if no agreement is made, a panel composed of representatives from the participating countries will discuss the issue, rendering a (nonbinding) recommendation on the matter; (c) failing both of these attempts, the issue would be forwarded to the WTO.

Intellectual Property Clause (IPC). The most frequent frictions between the United States and other Asia-Pacific countries relate to issues of intellectual property protection. The Uruguay Round agreement, as well as Intellectual Property Rights (IPR) conventions before it, lays out important improvements in international protection of intellectual property. However, problems will always surface, particularly in light of implementation of IPR laws. The IPC would specify clearly acceptable levels of effectiveness in the implementation of intellectual property protection in the participating countries. A study done on intellectual property rights in the United States and ASEAN[13] indicates clearly that changes can and should be made by all countries, including the United States. Consideration of joint patent offices among groups of countries (especially ASEAN) modelled after that of the EU should also be considered.

Augmented Bilateral Investment Treaty (ABIT). Under the ABIT, the participating countries would generalize individual country bilateral investment treaties and would go further in liberalizing trade-related investment measures, performance requirements, and issues pertaining to the employment of expatriate labor in foreign affiliates, as well as national treatment, guarantees against expropriation, and restrictions on the expatriation of profits. In addition to improving the investment climate in the region and stimulating joint ventures, the ABIT would also help economic integration and would reduce significantly any beggar-thy-neighbor policies in attempting to lure foreign investment.

Government Procurement. An agreement to reduce the minimum value of government contracts that could be bid on by foreign companies could be an important first step to deal with this issue. Moreover, a commitment could be made that any submissions by joint ventures or participating countries would be considered as domestic bids. Finally, a commitment could be made to ensure cooperation in "untying" foreign aid contracts in individual countries.

Services. The countries could pledge to work to expedite the implementation of GATT and to explore improvements in other areas, such as in definitions (e.g., what are "services"? what constitutes "national treatment"?) and data compilation, reducing hidden barriers to trade and investment in services, and exploring options to enhance joint ventures in the services sector. The agreement would ensure that any bilateral accord with third parties would be automatically extended to acceding partners.

Technology Transfer (this might be included under ABIT). The rapidly changing structure of comparative advantage in the region suggests tremendous opportunity for cooperation in the research, development, and production of a wide range of commodities of varying levels of technological development. Increasingly, ASEAN will need to improve its technical abilities to compete above low-cost nations like China and India. The United States will continue to require locational and skill advantages that ASEAN can offer. Hence, for both, greater dissemination of appropriate technologies is of the essence. An ASEAN–U.S. or APEC agreement would recognize the importance of this issue, and would create specific programs to encourage technology dissemination and research and development between the participating countries, through, for example, scholarly and technical exchanges, incentives for joint development, etc.

Tariffs. Under the agreement, the countries would pledge to implement rapidly the tariff reductions, conversions, and binding under the Uruguay Round. Also, it would commit the countries to develop a common customs classification and data base. Moreover, recognizing the importance of the Generalized System of Preference (GSP) to a number of ASEAN countries, the accord would spell out specifically the criteria for graduation or temporary withdrawal of privileges, guaranteeing that either would not be subject to arbitrary or protectionist motivations. It would also de-link GSP privileges from "social" issues, as has been done in the case of China for most-favored-nation treatment.

Nontariff Barriers. The countries would agree to:
- Dedicate all parties to the gradual rollback and eventual elimination of all NTBs to bilateral trade
- Eliminate all import licensing on intraregional trade
- Create special provisions for intraregional exports under rules of origin applicable to NAFTA and AFTA
- Specify clearly acceptable and unacceptable subsidies and methodologies to determine anti-dumping and countervailing duties
- Consolidate improvements under the Uruguay Round with respect to sanitary and phytosanitary measures, pledging to only restrict trade for clear, reasonable health reasons, foregoing arbitrary measures with protectionist intent.

Social Issues and Trade Barriers. Disagreement and frictions between the United States and several Asian countries with respect to various nontrade-related social issues have been increasing in importance and, perhaps, pose the most serious problems in U.S.–Asia relations. The agreement would recognize different social policies in each nation and the possibility of concern by other nations regarding these domestic policies. However, each country would pledge to address these issues through political and other diplomatic means, rather than through various types of economic sanctions.

Long-Term Commitments

The above accord would be implemented over the time horizon of the Uruguay Round, i.e., 10 to 15 years. Once implementation is in progress, the countries can simultaneously agree to schedules for further reductions of trade barriers. The wording in the clause would have to allow for flexibility, shunning strict commitments. While items A–J would have already led the countries down the road toward a comprehensive free-trade area through an evolutionary approach, the mention of a free-trade area has some semantic baggage, and must be treated carefully. We might also suggest that there be some "open regionalism" that would be inherent in any APEC accord, allowing conditional extension to other nations/groups and an accession clause (presumably for Indochina and, perhaps eventually, Burma or other South Asian countries).

CONCLUSIONS

Regional integration is a more difficult task among diverse countries. Questions of equity and distribution of gains become even more pressing when income levels diverge. The structural adjustments necessary when reducing tariff and nontariff barriers are apt to be more painful when levels of industrialization vary widely.

NOTES

1. Additionally, for political but also for economic reasons, the United States did work out preferential arrangements with strategic countries. For example, the U.S. Generalized System of Preference (GSP) scheme is, in effect, a preferential accord in favor of developing countries

(but is nonreciprocal). Also, in 1965, the United States and Canada agreed to free trade in automobile parts. However, these arrangements have proven to be exceptions to the rule.

2.   See the APEC Report of the Eminent Persons, 1993 and 1994. At the November 1994 Readers meeting in Indonesia, APEC leaders agreed to promote "free and open trade in the area" by the year 2020. However, concrete steps to fulfill this vision have yet to be decided.

3.   APEC includes the United States, Canada, Mexico, Chile, Japan, South Korea, China, Taiwan, Hong Kong, the ASEAN countries, Australia, New Zealand, and Papua New Guinea.

4.   Jacob Viner, *The Customs Union Issue* (New York: Carnegie Endowment for International Peace, 1950).

5.   Ippei Yamazawa, "On Pacific Economic Integration," *The Economic Journal* 102 (November 1992): 1519–29.

6.   Jan Tinbergen, *International Economic Integration* (Amsterdam: Elsevier, 1965).

7.   A more detailed review of policies is found in Pearl Imada-Iboshi, Michael G. Plummer, and Seiji Finch Naya, "Building Blocks of U.S.-ASEAN Economic Cooperation" (East-West Center, 1994).

8.   A large literature has emerged that considers the rationale for the United States' movement toward bilateralism. See, for example, Michael G. Plummer, "North American Economic Integration: Trade and Investment Issues," in *AFTA and Beyond: ASEAN Perspectives*, Wisarn Pupphavesa, ed. (Bangkok: Thailand Development Research Institute, 1994), and Jeffrey Schott, ed., *More Free Trade Areas?* (Washington, DC: Institute for International Economics, 1989).

9.   In 1989, Canada's share was actually greater than that of Latin America. U.S. Department of Commerce, Bureau of Economic Analysis (1993).

10. The Report (1993) notes: "To the extent necessary to achieve the ultimate goal of free-trade in the region, *APEC should also pursue an active program of regional trade liberalization.* All such efforts should proceed *on a GATT-consistent basis* and maximize their contribution to global openness. For example, APEC should seek regional agreement on proposals which had been considered in the GATT (e.g., during the Uruguay Round) but could not yet be adopted there. . .*The Asia Pacific Economic Community should seek to `ratchet up' the process of global trade liberalization"* (9, Executive Summary; emphasis from text).

11. Asia-Pacific Economic Cooperation, text of the APEC Final Declaration, 1994.

12. Imada-Iboshi, Plummer, and Naya.

13. Sumner J. La Croix, "Intellectual Property Rights in ASEAN and the United States: Harmonization and Controversy," *PITO Business Environment in ASEAN*, no. 14 (December 1994) (Honolulu, Hawaii: East-West Center).

IMPACT OF APEC
ON THE ASIA-PACIFIC REGION

Joun Yung Sun

POST-COLD WAR WORLD ORDER

T he end of the Cold War has exposed much of our conventional way of thinking to new challenges and rejuvenation. First of all, the power of nations is being redefined. Today, the economic strength of countries constitutes an increasingly important component of national power. Certainly, the pursuit of economic interests has always been implied in relations among nations. With much of the world freed from ideological preoccupations, however, economic issues have come to the forefront in the pursuit of national interests. More and more weight is placed upon the enhancement of international competitiveness of each nation. One can even say now that national security depends on economic strength, since it enables nations to acquire costly state-of-the-art military hardware, proven so crucial in modern warfare.

Economically, the collapse of communism has accelerated the transition of the former socialist countries to market economies and their integration into the global economy. This means that almost all the nations on the globe now compete under the same

Ambassador Joun Yung Sun, appointed Assistant Foreign Minister for Economic Affairs in March 1993, is responsible for directing the development of Korea's trade policies and negotiations on trade issues and general economic cooperation policies, both bilaterally and multilaterally. Prior to his current appointment, he represented his country as South Korea's first Ambassador to Czechoslovakia during 1990-1993. Upon his return, he served briefly as Ambassador-at-large for trade negotiations.

rule, namely, market principles.   This also means that the participants in the global marketplace have increased in number and diversity.

The rules and norms of the global marketplace have changed, too.   The launching of the WTO on the first day of this year signifies that national barriers to the flow of goods and services have been further dismantled, and that international traders and investors will compete in a freer and less restrained atmosphere. From an economic point of view, the significance of national boundaries is becoming less and less relevant.   International economic cooperation is now defined more in terms of interaction between individual enterprises than between nations.

Together, these trends will inevitably lead to unlimited competition on a global scale as well as ever-deepening interdependence among nations.   Such dramatic changes in the international economic environment provide all nations with both opportunities and challenges, which in turn pose uncertainty for their future.   To capitalize on those opportunities and to cope with such uncertainty, countries tend to form groups with like-minded or neighboring countries.   EU, NAFTA, and AFTA are examples of such groupings, although they differ in coverage, scope, and level of integration.   The apparent trend toward economic regionalism is in fact another salient feature of the post-Cold War international economic environment, along with the advent of enhanced globalism symbolized by the WTO.

We have witnessed that regional economic cooperation tends to expand in time into political and security cooperation.   The evolution of the European Economic Community (EEC) into the European Union (EU) is a case in point.   This is not a totally unexpected phenomenon.   Generally speaking, it is difficult to cooperate with any given foreign country economically while antagonizing it politically.   Cooperation or an alliance among states has usually meant cooperation in both political and economic aspects.   During the Cold War era, however, the separation of these two aspects was deemed possible and was actually practiced by some countries.   Yet, as economic considerations assume greater importance in international relations, nations find it increasingly difficult to differentiate between political and economic ties.   Moreover, unlike in the past when a political alliance usually preceded economic cooperation, economic interaction is now expected to pave the path toward political rapprochement. This is another reason why economic cooperation assumes today an even greater importance in international relations.

APEC'S CONTRIBUTION TO TRADE AND INVESTMENT LIBERALIZATION

Against this backdrop, it is beneficial to look at APEC in greater detail. In the last two decades, the Asia-Pacific region has achieved unprecedented economic growth. The total trade volume of APEC member economies in 1992 reached U.S. $3 trillion, representing about 41 percent of world trade. The region also represents 40 percent of the world's population and 50 percent of its global output. Economic relations among the APEC economies themselves have also improved dramatically. Trade among APEC member countries stood at 54 percent of their total trade in 1980, but increased to 66.8 percent in 1992. Intra-regional investment has demonstrated similar growth trends. This enormous economic stake was instrumental in giving birth to APEC in November 1989 as the first intragovernmental forum for regional economic cooperation in the Asia-Pacific region[1].

Since its inception, APEC has set out key principles for its activities, and these two principles have been adhered to faithfully. The first stresses that APEC recognize the diversity of the region, including the differences in member countries' social and economic systems as well as their levels of development. The second principle stresses that APEC, while pursuing its own regional cooperation, contribute to strengthening the open multilateral trading system and preclude the formation of an exclusive trading bloc. It is this second principle that leads naturally to open regionalism and GATT-consistency. The Bogor Declaration of November, 1994 took into account the economic diversity of the region when it set different target years for trade and investment liberalization for developed and developing members[2]. The Declaration also stressed that non-APEC developing countries would benefit from APEC trade and investment liberalization in conformity with GATT/WTO provisions.

Because regional trade arrangements contain both free trade and protectionist aspects vis-a-vis non-members, their compatibility with multilateral trading rules under the

GATT/WTO may be called into question. Although Article 24 of GATT explicitly endorses regional trade arrangements, preferential regional trading arrangements are *ipso facto* contradictory to the MFN rule, which is the bedrock of the multilateral trading system. Given these considerations, it is important to ensure that the benefits of trade and investment liberalization undertaken by regional arrangements be extended to non-members in conformity with GATT/WTO principles. This follows APEC's manifested principle of open regionalism and will ensure compatibility with the WTO system.

APEC is constantly expanding its activities and functions while interacting with subregional groupings within it. Particularly, trade liberalization through APEC provides favorable conditions for ASEAN's trade. The share of intra-regional trade among countries in Southeast Asia has remained stagnant over the past few decades, although the total amount of trade has increased. Intra-ASEAN trade constituted only 19.6 percent of the total trade of ASEAN member countries as of 1991—more or less the same level as 17 percent in 1971 and 18 percent in 1980. This is attributable to their relatively identical industrial structures and level of economic development. This shows that AFTA alone can hardly provide a sufficient framework for trade among its members, even though it may increase the competitiveness of its members in non-AFTA markets. APEC, regionally more expanded and encompassing major economic actors such as the United States, Japan, and China, is and will remain vital to ASEAN countries in increasing their trade. APEC is also expanding its geographic coverage, to perhaps include Indochina and additional Latin American countries in the Pacific rim. The Indian subcontinent is showing interest in establishing some kind of linkage with APEC, too.

APEC is also poised to develop close cooperation with other regional arrangements. All of the NAFTA member countries have joined APEC. It is expected that APEC will help discourage any inclination on the part of NAFTA to become inward-looking or exclusive toward non-members. The EU has recently made it known that a higher priority will be given to its relations with Asia-Pacific nations. The EU has expressed interest in establishing some type of involvement in APEC and is even floating the idea for a joint summit meeting with ASEAN and certain East Asian countries. Such an overture by the EU toward

ASEAN, with which Europeans have traditional ties, may in time lead to some kind of linkage with APEC itself. As the world's two largest economic groups, even though they are beyond comparison in terms of the magnitude of integration for the present moment, APEC and the EU can forge either cooperative or mutually exclusive relations in the future.

However, confrontational relations will benefit neither side. The Asia-Pacific region cannot stand on its own despite its economic dynamism. It is, therefore, important for APEC never to lose its open-minded posture. Once potential conflicts with the WTO, sub-regional groupings in the region, and other regional arrangements are avoided, APEC has a significant potential to function as a locomotive for world economic growth. Given the vast area and population covered and the participation of major world economic powers, APEC's trade and investment liberalization can accelerate trade liberalization at the global level and thus contribute to strengthening the multilateral trading system under the WTO.

APEC AND REGIONAL SECURITY

APEC has been expanding its activities and moving toward institutionalization, regardless of the reluctance on the part of some of its members. The APEC leaders' meetings have been *de facto* regularized, reinforcing high-level political support for APEC's activities and expanding its mandates. Cabinet ministers of different portfolios meet regularly and new committees are being established. For instance, the Committee on Trade and Investment (CTI) was established in 1993, and the Economic Committee in 1994.

Although APEC started mainly as an economy-oriented forum, we may not rule out the possibility of its evolving, in the long run, into a forum for comprehensive intergovernmental cooperation, where political and security issues are also handled. (Certainly, this possibility is contingent on consensus among the members.) The evolution of APEC in this direction may be implied in the difficulty of separating the concepts of economic and political cooperation among countries today.

Even before reaching that level in APEC's evolution, we may foresee the political implications of APEC's activities in the short term. APEC maintains multitiered channels for dialogue, ranging from the leaders' and ministerial meetings down to working level ones. The involvement of people with various backgrounds and portfolios may offer an unexpected but favorable byproduct by helping prevent and even resolve non-economic issues as well. In this respect, APEC is in a position to make significant contributions to confidence-building and preventive diplomacy in the region. The increased economic cooperation through APEC can also prevent economically-motivated disputes through checks and balances among its members, thereby contributing to regional security.

China is currently implementing wider ranging market-oriented reforms, while still maintaining its socialist political structure. Thus far, these reforms have proven successful, as demonstrated by China's annual economic growth of around 10 percent. And yet, no one can predict exactly how China will emerge in the 21st century in terms of economic and military might. Japan, with its defense budget second only to the United States, may opt to rebuild its military powers at some point in the future, as appropriate in light of its own security concerns.

The current state of the Russian Federation after the demise of the communist regime presents another source of uncertainty. When Russia recovers from its domestic economic and other difficulties, it may become more assertive in the region.

There is potential for ethnic conflicts as well. The end of the Cold War unveiled elements of traditional antagonisms and rivalries, creating uncertainty and the possibility of destabilization in the region. There is also uncertainty on the Korean peninsula, emanating from, among other things, the North Korean nuclear problem.

We have yet to devise a comprehensive framework for security that will replace the Cold War security arrangements in the Asia-Pacific region. In July 1994, a forum involving nearly all the countries in the Asia-Pacific region was created with a view to strengthening and enhancing political and security cooperation within the region through confidence and security building among the countries involved. The ASEAN Regional Forum (ARF) is an initial attempt at regional cooperation in political and security matters in addition to the already existing economic cooperation. Notwithstanding its importance, it is only in the early stages of development. It has not become fully organized enough to exert practical influence on security in the region.

Under these circumstances, if the United States reduces its presence in East Asia merely in consideration of its global strategy and the absence of rival military powers, it would seriously undermine stability in the region. For the future, the role of the United States will remain crucial in both sustaining economic growth and maintaining stability and security in the region. This is why no country in East Asia genuinely wants to see the United States disengage from the region. Moreover, given the enormous economic and security interests that the United States has in the Asia-Pacific region, it is less likely to disengage from the region.

CONCLUSION

In the new international environment, APEC member countries will continue to increase economic interactions among themselves and with non-member countries, while competing more vigorously than ever. Broader competition among countries in the Asia-Pacific region, if undertaken fairly under multilateral rules, will increase the region's overall economic efficiency and thus contribute to economic prosperity for the common good of the nations in the region. Moreover, given the uncertainties in the security situation in the region, it is very important for APEC member countries to direct their future efforts at mutual cooperation in such a manner as to promote security as well as economic prosperity in the region.

How do APEC, AFTA, and the WTO fit together? They are all relatively new and continuously evolving organizations and their structural development will merit close study by scholars and government officials for many years to come. Certainly there exists a potential for conflict among them, but it is overwhelmed by their potential for harmony. The reform and liberalization going on in the WTO on a global scale can spawn forward-thinking national policies among countries that wish to take their seats—and reap their rewards—as full members of the international community. Likewise, reform and liberalization at the regional level can prove to be the impetus for more rapid change on a global scale.

The manifest objectives and principles of APEC, AFTA, and the WTO are for freer trade and investment and closer economic cooperation. By their very nature, if these goals are accomplished —and they can be, simultaneously, on global, regional, and subregional levels—they can only lead to more secure political environment as well. Accordingly, the best policy direction for the countries of the Asia-Pacific region is to contribute to the development of open regionalism and to make efforts to help APEC and sub-regional arrangements complement the multilateral trading system under the WTO.

With all its diversity and vastness, the Asia-Pacific region cannot be totally exempt from the potential for conflicts and frictions caused by competing national interests. Nevertheless, motivations for cooperation and harmony far surpass the temptation for confrontation. After all, cooperation and harmony will ensure common prosperity for the nations in the region economically, while maintaining political stability. This is why I am confident that nations in the region will move toward greater harmony and cooperation rather than conflicts and disputes in the future.

NOTES

1. In fact, ideas for some sort of regional economic forum had already been floated since the 1960's. Such ideas were realized in part through the formation of the PBEC (Pacific Basin Economic Committee) and PECC (Pacific Economic Cooperation Council), yet without the involvement of governments in their full capacity.

2. Taking full account of the economic diversity of the region, it was agreed that the industrialized members should eliminate their trade barriers by 2010, and the developing members by 2020.

Part IV

HOW MUCH AND WHAT KIND OF MULTILATERALISM?

REFLECTIONS ON PROSPECTS OF ASIA-PACIFIC MULTILATERALISM

Kwa Chong Guan

SEARCHING FOR NEW STRUCTURES

The bipolar world of the Cold War is past. The structure and equilibrium of power the two superpowers managed to maintain for much of the past half century are irrelevant. The search for alternative structures within which we in the Asia Pacific can relate to each other anew started before the demolition of the Berlin Wall. Mikhail Gorbachev takes the credit for being the first to propose a new structure in his 1986 address at Vladivostok: "A Pacific conference along the lines of the Helsinki conference" to reduce the risk of superpower confrontation in North East Asia. Australian Foreign Minister Bill Hayden in August 1987 proposed a "superpower dialogue" and a series of Confidence Building Measures (CBMs) similar to those recommended by the Conference on Security and Cooperation in Europe (CSCE); he repeated the proposal a year later. All these, however, were rejected by the United States.

Today the need for alternative structures to cater to our different security priorities and concerns is perceived to be more

---

Dr. Kwa Chong Guan is Vice-Chairman of the Singapore Institute of International Affairs and a member of Singapore's CSCAP National Committee. Prior to his current appointment, he was Director of the Oral History Centre and, concurrently, the National Museum. Dr. Kwa has published in the field of Southeast Asian art history and archaeology.

urgent. High economic growth rates have enabled the armed forces of many countries to modernize their arms inventories.[1] The old concern that enlarging and improving arms inventories is destabilizing because it increases the probability of inadvertent conflict has been renewed. Calls for some form of arms control have followed.[2]

In 1990 Australian Foreign Minister Gareth Evans revived in a series of statements to Australian audiences his predecessor's call for establishing some form of common security through a process and institution that could be modelled after the CSCE.[3] His Canadian counterpart, Joe Clark, followed with broadly similar proposals for "a Pacific adaption of the Conference of Security and Cooperation in Europe." Not unexpectedly, both proposals were rejected by the United States.

Complementing these proposals for new structures and processes to negotiate our security and defense concerns in the Asia Pacific was also a growing need for alternative structures and processes to coordinate our growing economic interdependence.[4] The 1985 Plaza Agreement on currency realignment negotiated by the Group of Seven transformed Japan overnight into a capital surplus economy and released a new wave of Japanese investments into the region. Within ASEAN this new wave of Japanese investments threatened to integrate our economies in ways ASEAN had not anticipated.[5] The Four Modernizations launched by Deng Xiaoping is transforming the Chinese economy and creating the spectre of a Greater China.[6] The emergence of the four little dragons—South Korea, Taiwan, Hong Kong and to a lesser extent, Singapore—as net suppliers of capital to regional markets has increased further the complexity of regional economic interdependence.

CREATING AN ASIAN WAY TO PEACE IN THE 1960s

These proposals for multilateralism at the beginning of the 1990s recall an earlier series of proposals for regional cooperation in the 1960s. Malaysia, Thailand, and the Philippines in 1961 formed the Association of South East Asia [ASA) "to establish an effective machinery for friendly consultations, collaboration and mutual assistance in the economic, social, cultural, scientific and administrative fields." But negative Indonesian and Filipino responses to the inclusion of Malaysia aborted ASA taking off. However bilateral Malaysia-Thai and Philippine-Thai discussions on joint projects continued and by 1966 five project proposals reached funding status. The following Philippines proposal for a loose confederation of the Malay peoples of island South East Asia, Mushawarah Maphilindo, also never took off after its formation in 1963. More successful was the 1965 initiative by South East Asian Ministers of Education to form themselves into a Council and establish an Interim Secretariat to look into setting up regional centers of education with United States funding. Today SEAMEO is a thriving organization coordinating the work of nine regional centers.[7]

Complementing these South East Asian initiatives for multilateralism were a number of Japanese initiatives. The first of these initiatives was made as early as 1957, 2 years after the formal termination of the Allied Occupation of Japan, by Prime Minister Nobusuke Kishi. But these proposals raised the spectre of an earlier East Asian Co-Prosperity Sphere and were stillborn. More successful were Japanese initiatives for the establishment of an Asian Productivity Organization (APO) in 1961 and the Asian Parliamentarians' Union (APU) which by 1980 had widen to become the Asian-Pacific Parliamentarians' Union (APPAU). In the mid-1960s Japan, apparently inspired by its new "Asian diplomacy" launched two initiatives for multilateralism in the region. One was directed towards Korea, with whom Japan launched the Asian & Pacific Council, which in turn led to a number of subsidiary institutions. Most of these folded in 1972, when their members apparently thought the Cold War assumptions underlying the Asian & Pacific Council irrelevant after Nixon's visit to China. The other initiative was directed toward South East Asia, where Japan proposed the formation of a Ministerial Conference for the Economic Development of South East Asia (SEAMCED). With Japanese funding, some seven organizations were eventually set up, ranging from a Fisheries Development Centre to an Agency for Regional Transport and Communications and a Study Group on Asian Tax Administration and Research.[8]

It may be salutary to recall that an earlier series of initiatives for regional cooperation was made some four and a half decades ago, when an Economic Commission for Asia and the Far East was established in 1947 (and became the Economic and Social

Commission for Asia and the Pacific in 1974). Three years later the Colombo Plan for Co-Operative Economic Development was set up with British Commonwealth of Nations backing. And in 1954 the South-East Asia Collective Defense Treaty which brought SEATO into existence, was signed in Manila. The Federation of Malay, soon after it won its independence in 1957, signed with Britain the Anglo-Malayan Defence Agreement (AMDA) and confirmed Australian and New Zealand links with this Agreement in separate notes exchanged in 1959. The AMDA replaced an earlier ad hoc Australian, New Zealand and Malayan (ANZAM) Defence Committee which had been coordinating defence matters in Malaya since 1948.

DEFINING AN ASIAN WAY TO PEACE

If these earlier initiatives for regional cooperation were successful, it was because they followed an Asian way to peace, as Michael Haas documented.[9] This Asian way, Haas pointed out, is based upon building social relationships of solidarity founded upon affinity, affection, or kinship, *gemeinschaft* in the terminology of Ferdinand Tonnies, rather than upon contractual relations (*gesellschaft*) founded upon a division of labor. *Gemeinschaft* leads to mutual trust and consensus building, toward *mufakat* as ASEAN terms it, through a process of *mushawarah* between friends and brothers. In contrast, *gemeinschaft* is framed within Cartesian logic of individual self-interest that leads to formal contracting and institutionalization of relations.

This logic of institutionalizing relations assumes that creation of some kind of organization within which multilateralism can be practiced, and its progress monitored and measured, is preferred. If states and their governments rationally think through their interests, they must conclude that some construct of a more formal arrangement to cooperate is preferable. The Asian way, however, is more reflective, perceiving multilateralism more as a process which may, but does not necessarily have to lead to the creation of an organization. The Asian way recognizes the differences of values, norms, and practices among nations and therefore emphasizes the search for commonalities and understanding of each other, the building of confidence in each other.[10]

The Asian way, Haas further pointed out, prefers working toward shared objectives through informal incrementalism or "small steps rather than by drawing up grand blueprints or timetables." This Asian incrementalism, Haas described, "differs from Western incrementalism, notably of the Fabian variety. The latter sets up an institution and endows it with a mission in a carefully worded constitution or charter. Asian incrementalism instead stresses the utility of noninstitutional frameworks for discussion, while operational activities are entrusted to organizations without elaborate constitutional specifications."

Establishing norms and enunciating principles, is according to Haas, more important in the Asian way to peace than counting beans of what can or has been achieved. "Asian diplomacy," Haas noted, "contains a commitment to abstract goals first. . . . Implementation is assigned to administrative subordinates who are not supposed to throttle the attainment of political objectives. . . . The Western preference for making decisions only about matters that can be quickly and optimally translated into action is not part of the Asian way."

The Asian way to peace Haas has described corresponds to the main features of the strategic culture of the region. The key components of this strategic culture have been defined by Desmond Ball[11] as longer planning perspectives, reliance on bilateral rather than multilateral approaches, commitment to the principle of noninterference in other countries' internal affairs, more flexible and informal decisionmaking styles based upon pragmatism and consensus, and preference for a multidimensional approach to defence and security.

SECURITY: COMMON OR COMPREHENSIVE

This record of Asian experience in regional cooperation suggests that they are at the rather fundamental level of what constitutes regional cooperation for security. The Asian understanding differs from the recent proposals for some kind of CSCE form or architecture. Underlying the CSCE is the assumption that security is interdependent and common, that we share a common destiny. This concept that our security is interdependent and common is the central theme and structure of the Palme Commission's report, *Common Security: A Blueprint for Survival*.

The Commission called for "acceptance of common security as the organizing principle for efforts to reduce the risk of war, limit arms, and move towards disarmament means, in principle, that cooperation will replace confrontation in resolving conflicts."[12] The CSCE's first Basket of a group of three on security issues that need to be addressed is in effect an attempt to implement the Palme Commission's six principles of common security that:

- All nations have a legitimate right to security
- Military force is not a legitimate instrument for resolving disputes between nations
- Restraint is necessary in expressing national policy
- Security cannot be attained through military superiority
- The reduction and qualitative limitation of armaments are necessary for common security
- "Links" between arms negotiations and political events should be avoided.

But Asian experiences and memories of what constitutes our security differ from that of Europe. The Allied military administration of South East Asia and Japan after World War II fundamentally shaped the subsequent course of our development and security.[13] In Japan, post-war Prime Minister Yoshida Shigeru developed a "doctrine" emphasizing economic nationalism, restraining remilitarization, and close relations with the United States.[14] The legacy of Yoshida's stress on economic nationalism is clear today, as is the downplaying of the military. In 1980 these elements of national policy were reformulated into an overarching policy of comprehensive security.[15]

In South East Asia, allied attempts to reimpose a colonial order were challenged and the subsequent struggles for independence have shaped our concepts of security. In a number of cases external support for domestic political groups (in particular, Chinese Communist Party support for South East Asian Communist parties) complicated the struggle for independence and subsequent efforts to create new nations. These struggles for nationhood made a number of ASEAN countries recognize that domestic security of the state is as critical as its external security, leading them to adopt a wider, more comprehensive concept of security that goes beyond military capabilities to include economic, social, and other domestic capabilities structures.[16]

China's historical experience has also led it to different perceptions of security. The 1911 Revolution that deposed the last Qing emperor did not lead to a new era, as in Russia, but soon degenerated into warlordism followed by the Japanese invasion and occupation of China. China's experiences with alliances has not been congenial. It was forced during World War I to break with Germany to ally with the Allied Powers, but got nothing from that alliance at the end of the war nor support when Japan invaded Manchuria and subsequently China. And China's post-World War II alliance with the Soviet Union has not improved its confidence in alliances. Consequently China's attitude toward the current proposals for multilateralism that may lead to a multilateral security structure has been cautious, if not sceptical.[17]

Further, the experiences of developing nations have led a number of South East Asians to the perception that a primary cause of regional instability and insecurity is major power rivalry and intervention, and the region will be better if it can be isolated from the broader international system. Such perceptions appear to underlie the Malaysian proposal, made by its then Prime Minister Tun Abdul Razak at the 1970 Non-Aligned Summit, for the creation of a Zone of Peace, Freedom and Neutrality (ZOPFAN) in South East Asia. This was to be achieved by the United States, the Soviet Union and China guaranteeing the collective neutralization of the region by refraining from intervening in its affairs. Also, South East Asian countries were expected not to intervene in each other's affairs and not to become involved in the rivalry between the big powers. Response to the Malaysian proposal from its ASEAN partners was mixed and qualified. But the proposal for a ZOPFAN became a formal ASEAN policy when the ASEAN heads of government incorporated it in their Declaration of ASEAN Concord at their first meeting in 1976. The proposal for a ZOPFAN may have been idealistic and its assumptions not very well grounded, but it clearly indicates that as early as 1970, some of us in ASEAN were thinking of different alternatives to ensuring regional security.[18]

ARF AND CONFIDENCE- AND SECURITY - BUILDING MEASURES

Today the legacy of ZOPFAN lives on in ASEAN's search for alternatives to ensuring regional stability and security. At the fourth meeting of heads of government of ASEAN (in Singapore) in July 1993 it was agreed that the annual Post-Ministerial Conference should engage in a security dialogue. In July 1994 the ministers of the seven dialogue partners with whom ASEAN had been conducting bilateral sessions (the United States, Japan, South Korea, Australia, New Zealand, Canada and the European Union), the People's Republic of China, Russia, Vietnam, Laos and Papua New Guinea (the latter three were signatories of ASEAN's Treaty of Amity and Cooperation) for a 3-hour Regional Forum with their ASEAN counterparts.[19] A communique issued at the end of the meeting contained a comprehensive list of measures, including preventive diplomacy, confidence and security building measures (CSBMs) for conflict prevention, and conflict resolution, all of which the participants of the ASEAN Regional Forum thought worthy of further study.

How are these proposals to be further studied? One approach is to study the European experience of these measures in the CSCE and propose their applicability to Asia. But is the European experience that much of a model? Is there a clearly defined European experience? The records suggest there may not be an agreed European model but several evolving variants. And who is to participate in which measure is unclear.[20] Moreover, the strategic assumptions underpinning the CSCE—stabilization of a bipolar Cold War World and demarcation of the territorial and ideological boundaries of that Cold War world—are rather irrelevant in Asia. True, the CSCE fairly rapidly adapted to the post-Cold War world in shifting its priorities from arms control, confidence building and human rights to conflict prevention and resolution, peacekeeping and minority rights, but the CSCE failed its first critical test when confronted by the disintegration of one of its founder members, Yugoslavia, into military conflict. The European experience may be more relevant of what not to do.

THE TREATY OF AMITY AND COOPERATION

An alternative starting point to study the measures listed by the ARF is to build on the Asian experience and further develop the Asian way to peace. The ARF participants recognized this in endorsing the purposes and principles of ASEAN's Treaty of Amity and Cooperation as a code of conduct for governing regional relations. In the Asian context, the Grotian vision of an international community is not deeply ingrained in our social memories. Some of us in Asia continue to subscribe to a more Hobbesian view of the international system.

If some of us continue to perceive the world in Hobbesian perspectives, it is because our social notion of who we are as a community and how we respond to our changing world as a group are evolving much slower than the pace of political and especially economic and technological change. Some of us continue to perceive the world in Marxist-Leninist categories, others in terms of neutrality, but most from variant perspectives of realpolitik. The implications of growing economic interdependence are only beginning to impact on our social ideas of the sovereignty of a nation state. The concept that we may need to rethink our security as interdependent with others, rather than against them, is still new.

The Treaty of Amity and Cooperation as concluded by the heads of government of ASEAN, provides an established base upon which to review, affirm or, if necessary, build anew norms and principles for interstate relations in the Asia Pacific. Based largely on the United Nations charter and the sanctity of national sovereignty, the Treaty outlines a code of conduct for regional relations. A significant provision in the Treaty is for the specfic settlement of disputes among signatories by a High Council. The High Council consists of other signatories to the Treaty. The ASEAN heads deliberately made the Treaty open for accession by other regional states, especially the former Indochinese states which had just come under Communist rule. Brunei was the first new signatory in January 1984, upon joining ASEAN. Papua New Guinea, an observer at ASEAN meetings, affirmed the Treaty in July 1989.

The next step may well be to study how to open up the Treaty of Amity and Cooperation to other members of ARF by way of a protocol to support it as the legal base for regional order and conduct in the Asia Pacific. The alternative will be to draft a new Declaration on peace and cooperation for the Asia Pacific that may be based on the Treaty of Amity and Cooperation, but could also draw upon other agreements, declarations and treaties, among which could be the 1955 Bandung Conference Declaration on World Peace and Cooperation. The primary aim of such an exercise must be to think through fundamental principles and goals, to review and revise mental maps of the world,[21] for what we agree to will shape the nature and structure of the international society we want to live in.[22] Until we can agree to the kind of world we want to live in, we are unlikely to agree to much else.

CSBMS: THE ASIAN WAY

A number of assumptions defining the Asian Way to peace will determine which of the measures tabled by ARF are feasible and how they can be implemented. First and foremost is that proposed measures must not intrude into the domestic affairs of participating states. Until countries in the region are prepared to rethink fundamental assumptions underlying the classical concepts of sovereignty,[23] then measures seeking to constrain a state by reducing risk of accident and conflict, such as airspace and maritime control agreements or exclusion and separation measures such as a demilitarized zone for the South China Sea and the Spratly Islands, may be stillborn.

The second assumption is that proposed measures must be agreed to by all participants. It may sound trite, but it is worth reiterating that Asia Pacific countries are unlikely to participate and implement CSBMs until and unless they are convinced it is not a zero-sum game. There must be something to be gain from the exercise. Even the United States was not committed until recently; its experience with NATO allies led it to prefer bilateral ties with its Asian allies. [24] The idea that it may be in the interest of Asia-Pacific states to participate in some form of multilateralism, because the cost of not doing so may be higher,[25] may have taken root but does not appear to have flowered. Careful nurturing of these ideas of multilateralism is needed.

The third assumption is that our social ideas and experiences of earlier regional cooperation suggest that we start slowly and incrementally build up regional cooperation for security. Working informally rather than through channels is more suitable. Much depends upon our understanding of the different forms of cooperation in different fields. The South East Asian experience seems to be more comfortable with schemes for educational and technical cooperation, as in SEAMEO; or even economic cooperation as in the PECC or the Pacific Basin Economic Council and APEC today. The payoff from conforming to sets of explicit principles, norms, rules and decisionmaking procedures, from becoming a member of a "cooperation regime"[26] is clear, but the payoff from becoming a member of an international security regime is not. If Asia-Pacific states are cautious about participating in regional cooperation for security because the payoffs are uncertain, then the approach to regional cooperation must be to invite these cautious states into discussions with others in order to generate new ideas and approaches. Regional cooperation for security may need to be more reflective.[27]

CONCLUSIONS

The conceptual maps that guided us through the Cold War are increasingly irrelevant, but we do not have new conceptual maps to the post-Cold War strategic terrain. We continue to survey and chart. For a number of us in the Asia-Pacific it is not at all clear that we are moving into a unipolar world revolving around the United States.[28] Are we searching for a new balance of power in an increasingly fragmented and multipolar world? Who will be balancing whom in the post-Cold War World? Perhaps we are observing the emergence of a concert of powers, except that the forum to bring it together is absent.[29] Are we then left with variant concepts of our growing interdependent economies and security? Are these emerging concepts of common and comprehensive security going to be the landmarks of our new strategic landscape? It would appear increasingly so.

If these emerging ideas of comprehensive and common security are to drive our policy agendas, are they sufficiently clear, articulated, and widely shared? If, as it appears, these concepts are neither clear nor shared, that Asia-Pacific states are interpreting these concepts rather differently in the framework of their society and experiences, then who is to ensure that there is a meeting of minds and ideas? Perhaps this is where fora and especially the Council on Security Cooperation in the Asia Pacific (CSCAP) can play an critical role.[30]

NOTES

1. The complex link between economic growth and military procurement and deployment is explored by R. E. Looney & P. C. Frederiksen, "The economic determinants of military expenditure in selected East Asian countries," *Contemporary South East Asia* 11/iv (Mar

90), 274ff and A. L. Ross, "Growth, debt and military spending in South East Asia," *Contemporary South East Asia* 11/iv, 257-9.

2. The classic statement linking arms races to war is by L F Richardson, *Arms and insecurity* (Pittsburgh 1960). Proposals for arms controls have been made by R. Huisken, *Limitations of armaments in South East Asia: A Proposal*, Canberra Papers on Strategy & Defence no. 16 (Canberra: Strategic & Defence Studies Centre, Australian National University, 1977) and A. Acharya, *An Arms Race in Post-Cold War South East Asia? Prospects for Control,* Pacific Strategic Papers no. 8 (Singapore: Institute for South East Asian Studies, 1994).

3. The Australian proposal and related issues are examined by G. Wiseman, "Common security in the Asia-Pacific region," *Pacific Rev* 5/i (1992): 42-59; P. M Cronin, "Pacific rim security: Beyond bilateralism," *Pacific Rev* 5/iii (1992): 209-20 and G. Klintworth, "Asia-Pacific: More security, less uncertainty, new opportunities," *Pacific Rev* 5/iii, (1992): 221-31.

4. Further explored in R. Higgott, R. Leaver, and J. Ravenhill, eds., *Pacific Economic Relations in the 1990s Cooperation or conflict?* (St Leonards, New South Wales: Allen & Unwin, 1993). At a more fundamental level is the issue of whether Asia's development is only a "myth" as Paul Krugman, "The Myth of Asia's Miracle," *Foreign Affairs* 73/vi (1994): 62-78 argues, and the consequences when that "myth" breaks.

5. Discussed by Pasuk Phongpaichit, *The New Wave of Japanese Investment in ASEAN: Determinants and Prospects* (Singapore: Institute of South East Asian Studies ASEAN Economic Research Unit, 1990).

6. See in particular the contributions of H. Harding, "The Concept of 'Greater China': Themes, Variations and Reservations," R. Ash and Y. Y. Kueh, "Economic Integration Within Greater China: Trade and Investment Flows Between China, Hong Kong and Taiwan," and Wang Gungwu, "Greater China and Chinese Overseas," and other papers in *China Quarterly* 136 (Dec 93) on "Greater China."

7. The public documents of ASA and SEAMEO are in M. Haas, *Basic Documents of Asian Regional Organizations* 6, 287-88 for ASA, and 7, 28-118 for SEAMEO ((Dobbs Ferry,NY: Oceana Publs, 1979).

8. For documentation of SEAMCED and organizations it spawned, see Haas, 501.

9. M. Haas, *The Asian Way to Peace; A Story of Regional Cooperation* (New York: Praeger, 1989).

10. The difference between these two approaches corresponds to Robert O Keohane's distinction between a "rationalistic" and a "reflective" approach to international institutions in his "International Institutions: Two approaches," *International Studies Q* 32 (1988), 379-396.

11. Ball, *Strategic Culture in the Asia-Pacific Region (with some implications for regional security cooperation)*, Working Paper 3, 270 (Canberra: Strategic & Defence Stud Cent, Australian National Univ 1993), 11, and M. Haas, "Asian Culture and International Relations," in Jongsuk Chay, ed., *Culture and International Relations* (New York: Praeger, 1990), 172-190.

12. Olaf Palme, et al., *Common Security: A Blue Print for Survival* (New York: Simon & Schuster, 1982). See also Geoffrey Wiseman's *Common Ssecurity and Non-provocative Defence: Alternative Approaches to the Security Dilemma* (Canberra: Australian National Univ., Research Sch Pacific Stud., Peace Research Cent., 1989), for discussion of this and other concepts of security. David B Dewit distinguishes common security from cooperative security in his "Common, Comprehensive, and Cooperative Security in Asia-Pacific," *Pacific Review.*

13. British military administration is officially described in detail by F. S. V. Donnison, *British military administration in the Far East 1943-46* (London: HMSO, 1956). On the political legacy, see Louis Allen, *The End of the War in Asia* (London: Hart-Davis, MacGibbon, 1976).

14. J. W. Dower, *Empire and Aftermath; Yoshida Shigeru and the Japanese Experience 1878-1954* (Cambridge, Mass.: Council on East Asian Stud., Harvard Univ, 1979). The term "Yoshida Doctrine" is however a creation of the 1970s.

15. Umemoto Tetsuya, "Comprehensive security and the evolution of the Japanese security posture," in R. A. Scalapino et al., eds., *Asian Security Issues: Regional and Global* (Berkeley: Institute for East Asian Studies, Univ. California, 1988).

16. Muthiah Alagappa, "Comprehensive security: Interpretations in ASEAN countries," in Scalapino et al.

17. See Banning Garrett and Bonnie Glaser, "Multilateral security in the Asia-Pacific region and its impact on Chinese interests: Views from Beijing," *Contemporary SEAsia* 16/i (1994), 14-34, who attempt to sort out China's interest and stake in multilateralism.

18. Heiner Hanggi, *ASEAN and the ZOPFAN concept*, Pacific Strategic Papers 4 (S'pore: Instit SEAsian Stud., 1991). On attempts to neutralize the region, see Dick Wilson, *The Neutralization of South East Asia* (New York: Praeger, 1975), also Wolfgang Stargardt, "Neutrality within the Asian system of powers," in Lau Teik Soon, ed., *New Directions in the International Relations of South East Asia* (Singapore: Univ Press, 1973).

19. Pauline Kerr, "The Security Dialogue in the Asia-Pacific," *Pacific Rev.* 7/iv (1994), 397, provides a narrative of the events and forces leading to the formation of the ARF.

20. See Trevor Findlay, "Confidence-Building Measures for the Asia-Pacific: The relevance of the European experience," in Muthiah Alagappa, ed., *Building Confidence; Resolving Conflicts: Proceedings of*

the Second Asia-Pacific Roundtable, Kuala Lumpur, July 1-4, 1988 (New York/Lond.: Kegan Paul, 1989), 55-8. Stefan Lehne, *The CSCE in the 1990s: Common European House or Potemkin Village?* Laxenburg Papers 9 (Vienna: Austrian Institute for International Affairs, 1991) re-evaluates the European experience.

21. The impact of world views, beliefs and values on foreign policy is explored in Judit Goldstein and R. O. Keohane, eds., *Ideas and foreign policy; Beliefs, institutions, and political change* (Ithaca: Cornell Univ Press, 1993).

22. Hedley Bull was moving to explore this in his too-brief career. His ideas have been further developed in Bull and Adam Watson, eds., *The Expansion of International Society* (Oxford: Clarendon, 1984).

23. Described by F. H Hinsley, *Sovereignty,* 2nd ed. (Cambridge: Univ Press, 1986). But satellite dishes and stock markets today are eroding a state's claim to exclusive territorial control, see e.g. J. A. Camilleri and J. Falk, *The End of Sovereignty? The Politics of a Shrinking and Fragmenting World* (Aldershot: Edward Elgar, 1992).

24. Former U.S. Secretary of State James A. Baker III's statement, "America in Asia: Emerging Architecture for a Pacific Community," *Foreign Affairs* 70/i (Winter 1991-92): 1-18 appears to signal changing U.S. attitudes toward multilateralism. In this statement Baker proposed three pillars for a new Asia Pacific architecture: a framework for economic integration; a commitment to democratisation and a renewed defence structure for the region.

25. There is a growing literature attempting to explain why nations cooperate, much of it within the framework of game theory; see R. Alexrod, *The Evolution of Cooperation* (New York: Basic Bks, 1984); K. A. Oye, ed., *Cooperation Under Anarchy* (Princeton: Univ Press, 1986); A. A. Stein, *Why Nations Cooperate: Circumstances and Choice in International Relations* (Ithaca: Cornell Univ Press, 1990); and J. G. Stein & L. W. Pauly, eds., *Choosing to Co-operate: How States Avoid Loss* (Baltimore: John Hopkins Univ Press, 1993).

26. R. O. Keohane, *After Hegemony: Cooperation and Discord in the World Political Economy* (Princeton: Univ Press, 1984), argues for cooperation regimes based on mutual calculation of benefits to be gained.

27. Or, as Ernst B Haas argues, how to change the definition of the problem to be solved through either adaption or learning process in his *When Knowledge is Power: Three Models of Change in International Organizations* (Berkeley: Univ California Press, 1990).

28. As propounded by Joseph S. Nye, Jr., among others, in *Bound to Lead: The Changing Nature of American Power* (New York: Basic Bks, 1990), and critique by C. Layne, "The Unipolar Illusion; Why New Great Powers Will Rise," *International Security* 17/iv (1993).

29. The issues of organizing a concert and its underlying assumptions of collective security are discussed in C. A. Kupchan and C. A. Kupchan, "Concerts, Collective Security and the Future of Europe," *International Security* 16/i (1991), 114-61.

30. See the contributions to *Pacific Rev* 7/iv (1994) on ideas, identity and policy coordination in the Asia-Pacific coordinated by Richard Higgott.

MAKING MULTILATERALISM WORK:
ARF and Security in the Asia-Pacific

Amitav Acharya

OVERVIEW

T he launching of the ASEAN Regional Forum in Bangkok in July 1994 is a major milestone in the security environment of the Asia Pacific region.[1] ARF is an important and, in many respects, unique regional security institution. It is the first truly "multilateral" security forum covering the wider Asia-Pacific region. It is the only "regional" security framework in the world today in which all the great powers (including the United States, Russia, Japan, China, as well as Britain, France, and Germany as part of the European Union delegation) are represented. ARF is also a rare example of a security institution in which the great power members have willingly conceded leadership and agenda-setting functions to the less powerful developing member states (ASEAN). ARF thus represents a bold experiment in regionalism geared to addressing the uncertainties and anxieties associated with the post-Cold War security outlook in the Asia-Pacific region.

Dr. Amitav Acharya is Associate Professor, York University, and Senior Fellow, University of Toronto-York University Joint Centre for Asia Pacific Studies. From 1990 to 1992, he was Lecturer, Department of Political Science, National University of Singapore. He has published widely on South East Asia.

The emergence of ARF deserves careful scrutiny. This brief analysis is intended to examine some of the key questions related to the evolution, role and limitations of ARF.

At the outset, it is necessary to reflect on the "multilateral" character of ARF. Multilateralism in international relations is not just a question of numbers. In a multilateral setting, the nature of the relationship among the actors is a more important attribute than the number of actors involved. The key aspect of multilateralism is its "inclusive," or nondiscriminatory character. As Ruggie observes:

> In its pure form, a multilateral order embodies rules of conduct that are commonly applicable to countries, as opposed to discriminating among them, based on situational exigencies and particularistic preferences...The [multilateral] principle in economic relations prescribes an international economic order in which exclusive blocs of differential treatment of trading partners and currencies are forbidden, and in which point-of-entry barriers to transactions are minimized.[2]

As in the economic arena, security multilateralism involves an essentially equitable and nonexclusionary setting for cooperation in peace, conflict resolution, and order maintenance. ARF clearly fits this conception of multilateralism. In the words of Malaysia's Foreign Minister, Abdullah Badawi, the concept of ARF "requires the development of friendship rather than the identification of enemies. The nature of security problems in the Asia-Pacific are [sic] such that they do not lend themselves amenable for management through the old method of deterrence by countervailing force."[3] The membership of ARF is more "inclusive" than the ASEAN-PMC process on which it is based. Unlike the latter, ARF is not a dialogue among the like-minded; it engages regional actors having different and perhaps conflicting perspectives on regional security issues.[4] Thus, as the Foreign Minister of Australia points out, the purpose of ARF is to build "security with others rather than against them."[5]

Multilateralism as embodied in ARF can thus be defined *substantively* in direct opposition to the "exclusive bilateralism" of America's post-World War II security strategy in the region. U.S. strategy, as advocates of multilateralists would argue, focused primarily on a balance-of-power approach maintained by a regional network of bilateral military alliances. In contrast, multilateralists promise "common" or "cooperative" security institutions that would be "inclusive" in scope and political (nonmilitary) in content.[6]

THE EVOLUTION OF ARF

Why is the Asia-Pacific region now witnessing the emergence of multilateral security cooperation? In post-Second World War, multilateralism in regional security affairs found expression in a number of organizations such as the Organization of American States (OAS), the Arab League, and the Organization of African Unity (OAU) that were geared primarily to the pacific settlement of intraregional disputes. The Asia-Pacific region was noticeably lacking in such regional frameworks. To a large extent, this reflected U.S. policy preferences in the Cold War period. As the dominant global institution builder and the strongest Pacific military and economic power, the United States did not see multilateralism as a particularly necessary or desirable form of security institution in this region. American security objectives here were strongly oriented to ensuring the containment of the Soviet Union and China, which in turn required security arrangements with a collective defense function, rather than "inclusive" political institutions geared to the pacific settlement of intraregional conflicts. Thus, U.S. regional security approach focused heavily on forging a network of alliances aimed at countering the perceived threat of communism, but these alliances were mostly bilateral in scope (with the limited exception of the tripartite ANZUS Treaty involving Australia, New Zealand and the United States). Initial U.S. efforts to create a regionwide security structure were thwarted by the sheer diversity of security challenges (such as the salience of internal security concerns in Southeast Asia versus the more direct Soviet and Chinese threat in Northeast Asia) facing the region's pro-Western countries. In addition, serious limitations on the latter's military capabilities undermined the strategic coherence and deterrent value of any prospective NATO-type Pacific alliance and diminished U.S. interest in developing them. Testifying to this was America's weak commitment to the short-lived South East Asia Treaty Organization (SEATO), an eight-member defense arrangement that failed to make much impact on the region's security architecture. In contrast, the United States was able to establish a network of bilateral alliances involving Japan, South Korea, Thailand, the Philippines and the Republic of China. These bilateral arrangements promised greater U.S. control and flexibility in dealing with its regional allies and reduced the need for multilateral systems; together they amounted to what Dulles termed as a "mutual security system...[constituting] a defensive bulwark for freedom in that part of the world."[7]

The birth of the ASEAN in 1967 marked the emergence of the first indigenous framework for multilateral political and security cooperation in the Asia-Pacific. ASEAN, however, fearful of provoking its Indochinese adversaries, chose initially to downplay its political/security functions. Until the end of the Cold War, ASEAN remained an inward-looking and somewhat exclusionary subregional grouping with its members sharing a common suspicion of security arrangements with outside powers (even though all except Indonesia retained security ties with friendly Western powers).

The end of the Cold War led to a dramatic shift in the regional states' attitudes toward multilateralism for a number of reasons. First, it removes the overarching security cleavage that had hitherto sustained the appeal of deterrence-based security strategies. Second, multilateralism is seen as a necessary "insurance policy" by policymakers anticipating a steady and marked decline in the US regional military presence. While the actual extent of the US military retrenchement is not significant, there continues to be a general perception of the *relative* decline of the United States in a regional security milieu marked by the rise of several competing centers of power. The fact that the U.S. security umbrella can no longer be taken for granted has fuelled a search for alternative security strategies, including those based on a multilateral approach.

Third, multilateralism has been viewed in some quarters as a *desirable* long-term alternative to balance-of-power security concepts. These concepts, always regarded by their critics as conflict-aggravating and unreliable,[8] appeared to be particularly irrelevant and unhelpful at a time when the region's principal adversaries, such as the ASEAN states and Vietnam, Russia and Japan, and China and Russia were searching for a common ground to bury the Cold War hatchet. Fourth, the dramatic success of a particular form of security multilateralism, the Conference on

Security and Cooperation in Europe (CSCE), in ending the Cold War in Europe provided an initial impetus for some proposals for similar arrangements in the Asia-Pacific, despite the skepticism expressed by many regional countries about the feasibility of duplicating the CSCE here.

A final factor contributing to the perceived need for multilateralism is the growing economic and security interdependence between Northeast Asian economies and Southeast Asia. Problems such as the territorial disputes in the South China Sea or the potential for regional hegemonism by China and Japan transcend subregional dimensions. Regional security has become more indivisible than ever before since developments in one segment of the region can seriously affect the security of the other. In this context, bilateral and subregional approaches are deemed inadequate for ensuring regional stability.

The advocacy of security multilateralism since the late 1980s has taken many forms. Among the numerous proposals and positions that have marked the security debate in the Asia-Pacific region are:[9]

- Separate proposals made by the former Soviet Union (under Gorbachev) and Australia calling a new, broad-brush, macroregional security institution to facilitate confidence-building and conflict resolution within the region
- A Canadian initiative called the North Pacific Cooperative Security Dialogue (NPCSD), which envisaged a subregional membership, and called for the retention of bilateral security arrangements pending a gradual process of institutionalization addressed to both military and non-military threats;
- The notion of "ad hoc" or "flexible" multilateralism preferred by Japan and the United States. Essentially a reaction to the earlier proposals for a CSCE-type arrangement, it reflects U.S. opposition to the creation of any new security institution that might undermine the rationale for its existing alliances. This approach to multilateralism involved selective modes of cooperative action to deal with specific security problems by those most immediately affected by it
- An initiative by the ASEAN members to develop a regionwide dialogue on security issues that would follow their annual multilateral consultations (called the ASEAN post-ministerial conferences, or ASEAN-PMC) on economic and political matters with a number of "dialogue partners." The

idea of the "enhanced-PMC" later developed into ARF, a multilateral security dialogue focussing on transparency and confidence-building issues in the wider Asia-Pacific region.

THE POTENTIAL CONTRIBUTION OF ARF

To some extent, ARF came to reflect a compromise in the security debate between those who had called for a new multilateral security institution and those who, at least initially, had rejected the very notion of multilateralism, but ARF's potential to contribute to regional security goes well beyond its ability to take the middle ground. To begin with, ARF could claim to have "indigenous" roots, rather than being an implantation of supposedly "foreign" models of multilateralism such as the CSCE. As such, it is politically more acceptable to many regional countries, particularly ASEAN members, who retain a long-standing and deeply-ingrained suspicion of regional security proposals sponsored by outside powers. Moreover, being an extension of an *existing* and time-tested multilateral institution adds considerably to ARF's credibility and flexibility. It has precluded any controversy that would have inevitably marked attempts to form a new regional security institution. By requiring no new and binding commitments or sacrifices from its members, the ARF concept has proven to be most acceptable path to security multilateralism in the region.

ARF draws upon, and extends, those very norms that have already committed the ASEAN members to self-inhibiting and peaceful conduct in interstate relations and facilitated its evolution toward a regional security community. A key element of this process is the Treaty of Amity and Cooperation, ASEAN's chief normative framework for interstate behaviour. The first meeting of ARF held in Bangkok in July 1994 saw agreement by the member nations to "endorse the purposes and principles" of the Treaty "as a code of conduct governing relations between states and a unique diplomatic instrument for regional confidence building, preventive diplomacy and political and security cooperation."[10] In a dramatic concession to the principle of "inclusiveness," ASEAN, which had in the past been reluctant to let outside countries to sign the Treaty, is now preparing a protocol that might enable them to declare their support or adherence to the treaty's principles of co-operation.[11]

The stated aims of the ARF are predictably vague but clearly optimistic. These include a commitment "to work towards the strengthening and the enhancement of political and security cooperation within the region, as a means of ensuring lasting peace, stability, and prosperity for the region and its peoples." ARF's founders hope and expect that it "would be in a position to make significant contribution to efforts towards confidence-building and preventive diplomacy in the Asia-Pacific region."[12]

To assess what it can do to strengthen regional security, it is important to keep in mind what ARF does not aspire to be. First, ARF is not intended to be an alliance or collective defence institution. While military cooperation such as meetings of senior defence officials and exchange of military information is envisaged, these activities are clearly geared to confidence building among the ARF members, rather than to developing a collective capability against any common enemy. Neither are the founders of the ARF developing a collective security arrangement in the strict sense of the term. A collective security framework provides that aggression by one member state against another would be punished through an automatic and collective response by all the other members of the grouping. Such a system requires commitments, resources, and capabilities the ARF framework cannot realistically muster for the foreseeable future.[13] While a major goal of ARF is to discourage the use of force by its member states to settle disputes, it does not make any provision for common action to punish an act of aggression.

Unlike in collective security or balance of power models of security cooperation, ARF relies largely on a political instrument. As Michael Leifer points out, members of ARF are "hostages of fortune" in a multilateral framework in which "those who might appear to violate it must calculate the [political] cost of violation."[14] Through its largely consultative agenda, ARF aims to contribute to regional security in three important ways:

- By promoting transparency in strategic intent and threat perceptions
- By building mutual trust and confidence with regard to military capabilities and deployments
- By developing a "habit" of cooperation that will facilitate peaceful resolution of conflicts.

Some of the measures that have already been proposed and debated within the ARF framework (including supporting semi-governmental tracks such as the ASEAN Institutes of Strategic and International Studies and the Council for Security Cooperation in the Asia-Pacific) include enhanced transparency in military activities, creation of a regional arms register, exchange of defence white papers, allowing the presence of observers in military exercises, greater exchanges of military personnel and the establishment of a regional peacekeeping centre.[15]

OBSTACLES AND LIMITATIONS

Despite an enthusiastic start, ARF faces a number of uncertainties and constraints. One likely source of problem concerns ASEAN's central role within ARF. ASEAN members leave no doubt as to who will "dominate and set the pace" of ARF; in the words of Thai Deputy Foreign Minister Surin Pitsuwan, "ASEAN will always have the driver's seat." Although ASEAN promises to "recognize the concerns and interests of" outside powers, including the four major powers (the United States, Japan, China, and Russia), it clearly expects the latter to accept ASEAN's leadership of the forum and the norms and principles that are specified by ASEAN.[16]

But ASEAN's hold over the pace- and agenda-setting processes in ARF may prove divisive. ARF embodies ASEAN's extremely cautious approach to institution building, including a preference for informal and ad hoc consultations to formal and structured cooperation. From the very outset, ASEAN members (particularly Singapore and Thailand) as well as China, Vietnam and Russia, have clearly stressed the need for a gradual, step-by-step approach in developing ARF, one that establishes a "comfortable relationship among participants" before embarking on ambitious initiatives. This position contrasts with that of some Western members, notably, Australia, and the United States who would like ARF to develop quickly and adopt concrete measures.[17] There are some concerns that ASEAN's cautious approach will make it difficult for ARF to develop concrete initiatives in the areas of conflict resolution, confidence building, and arms control.

If the first ARF meeting is any indication, ARF's ability to move beyond a consultative agenda and to address the region's myriad conflicts is by no means assured. Of the four major conflicts that attracted most attention at the meeting, i.e., territorial claims in the South China Sea, Cambodia, Burma and North Korea, only the last item merited a mention in the final Chairman's statement. This prompted a comment by a Thai newspaper that, "Despite blithe official pronouncements of the conviviality of the three-hour meeting, it was obvious that the dialogue had exposed irreconcilable differences, especially on territorial disputes."[18] Indicative of the differing priorities of ARF members and the resistance of some to quick movement was the fact that the finalization of the statement required "at least 12 attempts." After a debate on a host of specific proposals, especially from Australia and Canada, several items had to be dropped from the list of possible initiatives. Among these were proposals for a regional security studies center, establishing the practice of sending observers to military exercises, exchange of defense white papers, and creating a maritime information database. The final list of approved items to be subjected to "further study" included ideas on "confidence and security building, nuclear nonproliferation, peacekeeping cooperation including [the creation of a] regional peacekeeping training centre, exchanges of non-classified military information, maritime security and preventive diplomacy."[19] As the chairman of the 1995 meeting of ARF, Brunei was tasked to undertake consultations on these proposals and to report to the next meeting, which will then make decisions on the specific measures to be implemented.[20]

ARF's contribution to preventive diplomacy and conflict-resolution is constrained by another factor. As currently constituted, ARF is not inclusive enough. It does not include parties to major regional conflict situations such as Taiwan (a Spratly claimant) and North Korea. The United States seems opposed to the early inclusion of North Korea into the ARF framework. U.S. Assistant Secretary of State Winston Lord responded to North Korea's reported request (Pyongyang had apparently indicated a desire to join ARF through the Australian embassy in Bangkok)[21] for inclusion in ARF "interesting," but "a little premature," insisting that North Korean membership was conditional upon a satisfactory resolution to the nuclear proliferation issue.[22] Also excluded from ARF is India, although its growing power projection capabilities is a source of concern for some ASEAN states.

Another important question about ARF's effectiveness concerns the relevance of ASEAN subregionally conceived norms in a larger and, in many respects, a more complex security arena. The "ASEAN way" of problem solving, which involves consultations and consensus and a habit of avoiding direct, public confrontation in the interest of corporate solidarity,[23] was developed when the threat of Communist expansion served as a cementing factor for its otherwise divided membership. It is doubtful whether these norms and practices (which relies heavily on interpersonal and informal ties within the ASEAN grouping) can be successfully duplicated within a wider regional setting. Of particular concern here is whether ARF is the appropriate framework for handling security issues in Northeast Asia; many doubt that it is. Thus, there have been suggestions for the creation of a subregional forum in Northeast Asia that would be more sensitive to security issues specific to that particular subregion. At the first ARF meeting, then South Korean Foreign Minister Han Sung-Joo argued, "Countries in the Northeast Asian subregion are in need of a framework for security dialogue and cooperation," and "The remaining vestige of the Cold War structure warrants a Northeast Asia security dialogue".[24]

Finally, ARF faces a significant challenge in securing meaningful support from its largest Asian member, China. China's hitherto opposition to multilateralism is particularly debilitating for ARF. China sees multilateralism as a way for lesser regional actors to "gang up" against Chinese interests and objectives in the region. It is also suspicious that ARF may develop into a tool in the hands of the Western powers for interfering in the domestic affairs of the Asian member states. Indicative of this is a warning by the Chinese Foreign Minister, Qian Qichen, that "no attempts should be made to use confidence-building measures and preventive diplomacy to resolve internal conflict or problems of a country."[25] Beijing prefers bilateral solutions to the territorial dispute in the South China Sea. It has also taken a particularly hardline stand against Taiwanese participation in any regional security discussions (including Track-II fora such as CSCAP)

The Chinese position at the first meeting of ARF was particularly revealing. While the Chinese Foreign Minister stated that "China does not . . . have a single soldier stationed on foreign soil, nor does it have any military base abroad," this had the paradoxical effect in affirming Beijing's hardline position on the

South China Sea dispute, since Qichen's assertion can only be valid if one considered China's stationing of troops on the Spratly Islands as an "internal" military presence.[26] China also successfully opposed a proposal that working groups be set up within the ARF framework to deal with specific issues in between ministerial meetings. Indeed, China's rejection of a number of initiatives proposed by other ARF members prompted one media observer to comment that "China had taken control of the agenda and the other delegates, including the US, Russia and Japan, were forced to go along with Beijing."[27]

These questions about the effectiveness of ARF explain the continuing preference of many ARF members for bilateral mechanisms for conflict management. For example, the management of the recent North Korean proliferation crisis consisted of a series of bilateral exchanges between the United States and North Korea, North Korea and South Korea, China and North Korea, Japan and South Korea and, at least initially, Japan and North Korea. Within ASEAN too, bilateral mechanisms (such as joint border committees between Indonesia and Malaysia and Malaysia and Thailand) continue to play a critical role in dealing with contentious territorial disputes. Obviously, multilateralism is not expected to replace these time-tested bilateral mechanisms for regional conflict management.

CONCLUSION

Given the uncertainties and limitations facing ARF, some analysts have dismissed multilateralism as the answer to the region's post-Cold War security challenges; yet, such a judgment is premature. For all its limitations, there are no viable alternatives to ARF in the region's current security climate. Critics of ARF paint a grim picture of the region developing a Hobbesian anarchy marked by competitive alignments and balancing behavior,[28] but a Realist understanding of Asia-Pacific security does not provide any concrete ideas about an alternative security architecture for the region, except for vague prescriptions about the need for a balance-of-power structure.

Theoretically, existing U.S. alliances in the region can be seen as providing the basis for such a structure, but the US role as a "regional balancer" remains ill defined and is marked by several uncertainties. Three sets of problems are particularly noteworthy.

Military-strategic uncertainties relating to the future of U.S. regional military presence have already created serious doubts about the credibility of the U.S. balancing role. Economic-trade frictions threaten the stability and longevity of U.S. alliances that underpin its role as a regional balancer. Political-diplomatic problems relating to human rights and democracy are also causing strains in the relations between the United States and some of its regional allies. Managing these problems would be a key test for American policy makers in the post-Cold War era.

If the U.S. role as a "regional balancer" lacks credibility, the region may see its weaker states "bandwagoning" with its emerging regional powers, China and Japan. Such a scenario will lead to the exclusion or isolation of the United States and the further enhancement of the political and military position of the former—but neither China nor Japan is politically acceptable in the region as a partner to bandwagon with. Neither can muster the right combination of military and economic power (with Japan lacking in the former and China lacking in the latter) that might secure the allegiance of their lesser neighbors.

Against this backdrop, multilateralism as embodied in ARF remains an essential element of the post-Cold War security architecture of the Asia-Pacific region. Many analysts posit a false dichotomy between a balance-of-power approach underlying America's bilateral alliances and the norms of security multilateralism as embodied in ARF. In reality, the two can be complementary. U.S. alliances still provide the best guarantee against regional hegemony; indeed, U.S. security posture seems to be already being geared to this objective. If this is the case, it ought to contribute to the development of multilateral conflict-control and order-maintenance mechanisms within ARF. If the emerging regional powers are persuaded that their use of force to extend regional influence will be promptly resisted by the United States, then they are more likely to accept the logic of multilateralism.

To be sure, in the short term multilateralism cannot, be expected to address the full range of security problems that could arise in East Asia in the post-Cold War milieu. For the time being, multilateral security institutions will remain acceptable only as a complement to, rather than substitute for, existing bilateral arrangements. But the security dialogues as currently envisaged under ARF could prove useful in clarifying threat scenarios and establishing norms for the pacific settlement of conflicts. They could, over the long term, promote transparency, confidence building, and other forms of security cooperation.

NOTES

1. ARF members include the six ASEAN members (Malaysia, Indonesia, Brunei, Singapore, Thailand, and the Philippines), their seven dialogue partners (the United States, Canada, Japan, South Korea, Australia, New Zealand, and the European Union), two consultative partners (Russia and China) and three countries with observer status in ASEAN (Papua New Guinea, Vietnam and Laos).

2. John Gerrard Ruggie, "Third Try at World Order: America and Multilateralism after the Cold War," *Political Science Quarterly* 109, no.4 (Fall 1994): 556-557.

3. "ARF: S'pore proposes a gradual approach," *The Straits Times,* July 23, 1994, 1.

4. Peter Ho Hak Ean, "The ASEAN Regional Forum: The Way Forward," Paper Presented to the Third Workshop on ASEAN-UN Cooperation in Peace and Preventive Diplomacy, Bangkok, 17-18 February 1994.

5. *The Straits Times,* August 4, 1994, 2.

6. On the concept of common and cooperative security, see: Dewitt, David B., "Common, Comprehensive and Cooperative Security," *Pacific Review* 7, no.1 (1994): 1-15.

7. For a historical survey of the impact of the US-Soviet rivalry in Asia on the development of their alliances, see: Akira Iriye, *The Cold War in Asia: A Historical Introduction* (Englewood Cliffs, Prentice Hall, 1974). An excellent analysis of the relative importance of bilateralism and multilateralism in the US security policy towards Eastern Asia can be found in Bernard K. Gordon, *Toward Disengagement in Asia: A Strategy for American Foreign Policy* (Englewood Cliffs, Prentice Hall, 1974).

8. For a critique, see: Geoffrey Wiseman, "Common Security in the Asia-Pacific Region," *Pacific Review* 5, no.2 (1992).

9. For a discussion of the evolution of ideas and initiatives concerning a multilateral security system in the Asia-Pacific region, see: Amitav Acharya, *A New Regional Order in Southeast Asia: ASEAN in the Post-Cold War Era,* Adelphi Paper no. 279 (London: International Institute for Strategic Studies, 1993).

10. "Chairman's Statement: The First Meeting of the ASEAN Regional Forum (ARF)," 25 July 1994, Bangkok, 2.

11. Lee Kim Chew, "Asean 'has entered new phase in development'," *The Straits Times,* July 28, 1994.

12. "Chairman's Statement, 2-3.

13. On collective security, see Charles A. Kupchan and Clifford A. Kupchan, "Concerts, Collective Security, and the Future of Europe," *International Security* 16, no.1 (Summer 1991): 114-161.

14. Leah Makabenta, "Asia-Pacific: better ARF than war," *Inter Press Service*, July 30, 1994.

15. "New framework for security," *The Straits Times*, July 26, 1994, 15.

16. Yang Razali Kassim, "Minister: Asean will always have driver's seat in forum,"*Business Times*, July 25, 1994, 3.

17. "New framework for security," 15.

18. Makabenta.

19. "Chairman's Statement," 3; "ASEAN: ARF will work if given the chance", Reuter Textline, *Bangkok Post*, July 27, 1994.

20. Reg Gratton, "ARF is born, but will it be all bark and no bite," Reuters World Service, July 29, 1994.

21. *Business Times (Malaysia)*, July 30, 1994.

22. "N. Korea not yet ready for security forum, U.S. says," Kyodo News Service, Japan Economic Newswire, July 29, 1994.

23. Michele Cooper, "ASEAN seizes role in post-Cold War diplomacy," Agence France Presse, July 28, 1994. For a fuller discussion of "the ASEAN way" see: Arnafin Jorgensen-Dahl, *Regional Organisation and Order in Southeast Asia* (London: Macmillan, 1982); Noordin Sopiee, "ASEAN and Regional Security," in Mohammed Ayoob, ed., *Regional Security in the Third World* (London: Croom Helm, 1986), 221-231; Donald Weatherbee, "ASEAN Regionalism: The Salient Dimension," in Karl D. Jackson, and M. Hadi Sosastro, eds., *ASEAN Security and Economic Development* (Berkeley, CA: Institute of East Asian Studies, University of California, 1984), 259-268.

24. Valerie Lee, "US hails defence forum, warns Korea problem urgent,"Reuters World Service, July 26, 1994.

25. Michael Richardson, "A step ahead on Asian security," *International Herald Tribune*, 26 July 1994, 2. At the inaugural ARF meeting, China proposed a five-point approach towards regional security and confidence building.

    *   A new type of state-to state relations characterized by mutual respect and amicable co-existence on the basis of the UN Charter and the Five Principles of Peaceful Co-existence;
    *   Economic ties on the basis of equality and mutual benefit and mutual assistance, with a view of promoting economic development;
    *   Consultations on an equal footing and peaceful settlement, which should serve as norms in handling disputes between countries in the Asia-Pacific so as to gradually remove the destabilising factors in the region;
    *   The principles that armament should be used for defensive purposes should be adhered to and arms race of any form should be

averted. There should also be no nuclear proliferation. Nuclear states should undertake not to be the first to use nuclear weapons and not to use or threaten to use them against nonnuclear-weapon states or nuclear-free zones; and

    *   Bilateral and multilateral society dialogues and consultations in various forms should be promoted in order to enhance understanding and confidence.

Ahirudin Attan and Lokman Mansor, "Thailand: ASEAN Forum hailed as force for regional peace," *Business Times (Malaysia),* July 26, 1994.

26. Makabenta.

27. According to the same report, "Well before the conference, Chinese diplomats in South-East Asian capitals had called on the foreign ministries in their host countries to pass on Beijing's desire for the forum to reject any ambitious security agenda." David Hague, "ASEAN: China flexes its muscles," *Sydney Morning Herald,* July 28, 1994.

28. Gerald Segal and Barry Buzan, "Rethinking East Asian Security," *Survival* (1994).

ASIA-PACIFIC AND REGIONAL SECURITY COOPERATION

Dao Huy Ngoc

Asia Pacific has not been as fundamentally affected as has Europe by the end of the Cold War, but the region did witness drastic changes in security problems, with a special concern regarding the possibility of the United States withdrawing many of its forces from the area.

In this paper we look at the situation in Asia-Pacific with its radical changes, emphasizing the relations between major powers and the new approaches to security in the region by small and medium-sized countries.

PRESENT SITUATION IN ASIA PACIFIC

Since 1989, strategic transformations have swept across the world. The most striking and unexpected was the collapse and disintegration of the former Soviet Union, which had profound impacts on the development of international relations and on security problems in various regions, including East Asia Pacific.

The end of the Cold War of course futhered the trend toward peace, development, and cooperation on a global scale, but it also generated many uncertainties, where nationalism and state economic interests once relegated to the background of international politics have repositioned to the forefront.

Ambassador Dao Huy Ngoc is Assistant Foreign Minister and Director General of the Institute for International Relations, Hanoi. Previously he served as Ambassador to Japan. Ambassador Ngoc's major publications include a textbook on the history of international relations.

Efforts aimed at sustained development in politics, economics, and security are underway within Asia-Pacific. All of which help maintain stability. The economic vitality and dynamism, the progress achieved, the realization of vital forces undiscovered until now in economy, in culture, and especially in traditional values . . . all of these have led to a growing self-confidence that will play an important role in shaping the new order emerging after the Cold War.

No one could have predicted a few years ago that China would be the world's hottest investment prospect, or that the most dynamic trade group in the world would be the Asia Pacific Economic Cooperation (APEC) forum, or that political reform could suddenly shove from power the post-World War II ruling party in Japan. Even recently one couldn't imagine that after decades of confrontation during the Cold War period, a new era for all the nations and the peoples of South East Asia has appeared, an era where all countries of South East Asia—big and small, strong and weak, rich and poor—could live in close proximity with one another and share a common destiny.[1] But along with these opportunities came challenges:

- Each country in the region is facing many domestic economic changes. Eonomic growth in South Korea has already begun to slow; Taiwan has come to increase its economic dependence on mainland China, both in terms of trade and investment; ASEAN industrial entrepreneurs have not yet reached the point where they can continue their development without the assistance of enterprises in more developed countries; and China has to resolve major problems concerning infrastructure, environment, energy resources before achieving its economic modernization program. Moreover the nations in Asia still fear the fragmentation of the world market into regional economic blocs, so they expect the Asia Pacific Economic Cooperation will play a leading role in maintaining the international free-trade system.
- Potential interstate conflict still exists. Ensuring that North Korea does not continue to try to develop nuclear weapons is a matter of concern of almost all countries in Asia Pacific; ownership of islands in the South China Seas is contested by many nations, including China and Vietnam, because these islands have potentially rich oil deposits in the

area; and the military modernization programs of some states
have caused concern and anxiety among others in the region.

• The relationship among the United States, Japan, China,
and Russia is crucial for stability and peace in the region. This
relationship is in the process of being shaped. This situation
is complicated because multilateral Asia-Pacific security
cooperation is still problematic and there still exists an urgent
need to find some new mechanisms to handle outstanding and
developing problems.

Despite all the above-mentioned challenges, it is encouraging
that for the first time in history almost all states and peoples in
Asia-Pacific have real opportunities to concentrate efforts, to forge
positive changes, to achieve prosperity, and to integrate positively
in world politics and economics.

SOME BASIC PROBLEMS IN ASIA PACIFIC

How to Define National Security

For decades the term *national security* has meant by and large
military security, and it is understandable that in the years of the
Cold War the United States and the former Soviet Union pursued
a national security strategy focused on one goal : By every possible
means strengthen military capability to contain the principal
enemy and preserve a leading role in world affairs. With the end
of the Cold War, however, the doctrine of containment has become
a victim of its own success.

There is little doubt that in the years to come military power
and politics are and will still be of paramount importance in
national security, but economic well-being also seems to be a *sine
qua non* of a nation's security. The debate over what problems
constitute a threat to national security has been renewed not only
by major powers but also by medium-sized and small countries as
well. In America, for example, analysts from a variety of fields
have identified new threats: budget and trade deficits, stagnation
of American wages in the face of global economic competition, and
degradation of the environment.[2]

To quote the definition of national security given by Charles
Maier, a concept shared by many scientists:

National Security is best defined as the capacity to control those
domestic and foreign conditions that the public opinion of a given

community believes necessary to enjoy its own self-determination, or autonomy, prosperity, and well-being.[3]

From our ASEAN friends' thinking, the most probable and therefore most serious threat for each country is internal turmoil, political as well as economic. This fear has been largely shared by the Vietnamese people.

Since our VI Party Congress we have pointed out that the highest interest of the Party and people of Vietnam is to consolidate and firmly preserve peace by economic development growth, a decisive factor for solidifying and maintaining our national security. The political bureau of the CPC in its 13th Resolution has further clarified our policy of national security: "With a strong economy and . . . sufficient . . . national defence coupled with the expansion of international cooperation, the country will have more abilities to firmly maintain the independence and successfully build up socialism." [4]

When discussing national security we must be aware that when the transnational technological changes in communications and transportation are making the world smaller. The market economy has a decisive role in economic development all over the world. The trend toward interdependence in the international system—interdependence in fates, security, and well-being—has become irreversibly linked to domestic and foreign policy more than at any time in history. In this case a nation's security policy, both military and economic, could have direct or indirect impacts on other regional countries; hence this situation becomes a matter of concern.

Some Asian Characteristics

After the Cold War, some new thinking about Asia flourished among politicians as well as scientists, as shown in articles written by Yoichi Funabashi,[5] and Morinosuke Kajima.[6] The main idea of the new thinking is that Asian peoples are in the process of rediscovering themselves through several ways:

 • The economic vitality and successful economic performance in some recent decades of most of the countries in the region have given Asia more confidence. The days when the United States sneezed and Asia caught cold are forever in the past. In the Asia-Pacific we have to work with nations who have long grown up and just discovered their vital forces in economy, in culture, and especially in their traditional values. These nations believe that in the years to come power and influence will have shifted decisively to the east side of the Pacific. Right now they are framing their thinking and their policies to conform with this radically changing situation.

• The Asia-Pacific has entered an era, with a new framework, in which all nations in various regions can participate and discuss on equal footing all issues relating to peace, stability, and development. In this new framework, although political and military power still play an important role, economic priorities, historical background, and Asian culture and values are increasingly becoming instrumental forces in the evolution of international politics.

• These traditional values will continue to play an important role in Asian societies, but it does not mean that particularistic nationalism has come to the forefront in the foreign policy of Asian countries or there exists now a "Great Wall of China" between Asia and America and Europe. This characteristic does mean that it is extremely important to recognize the pluralistic nature of civilization and the diversity of human life styles, that every nation has the right to advance its own living standards. Extreme nationalism in imposing democratization and industrial development on other countries will have harmful side effects and will surely end in failure. People in Asia are aware that it took America and Western European countries about two centuries to go from an undeveloped nation to the countries they are today. Japan took about one century.

One conclusion could be drawn from the above points. When economic developments have already energized important political and social changes and will surely cause more in the region, it is vital that major powers—like the United States, Japan, China, Russia, and other countries—face these changes cooperatively and not competitively, constructively and not negatively.

Relationships Among Regional Power Centers

During the Cold War, although the situation in the Asia Pacific region was mainly affected by the rivalry between two superpowers, regional power structure underwent changes over time. In the 1950s and early 1960s, the balance in the region was essentially bipolar, involving hostile confrontations between China (with the support from the Soviet Union) and the United States. As a result of Sino-Soviet split, the balance became increasingly triangular in the late 1960s and 1970s, involving the United States, the Soviet Union, and China. Then, in the 1980s, with the rapid emergence of Japan's economic power and influence, a four-power balance gradually took shape. Looking at the foreign policy of major powers some possible trends can be discerned:

- Balance-of-power policies may be used more than they were in the past as national power and national interests become more relative in a world of greater interdependence.
- Economic interdependence will increase and may become a more important factor in world politics than policies designed to prevent alliances aimed at forming overwhelming power bases.
- In the near future, it is certain that Russia will be preoccupied with internal transformation. To the extent that Russian foreign policy focuses on Asia, it is focused much less on East Asia than on Central Asia and the multiple disorders on Russia's Southern borders. In the long term, if Russia solves its problems, it will inevitably be a strategic player in the region. This is unlikely until the turn of this century. Therefore, in the time frame of this paper, Russia can be temporarily left aside, though recently it has participated in the ASEAN Regional Forum and has shown interest in retaining its position in the region.

In short, at least until the end of this century, the United States, Japan, and China will be power centers with increasing influence in the Asia Pacific. The pattern of relationships among them has profound implications for the South East Asia region.

Sino-US Relations. Since 1949 Sino-U.S. relations have gone through several periods of transition: hostility (1950-1970), rapprochement (1971-1972), pessimism (1972-1978), optimism (1979), disillusionment and disagreement (the last 8 years). Until 1990, the Cold War and "Soviet threat" had a significant impact on Sino-U.S. relations. The security factor dominated the thinking of leaders in both the United States and China with regards to their bilateral relationship.

Now that the Cold War has ended, making the concept of the "strategic triangle" obsolete, Sino-U.S. relations have reached a new point. Today the Russian factor has much less influence on relations between the two. Other more fundamental factors arise: How does the United States evaluate China's increased economic and military strength—is it an opportunity or a threat to regional security ? Does Japan pose an economic threat to the United States? What role should the United States play in the region? Until there are clear answers to these questions, the pattern of the Sino-US relationship in the post-Cold War era is still characterized by uncertainties and a series of ad hoc responses from both sides.

Events in the past few years illustrated this point. Sino-American relations deteriorated after Tianamen Square. They seemed to improve somewhat after the changes that took place in Eastern Europe and the Soviet Union in late 1989-1990, as well as the development of the Persian Gulf war and peace settlement in Cambodia. However, they remained tense and sometimes came to deadlock as the Americans continued to refrain from high level contacts with their Chinese counterparts and highlighted the issue of human rights in dealing with China. There was a breakthrough in the relations between the two countries in late 1993, when the Clinton administration decided to follow a policy of active engagement with China. Under this policy, the United States recognized China's important role in the Asia-Pacific, and expects to incorporate China into regional security and economic framework through cooperation with China. On the other hand, there is an indication that the United States is acting in concert with its allies to constrain China.

In May, 1994, President Clinton announced the separation of economic issues from human rights in extending most-favored nation status to China. Sino-U.S. relations improved remarkably in 1994 by a series of exchanges between high-ranking officials from the two countries. Meanwhile, the United States decided to upgrade its relations with Taiwan, which caused resentment in China. Economic relations is another source of tension that must be handled carefully in the coming years.

Sino-Japanese relations. Since their normalization in 1972, Sino-Japanese relations have developed rapidly, especially in economics. With Japan being China's top loan source and its second-ranking trading partner, and with neither country threatening the other militarily, the two countries have the ingredients for building a positive relationship. Tokyo believed

China's economic reform would have a favorable impact on their mutual ties.

However, during the past 22 years, there were quite a few thorny problems troubling Sino-Japanese relations. These could be divided into two groups: one was related to historical issues, for example Japanese attitude toward past crimes of aggression or Japan's territorial claims to the Sensaku; the other was related to current issues, such as the Japanese attitude towards Taiwan, or China's objection to the widening bilateral trade gap in Japan's favor and to lagging technology transfers from Japan. So long as the Japanese leaders are cautious about trying to assert any role of political leadership in Asia, these problems between Japan and China may not develop to a break point.

The end of the Cold War raised several important questions that would affect Sino-Japanese relations:

- How will Japan manage its security relationship with the United States? Will Japan become a "normal state," developing a ratio of military to economic power comparable to that of other large, rich countries ?
- How would both China and Japan respond to an accelerated pace of international and regional development ? Will China try to fill the "vacuum" left by the Russian withdrawal and US reduction of forces in the region ?

Until the answers to these questions become clear, Sino-Japanese relations are best regarded as in a transitional phase. On the one hand, Japan approved a ¥810 billion loan package for China, but would provide funds annually and require China make public its defense spending. In return, Japan is seeking China's support for permanent membership in the U.N. Security Council. Meanwhile, Japan tacitly increased its exchange with Taiwan, which raised strong objections from China. We can say only that Sino-Japanese relations are now perhaps better than at any point in their long history and we can expect them to be both cooperative and competitive.

U.S.-Japan relations. The pattern of relationship between America and Japan in the past four decades was characterized by political and security stability. There have been repeated trade tensions as Japan quickly recovered from the devastation of World War II. By the 1980s, Japan had become America's major creditor, accounting for approximately 30 percent of all purchases of U.S. Treasury obligations. By the beginning of the 1990s, every aspect of American life had some connection to Japan. Meanwhile, Japan until now, has benefitted greatly from the American security umbrella.

The end of the Cold War has brought about new challenges for U.S.-Japanese relations. How would America and Japan respond to the changes in the former Soviet Union and Eastern Europe? How should the U.S.-Japanese security relationship be redefined? Without U.S.-Russian military domination of Asia, can China avoid becoming a potential threat to regional security? Is Japanese economic might becoming a threat (replacing the former Soviet threat) to American security? The real problem for post-Cold War U.S.-Japanese relations is that whereas trade and national security policy between the two countries were kept on separate tracks in the Cold War years, now they are overlapping. Why should American troops protect its major trade rival is not an uncommon question posed by Americans nowadays. The United States may continue to provide the security guarantee that allows Japan to remain militarily limited, but the reason to do so will steadily become less obvious as time goes on. Japan-U.S. ties will remain much stronger than the Japan-China relationship or the U.S.-China relationship, but there already exist differences in the China policies of Japan. Japan needs to make greater efforts to improve its ties with the United States to maintain the bilateral security treaty; at the same time, Japan must do its best to compete with the United States for the Chinese market.

REGIONAL SECURITY COOPERATION

A perspective of peace and security has opened to all nations in East Asia Pacific and the durability of this possibility is the first pre-condition for the comprehensive advancement that Asia must have.

In our time different states may have different priorities and may seek to emphasize different aspects or details of their national interests but it is also in the interests of all states in east Asia-Pacific to cooperate in making peace and security durable. Cooperation must be the key.

In Asia, as in the global environment, opportunities for cooperation exist in juxtaposition with a number of challenges as traditional sources of suspicions and tensions still abound. This juxtaposed situation requires government leaders and policy makers to respond with vision and boldness. It is desirable to notice that over the last few years, leadership in South East Asia has constructively responded to the rapid and far-reaching changes in the global and regional environments. Leaders have made great progress in their efforts to promote regional cooperation.

Many historians will see the October 1991 Paris Peace Agreement on Cambodia, the January 1992 agreement by the members of the Association of Southeast Asian Nations (ASEAN) to establish the Asian Free Trade Area (AFTA), Vietnam's and Laos' adherence to the Treaty of Amity and Cooperation in July 1992, and the first ARF, held in July 1994, as key landmarks on the road toward lasting peace and prosperity not only in South East Asia but in the whole region as well. Certainly the burdens of yesterday will not simply disappear overnight. Nations in this region must do their best in the years to come to promote mutual understanding and enhance cooperation in order to find a number of interrelated components, which should be considered integral to the structure of regional security.

Some guiding ideas concerning security cooperation in Asia Pacific:

● A pluralistic community: Asia Pacific must strive not to be a supranational community as envisaged by proponents of the European Community's Maastricht Treaty, but a pluralistic community of different peoples with their own identities, their own domestic arrangements and economic development, their own patterns of external affiliations and connections. This community requires economic performance and social capabilities in each country adequate to satisfy not only basic needs but also rising expectations and reduction of socioeconomic inequities. Laws and institutions have to be in place to prevent excesses and abuses, to dispense justice, to maintain peace and preserve law and order. The process of basic nation building may be completed in all Asian States.

● Foster and fortify good bilateral relations: The fostering of cooperative bilateral relations is an essential building block for regional and international security. Good neighborliness is a prerequisite for a truly peaceful town. At the same time we do believe that a multilateral approach on the basis of bilateral relations will promote the process of developing more formal structures of cooperative relationships in a variety of economic and related fields.

• Consensus regarding the rules of the game to govern the regional states relations with one another in both security and nonsecurity issue areas should be accepted by all regional states. The ASEAN way of solving or controlling bilateral problems among themselves not referring to the High Council of the 1976 Treaty of Amity and Cooperation (TAC) is worthy of consideration. Certainly not all problems have been solved, but many, including border disputes, have been successfully settled while keeping the bilateral relations intact.

• Regional security activities must be conducted within the frameworks and in accordance with the Charter of the United Nations. The need for reform is self-evident as the world has been drastically changed since its establishment.

• In Asia there is a great need to engage the United States, Japan, China, Russia, and India in effective and productive sub-regional and regional processes. These major powers could play more prominent and constructive roles in regional security affairs and dilute suspicions and tensions in the area. Extraregional economic partners should be welcomed particularly where trade, investment and infrastructure-building are concerned. Though we give great importance to the involvement of internal as well as external powers in regional affairs, we are also aware that great power politics would no longer be predominant, thus allowing the regional states to pursue their own interests and aspirations in a freer and more flexible manner.

SETTING UP A MULTILATERAL FRAMEWORK

The proponents for institutionalization of CSBMs in the Asia-Pacific have come from Canada and Australia. Taking into consideration the great diversity of the Asian strategic culture, and even the balance of power in the Asia-Pacific, we do think that the European experience should be evaluated. It is of vital importance, however, for Asian nations to find their own multilateral framework that can help to define the direction for economic, political and security cooperation. This security framework (or security system) also has the task to engage more major powers inside and outside the region whose actions can threaten or promote peace and security in our common efforts to enhance peace and security.

In our view, ARF is considered by ASEAN and non-ASEAN participants as an effective system to discuss many important problems relating to security cooperation in Asia Pacific, such as confidence-building measures, preventive diplomacy, non-proliferation, and arms control. A lesson which can be drawn from the activities of the ASEAN is that regional security is to be attained step by step through fruitful cooperation between states and not confrontation. Friendship, mutual understanding and good neighborliness, as in the case of the relations between ASEAN and Vietnam, are essential components of interstate cooperation.

During the past 40 years a number of multilateral agreements, treaties and declarations have been signed by many Asian States. The norms and principles in these documents, which are in conformity to the principles of the U.N Charter, might be considered useful for the purposes of regional, political, and security cooperation in the Asia Pacific. We can mention the most important documents among them for consideration:

- The Five Principles of Peaceful Coexistence (1954)
- The Declaration on World Peace and Cooperation (Bangdung Conference), 1955
- The ASEAN Declaration (Bangkok Declaration), 1967
- The Zone of peace, freedom and Neutrality Declaration (Kuala Lumpur Declaration), 1971
- The Treaty of Amity and Cooperation in Southeast Asia, 1976
- The South Asian Association for Regional Cooperation (SAARC), 1985
- The ASEAN Declaration on the South China Sea, (Manila), 1992
- The Charter of the Council for Security Cooperation in the Asia Pacific (CSCAP), 1993

From these documents we believe the following norms and principles are worthy of consideration:

- The right for every country to choose, independently, its own political economic and social system and road for development in accordance with its particular national conditions.

- Respect and strictly abiding by the principle of noninterference in the internal affairs of other countries and refrain from imposing their own values, ideology and development models on others.
- Respect for the sovereignty and territorial integrity of all nations.
- The settlement of all disputes, international, regional multilateral or bilateral strictly by peaceful means as opposed to resorting to forces or threatening to use forces.
- The right to participate in international affairs of all countries big or small, strong or weak, through consultation on an equal footing. No countries should be allowed to seek hegemony or practice power politics.
- Respect for the right of each nation to defend itself singly or collectively, in conformity with the Charter of the United Nations.

The above mentioned norms and principles possibly reflect the values and aspirations of Asian peoples and it is understandable that they could be acceptable to Asia Pacific States.

From ASEAN to ARF, people in South East Asia have to overcome a few obstacles. During this period they have achieved both successes and failures on the way to finding some possible solutions for regional security arrangements. The establishment of a multilaterial framework in the Asia-Pacific for security cooperation still has a long way to go, and needs not only time but also patience and good will.

NOTES

1. *Shared Destiny—Southeast Asia in the 21st Century,* Report of the ASEAN Vietnam study group, February 1993, 14.

2. Joseph. J. Room, *Defining National Security Council of Foreign Relations Press*, 1.

3. Room, 6.

4. Sixth Party Congress, Resolutions and Documents, NXBND Hanoi May 1988.

5. Yoichi Funabashi, *The Asianization of Asia*, NN/Dec. 1993.

6. Morinosuke Kajima, *The Road to Pan-Asia.*

U.S. PERSPECTIVES:
Multilateral Activities in Asia

Paul Bracken

Multilateral approaches to economics, security, and politics are obviously not new to U.S. foreign policy. While formal institutionalized activities may have been rare before World War II, coordinated international support to further American interests has been a long standing part of this nation's foreign policy. The end of the Cold War has brought multilateralism to the fore once again, this time with grand expectations.

Many of the discussions surrounding multilateralism and U.S. foreign policy center on whether the United States should go it alone, or should rely on international cooperation. Stated in these terms the matter is not terribly interesting, as it is clear that multilateralism will continue. Also debated is the likely increase or decrease of multilateralism, both with American involvement and among foreign nations. It appears clear that multilateralism will continue and is more likely to increase than it is to decrease. Rather than dwell on either of these aspects of multilateralism, the thrust of this paper will be on multilateral fora as arenas for competition among the actors in them. That is, in every multilateral institution or activity there is a differential power

Paul Bracken is Professor of Political Science and Professor of International Business, Yale University. He is the author of The Command and Control of Nuclear Forces, Reforging European Security *(with Kurt Gottfried),* The Diffusion of Advanced Weaponry, *and many journal articles dealing with European defense, Asian security, and defense planning. Professor Bracken is a member of the Council on Foreign Relations.*

distribution. Strong countries get their way more of the time than not, yet the structure and kind of multilateral activity also matter.

During the Cold War the U.S. approach in these matters may best be described as technically multilateral—that is, in the security field through U.S.-created organizations such as NATO, SEATO, and others to advance its interests. These initiatives were not a cooperative effort among partners of equal status. Rather, they originated in U.S. thinking, were underwritten by U.S. military power, and were governed with an attitude that while we had to be sensitive to allied interests it was always understood that the United States was bearing the larger share of the risks, and therefore should have its way on important matters. This was especially true in the early stages of Cold War alliances and multilateralism. During the late stages of the Cold War, friction among allies increased, as the sense of threat diminished and as our allies perceived Washington to be hanging on to these structures for their strategic benefit rather than for their collective good.

Yet despite allied concerns that U.S. multilateralism was one-sided in its advancing U.S. interests, and despite private complaints, it is remarkable how much the United States gets it way still on security and military matters that come before NATO, the United Nations, and other multilateral bodies. What is remarkable is how *little* American power has declined in the multilateral arena, not how much. We are now in the fourth decade where predictions of imminent decline of American power are offered, whereas what really needs explanation is how the United States has skillfully used NATO, the United Nations, the World Bank, the G-7, and many other multilateral activities to preserve a status and power which does not match the relative decline of economic and political indicators. For 40 years the relative U.S. share of GNP in the world, our contributions to the United Nations and the World Bank, and our military contributions to NATO have fallen, leading observers to erroneously forecast the United States would have to share leadership of these organizations with other allies. Yet while some of this happened, no shift to multilateral leadership has occurred, only continued American leadership with more griping.

Even in economic multilateralism a similar pattern predominated. Until 1971 the United States basically wrote the rules of the international financial system. The World Bank was far more likely to follow Washington's directions than that of any other country. And while it is true that power shifted to a greater set of actors, in particular Japan and the G-7 countries, it has not been difficult for the United States to live off the legacy of these multilateral systems to get its way more often than not. The recent financial accord to salvage the Mexican economy was unilaterally decided upon in Washington, with its financial allies in Europe and Japan presented with a virtual fait accompli concerning their level of contribution to support the Mexican peso. This case is all the more remarkable because the benefits of this aid package so disproportionately benefit the United States over Europe and Japan. Not only were the G-7 told how much to contribute, but their contributions saved far more U.S. than European or Japanese jobs.

In both the security and the economic areas, skillful U.S. diplomacy deserves credit for this state of affairs, but there is more to the issue than skillful diplomacy. One can go back to academic studies beginning in the early 1970s for predictions of imminent decline of U.S. clout in multilateral organizations, formal and informal, but while declines have taken place, they are surprisingly small because institutionalized multilateral activities create a set of norms whose preservation transcends the importance of any single issue. Not being consulted on an economic assistance plan for Mexico is galling to our friends, especially when it benefits the United States more than it does them, but this is dwarfed by the need to preserve the G-7 system, and our allies understand this. Drawing the line on any single issue gives fewer benefits than continuation of a multilateral system of cooperation which basically works, and which allows all of the involved parties to avoid the inevitable disagreements about the shape and size of new replacement multilateral systems. Arguments about the structure of a new system would truly be disruptive and could result in anarchy more than order.

It is this that makes new multilateral initiatives and organizations like those appearing in South East Asia so interesting. That is, these can be examined and analyzed in terms of the immediate problems that they solve, or purport to solve. This is where most of the attention goes. Will the ASEAN Regional Forum be a useful instrument for helping implementation of the North Korean nuclear accord? This is an important question, but there is another as well—do these new efforts at multilateralism offer opportunities to shift established power balances in multilateral activities? There could be enormous difference between *new* multilateral efforts versus reform and patchwork repair of old ones. Reform of the United Nations, NATO, the World Bank, and most other multilateral activities could be undertaken in a way that better preserves U.S. interests and advantages than does creation of new fora. New multilateral activities do not have the legacy of decades worth of norms whose value it pays everyone to preserve.

Multilateralism in Asia is thus especially important to the United States for two reasons. First, Asia's dynamism means that it is an extraordinarily important region, and our capacity to shape the rules of the game is clearly at issue. Second, the appearance of new initiatives and activities creates opportunities to work around old structures of multilateralism, thereby undermining their universality and uniqueness. In the 1940s and 1950s, the United States used its unique position in Europe as security guarantor and chief supplier of economic assistance to get our European friends to fundamentally alter the way they did business. These American efforts culminated in the 1958 Treaty of Rome establishing the European Economic Community. This Treaty, although the United States was not a signator, enshrined the principle of comparative advantage—basically free trade—into European international relations.

U.S. efforts today toward bolstering free trade in Asia have many successes, but nothing comparable to the fundamental rewriting of the old European order of cartels and exclusion in economic affairs. The goals for the United States in Asia are clear enough, as economic liberalism is a part of the message of every speech given by American officials traveling in the region, but examples of resistance are manifest even in this area. When one turns to security matters, human rights, environmental protection, and other matters, successes are more limited, and new multilateral initiatives may solve the problems they are designed to address while creating new structures that weaken American power.

What the likely outcome of new multilateral activities in Asia will be is impossible to say. A look toward the future in this particular area of international affairs is clouded by the usual uncertainties of prediction, but also by issues of scale. Scale here refers to distance, population, cultural diversity, and degrees of social and economic transformation. It may be almost mundane to say so, but the fact that multilateralism during the Cold War was largely Eurocentric meant that the scale of the problem was confined in geography, population, and cultural diversity. This made it far easier to implement.

While any look at the future in the field is uncertain, it is nonetheless possible to distinguish factors that favor successful multilateralism, and those that work against it. Such distinctions can be useful contributions toward a conversation about multilateralism in Asia, and about its strengths and weaknesses.

FACTORS ENCOURAGING MULTILATERALISM IN ASIA

Probably the most important single factor encouraging multilateral approaches to security, economic, and other problems in Asia is the importance of the subject. This has several aspects to it. With Asia the most economically dynamic region of the world, it is essential that it turn out right, because of the dire negative consequences if it does not. The most negative outcomes arising from current Asian developments are not things it is useful to dwell on. If the outcome of current developments, however, were to even remotely approach the outcomes from the European experience with its industrial and capitalist transformation of the 19th century, the world might well see "the end of history" in the literal sense of the term.

People who follow these matters seem to understand this, at least at an intuitive level. One of the curious features of proposals for increased use of confidence measures throughout Asia is that they come at a time when Asia is remarkably free of conflict. Territorial disputes remain, to be sure, but these are of a kind that it is hard to imagine Asian states going to war over. No one, I think, can plausibly imagine that the militarily strong nations of Asia will resolve a territorial dispute with overt military force. The effects would be catalyzing, upsetting so many expectations and drawing in so many other issues that whatever gains were had from possession would be more than offset by its negative consequences. To be fair, this statement applies with greater truth to the larger stronger powers in Asia. Despite this, what explains the emphasis on confidence-building measures?

The most plausible answer arises from the recognition that

creation of new security structures can shape behavior, making their upset expensive. It raises the cost of military action. Multilateral confidence building regimes entail recognition of the interests of foreign states. This induces not only caution and calculation over what their response will be, but also delay and incrementalism, these are sources of international stability. Thus, one way to interpret the growing interest in confidence-building measures is a way to construct a web of interactions that it will be costly to break. Seen this way these proposals make a great deal of sense even in the absence of intense military interactions of the present time.

Another factor favoring multilateralism in Asia is the recognition of great powers not in Asia that their stable futures are vital to their own interests. This factor has several manifestations. In the United States it is quite striking that recent administrations have seen U.S. public education as an important component of their Asian policies. It cannot truthfully be argued that America is playing catch-up, only lately recognizing the importance of Asia. Rather there is a conscious attempt to direct attention away from a Eurocentric view of the world. This domestic educational component of U.S. policy should not be underestimated. It is a case of the government raising the level of discussion at home, something which is enormously important as a precondition for American action if new demands are placed on us in Asia. It is being copied by European governments, but here I think it safe to say that Washington has been far ahead of our European friends in raising the presence of Asian issues among the educated public.

Another manifestation of this non-Asian awareness of multilateralism in Asia comes from U.S. and European business communities. Broadly speaking, large multinationals based in North America and Western Europe have major expansion plans for Asia, as some of these leading firms are recreating themselves in a way that places the future of their companies on their operations in Asia. Asia is not only a target of foreign direct investment, it is the foundation for a future where foreign operations dominate those in the home base. What this means is a keen interest in multilateral economic activities of ASEAN, APEC, and the WTO as applied to Asia. It means that the most important U.S. and European multinationals have done their homework on such diverse issues such as Chinese entry to the

WTO, ASEAN trade practices, and the business opportunities of a unified Korea. Clearly, these corporations have a major voice in the policies of their home governments. The chance that a non-Asian government will make a shortsighted move without due consideration of its long term consequences declines as firms bring information daily to their governments.

There is great awareness in the world over the importance of the new issues of international relations. It may well be true to say that international narcotics traffic, cross-border environmental degradation, uncontrolled population growth, and the spread of AIDS are recognized examples of increasing international interdependence, but however much the term interdependence has become a cliché, it should not divert attention from the validity of the fundamental argument. Interdependence is increasing in Asia and between Asia and the rest of the world, and it is no small accomplishment that this fact is recognized. Of direct relevance to multilateral approaches it is clear that bilateral approaches to these problems are inadequate. Increased interdependence may not force solution of these problems, but it will force their discussion and analysis in multilateral settings. It is hardly conceivable that nations could ignore coordinated attempts to talk about solutions to these problems.

Finally, the existence of multiple overlapping formal and informal vehicles for multilateralism are a positive factor in its continued effectiveness. This has special significance for the United States. At this stage it may seem that duplication of effort is wasted effort, but politically this is not so. The United States is wary of being locked into a single vehicle for its multilateral activities, as it can retain the freedom to switch fora if it is not reaching the conclusions that it would like. This makes early successes all the more likely, and it provides Asian states many face saving alternatives that may well complicate the daily life of the diplomat, but which make national commitment to multilateral activities easier to sustain.

FACTORS LIMITING MULTILATERAL APPROACHES

The arguments so far could be read to say that necessity is the mother of invention. The importance, recognition, and self-interest that encourage multilateralism are only part of the story. Other considerations weigh against it, or serve to set up multilateralism for a fall. Several of the key problems can be identified, although their resolution is not an easy matter.

A recent book by Henry Kissinger identifies an important factor underlying successful international diplomacy in all areas. In *Diplomacy,* Dr. Kissinger argues that it was the common cultural heritage created over the centuries in Europe that made diplomacy possible, and which in the 20th century made NATO and the EC possible. Self-interest, calculation, and rational behavior can only go so far in sustaining international cooperation, however. There is an unrecognized dependence on common historical experiences, cultures, language, and social and economic development that is also important. Interestingly, Kissinger argues, a history of cooperation is not absolutely necessary for multilateralism to develop, as the experience of France and Germany demonstrates; but what is essential is shared expectations about behavior, and these are slow to develop.

It seems fair to say that the enormous cultural diversity resident in Asia could work against any deep form of multilateralism. The idea of an integrated Asia resembling anything like an integrated Europe is very far off indeed. The U.S. Government recognizes this in its many attempts to increase communication and dialogue within Asia and between Asia and the United States, but the way history has developed in this century has not induced the positive interactions in Asia that have occurred elsewhere. For whatever reasons, even the United States did not embrace political understanding there until after the Vietnam war. It is quite remarkable that the United States was willing to fight two Asian ground wars indirectly aimed at a country with which we did not have diplomatic relations. Indeed, the earliest think tank studies in the 1950s of our relations with Moscow all concluded that diplomatic relations had to be maintained—could not be broken whatever the crisis or provocation—and yet we did not maintain relations with a country that we were in conflict against.

Obviously there has been an intellectual transformation on this in the United States, yet the fact that it occurred so recently illustrates the relative lack of common and shared understandings between the United States and Asia relative to other parts of the world. Even today it is apparent that the United States sees Asian security in maritime terms, not in continental terms, and is thus disadvantaged in seeing trends the way many Asians do.

Another limitation on multilateralism from an American perspective arises from our extraordinary belief in assumptions of community in international affairs when it is not clear that these do not arise from our own inchoate needs and desires. The historian Eric Hobsbawm, in his recent book *The Age of Extremes*, describes an American tendency to see the world in terms of "communities," but these are often vapid phrases with little meaning other than a utopian wish to put into place the structures of a long bygone era. Hobsbawm may be too pessimistic, but the frequency with which the phrase "Asian community" is used in American foreign policy without any reciprocal use by Asians themselves is quite remarkable. It may represent a desire to project on to the outside world some deep American longing more relevant to an age that is passed than to one that is emerging. It would be an extremely worthwhile exercise to look at Asia, the United States, and multilateralism as they might develop in the *absence* of any real community other, than the one defined by high levels of GNP growth.

With regards to security matters there is a negative factor limiting multilateralism that has received much less attention than it deserves. Our understanding of defense structures, their transparency, and their evolution is actually quite limited. Consequently, calls for confidence-building measures, greater transparency among defense establishments, and restraints on defense expenditures may not be focusing on the new capacities and developments which are potentially the most destabilizing.

Throughout much of Asia today, published defense expenditures are meaningless. They do not account for actual expenditures, self-financing activities of the armed forces, or the structural transformation that is going on throughout the region. In many countries there is now a shift underway to transform the armed forces from an instrument of internal nation building and political control to an externally looking force with modern advanced technology weapons. In terms of force structures, what is taking place is a reduction in mass peasant infantry hierarchies to forces with the beginnings of external power-projection capacities. Judged in strict numerical terms this conversion is frequently described as an arms limitation or even a reduction; nothing could be further from reality.

Focusing on defense expenditures can muddle more than it clarifies. Throughout much of Asia today there is a profound restructuring of armed forces taking place that basically is turning internally looking forces with very limited cross border reach into more effective outward-looking ones with some crude capacity for operating outside of national boundaries. New technologies are being adapted, older infantry ones shed, and new high-command arrangements are being implemented to manage the more differentiated and complex military structures.

These trends are hardly surprising and represent what is probably a simple imperative of military modernization accompanied by increased disutility of the mass infantry format of arms. As Asian economies turn capitalist, there is a need to get the army out of business. Also, social control is achieved less by coercion, as it was during the nation building era, than by labor markets. Yet these important transformations do not seem to be a part of the many proposals for restraining the armed forces of Asian nations. It is entirely possible the future may see a thin shell of arms control restraints emplaced on far more lethal defense organizations than have appeared in Asia, at least during the last 50 years.

CONCLUSIONS

The growing attractiveness of multilateral activities in Asia is something with a strong foundation for the reasons described here. The need for them is considerable, and this is recognized by most states in and outside of the region. But these factors, as important as they are, should not obscure some of the serious factors working to limit multilateralism, or channel it into areas that do not deal with the fundamentals of security and economics.

Predictions are possible but do not seem especially helpful in how the positive and negative factors will interact to produce an outcome. It does seem clear that multilateralism will be an important factor of international relations in the coming years in Asia, and it may well be that the negative factors raised here will either turn out to be less important, or that their significance will be dwarfed by the positive developments in Asian international relations. However, this benign outcome cannot be assumed, and it would be worthwhile to consider a broader range of future possibilities which involve more limited successes and the possibility for setbacks to multilateral activities. The robustness of multilateral activities may be the true defining test of their ability to forestall negative developments.

Part V
A LOOK TOWARD
THE FUTURE

SOUTH EAST ASIA
AT A CROSSROADS

Kenneth S. Courtis

INTRODUCTION

Three forces are shaping a new economic agenda, not just for the Asia-Pacific, but for the world economy. These forces continue to develop, but they have begun already in many ways to shape the issues now moving to the top of the agenda for South East Asia. In addressing these new issues, the countries of the region will be led to take approaches that are increasingly multilateral in nature.

Three forces shaped the new global economic agenda: the end of the Cold War, the peaking of the global debt cycle, and the accelerating pace and widening scope of technological change. The effect of these forces on South East Asia is occurring within the broader framework of a fundamental shift in the center of gravity of the world economy to Asia. That shift will begin to take on its full impact over the coming decade, a period during which East Asia will generate more than half of the growth of the world economy. Let's examine these forces for change and then explore their impact on South East Asia and the issues that result.

Professor Kenneth S. Courtis is First Vice President of Deutsche Bank Capital Markets, Asia, where he conducts economic and policy research and investment and strategic analysis for the group in the Pacific. He lectures at Keio and Tokyo Universities and is a Visiting Professor at the Stockholm School of Economics. He also serves on the International Research Council of the Center for Strategic and International Studies (CSIS) in Washington.

THE CONTINUING EFFECTS OF THE END OF THE COLD WAR

The first of these forces is the continuing effect of the end of the Cold War. This is not just the disintegration of the Soviet Union, or the collapse of its Eastern European Empire; the consequences are much broader and deeper. The United States, for example, ends the Cold War financially fragile. Today the American economy carries just over $16 trillion in combined household, corporate, and public sector debt—in other words, $2.60 of debt in the America economy for every dollar of economic activity. The last time we saw that level of leverage was at the beginning of the Great Depression.

This means that the next time the United States slides into recession, it will be unable to get out of it by cutting taxes. Indeed the recent adoption of new budgetary laws means that the United States will have to raise taxes during the next recession, and so intensify the effects of recession. Similarly, it will not only be unable to increase spending, it will have to cut it. With a 3 to 4 percent net savings rate, the country will be unable to count on the consumer to spend the economy out of recession. There is but one option left—exports—and so the United States will be led to struggle even harder than is the case today for exports and foreign market share.

With the region from Beijing to Bangkok to Bombay booming ahead at 6 to 12 percent a year, and massive new markets emerging across the region, it is very likely that South East Asia will see more, much more pressure from America for exports to the region. Interestingly, all South East Asia, like all members of NAFTA, continue to run major trade deficits with Japan. This increased pressure from America, and the need for the countries of East Asia—all with export-led growth strategies—to find new markets, will create conditions that could also lead to a convergence of pressure from both sides of the Pacific on Japan. Thus the period ahead will also be very troubling for Tokyo.

Another adjustment the end of the Cold War engenders is a sharp decline everywhere in military spending, but problematically *not* in Asia. For example, since 1990, one million soldiers, formerly stationed in Germany (East and West) together with the civilian work force that went with them have been decommissioned. Equivalent military cuts have occurred in Russia,

Eastern Europe and of course in the United States, all of which have a depressing effect on Western economies. South East Asia has moved in the opposite direction with military budgets higher everywhere. So in a very simple sense, as issues of economic development become more complex, so the question of security becomes more complicated for the region.

These changes are occurring at the very moment when the social welfare systems of North America and Europe are unraveling. These systems were in large part developed during the Cold War and acted as glue holding social coalitions together during that epic confrontation, but today they are no longer fiscally nor politically sustainable. As governments confront the politics of unwinding these commitments, the will to keep markets open will be severely tested. The implications of these developments are deeply problematic for South East Asia, so dependent is the region on trade. As a result, the region will need to speak with a much stronger and unified voice in the new World Trade Organization if it is going to be able to protect and promote its own interests.

A further consequence of the end of the Cold War for South East Asia is still more important, and that is that it has transformed the very nature of the world economy. During the Cold War, when we spoke of the world economy, we actually talked about only a part of it. Great portions were excluded. China and the Soviet Union were excluded, and India excluded itself. Think of it: 920 million Indians today export less than the 6 million people of Hong Kong. But with the end of the Cold War, these countries have all come into the world economy. As a result, we not only find ourselves increasingly in a world market for goods, food, services, and capital, but also for labour. At a similar level of technology, labour everywhere is in direct competition. What then will increasingly differentiate labour is the management structure and practice within which it works, its level of training, and the capital that allows it to work. The implications of these changes are only beginning to make themselves felt on South East Asia. The inescapable reality that these dynamics create is that there is simply no low wage strategy for the more advanced countries in the region, as a response to the new competitive challenges that the integration of China and India into the world economy create.

Think of China. In the next decade, some 17 million young people will enter the urban labour market every year. An additional 8 to 10 million people leave the country legally to work in the cities. That means that over the next decade, China must create over 270 million new jobs just to keep unemployment where it is. And these 270+ million people are in that part of China being integrated into the world economy. Clearly there will be much more downward pressure on wages during the period ahead. South East Asia will have to move up the value-added ladder, and quickly. The adjustments—new infrastructure, increased risks, market size, technological innovation—are simply too large for individual countries of the region to carry on their own. A coordinated, multilateral, regional approach is required.

THE GLOBAL DEBT CYCLE

The second major force driving change in the world economy is the debt cycle. Debt is building everywhere. At the same time, in North America and Europe savings rates continue to fall. In the decade of the 1960s, the net savings rate of the six western members of the G-7 was 13.8 percent. It fell to 12.2 percent in the decade of the 1970s, to 10.1 percent in the 1980s, and to 7.8 percent in 1994. Asia, where the net savings rates exceed 25 percent of the GNP. These higher savings rates to sustain very high investment levels, which in turn generate higher growth and superior market returns. With the integration of world financial markets, money can now move, and does move, from low-return markets to the higher returns of South East Asia. What are the implications of these developments?

First, the debt-ridden governments of the West will find themselves increasingly in direct competition with South East Asia for what will be a relatively smaller pool of excess global savings. As a result, in order to attract funds, these higher indebted economies will have to run higher real interest rates. Indeed, such is already happening, as the dominant characteristic to emerge in global bond markets during the past year is that highly indebted economies such as Mexico, Italy, Canada, Australia, and the United States, have seen their interest rates climb substantially more than have the high savings economies such as Japan, Germany, Switzerland, Hong Kong, Taiwan, and the core economies of South East Asia. Where interest rates for such countries have not climbed enough, their currencies have been forced lower.

But more than interest rates and currencies are at stake. It is the question of the very availability of capital that is at stake. Think back to February 1994, and the collapse of the United States-Japan trade negotiations. Many expected Japan to return quickly to the table, but it did not. It waited for America to move, and with a gross savings rate in excess of 30 percent of the GNP, and a $130 billion current surplus, Japan could afford to wait. While the government waited, Japanese investors simply went on strike, and virtually stopped buying U.S. bonds for the next 6 months. By late May, the U.S. Treasury, Federal Reserve, and the National Economic Council all had become extremely concerned that the United States would be forced to raise interest rates in order to support the dollar. As pressures were already building on interest rates, the administration found itself forced to moderate its trade demands in order to achieve an agreement with Japan and to entice Japanese investors back into U.S. markets. In effect, with the United States now requiring upwards of $160 billion dollars a year in order to finance its external deficit, capital flows have become a critical constraint in trade negotiation. But capital flow constraints, and higher real interest rates mean slower growth, and slower growth in turn will mean more difficulty in making the complex political transitions that must come for Europe and the North America.

It will require the most adroit political leadership throughout South East Asia to navigate its way through this period of developing economic challenges and political complexity that lies ahead. It is only through a multilateral approach that the region could generate the weight, and position to promote and protect its interests during what will be for the region a period of substantially higher risk.

TECHNOLOGICAL CHANGE

The third major force driving change in the world economy is the torrid pace of technological innovation. We have yet to see the peak of its power or its full breathtaking scope. It will involve all aspects of our corporate and national lives. Recently, I was in Arizona working with one of the world's leading semiconductor producers. From this company I learned that in the past 8 years the size and power of the microchip relative to its cost have moved exponentially. Today, we have 25 times more computing power on a 25-times-smaller chip, at one 25th the cost of what we had but 8 years ago.

What does this change mean for East Asia? First, it means that capital stock will have to be renewed at an increasing speed. So great are the productivity gains the most recent capital equipment permits, that a competitor who falls behind will rapidly find his disadvantages compounding. That means that capital stock in Europe and North America, where investment levels are considerably lower, is set to become much more quickly outdated than many yet understand. As a result, South East Asia, with its much higher investment levels, is now positioned to move ahead relatively much faster than it has over the past two decades.

Thailand is typical of this broader process. In 1984, Thailand's per capita income was about one-sixteenth of that of the United States, and America invested some 10 times more per capita than Thailand did. In 1994, Thailand's per capita income was about a ninth that of America, while the United States committed only five times more per capita to capital investment than Thailand did. The implication of those trends—should they continue for another 15 to 20 years— would be a substantial transformation of the competitive balance between North America and East Asia, similar to the one that has occurred between America and Japan during the past half decade. But the real implications of this technological change are much deeper, and more powerful. Two issues in particular emerge:

• *Productivity, production, and wealth creation*: Today, through new technology and information, you see tremendous increase in productivity. That is the story of Guangdon province, which had 16 percent average annual growth over the past 15 years. That economic growth rate makes you eight to nine time bigger than you were when you started. For a city like Bangkok, which had 12 percent annual growth over the past 14 years, it means that the metropolis is today five to six times richer than it was a little more than a decade ago. A similar dynamic of change characterizes what is occurring in the region surrounding Singapore, and for many of the other great cities of South East Asia. More fundamentally, what is at work is that there is a shift of where production will occur, where wealth will be created, where return will be higher, and where capital will be moving.

Japan is set to play a critical role in this process through its massive investment in the region. It is useful to consider the numbers in this regard. Over the decade of the 1980s, Japan's current-account surplus was some $400 billion, of which approximately $160 billion was recycled to the world economy through direct foreign investment. Of that amount, some 12 percent, or approximately $18 to $19 billion, was channeled to East Asia. That means that Japan's direct investment in the region will be eight to nine times larger in the decade ahead than it was in the past 10 years.

More broadly, what we will witness is a whole new way of integrating Japanese capital, management, and technology with Asian demographics and labor costs. This investment is one of the forces that will keep South East Asia growing faster than is widely understood. What is at stake is the balance of international competition, which is shifting to the region at a pace that, for many, will be seen later as stunning.

• *Information Technology and Jurassic Park*: The second critical issue driven by technological change—one that will destroy any organization that fails to understand and act on it—is the way information is processed, and managed. The new technology allows us to amass mountains of information and to analyze it at lightning speed. As a result, the technology empowers people at the base of organizations. Enfranchised by the new technology as never before in history, the base can lead the decisions. Decisions, as a result, can be made quicker, will have to be made quicker, and still quicker—at the point of production, of sales, and of engagement with the market, and more broadly at the point of engagement with society.

Traditional organizations have been structured in a way that enables them to gather information horizontally, run it up the hierarchy, analyze it at the top, make a decision, and then send the decision back down to be implemented horizontally. Today that's too slow. Organizations that continue to operate that way will die. Societies that have government organized to operate in that manner will also find themselves in much trouble. In fact, the biggest and most vulnerable institutions in this tumultuous change driven by technology, I believe, are state structures—the great bureaucracies, the Jurassic icons of another era—and political parties. They are set to share the same destiny as the dinosaur. Here South East Asia faces a very major test of transition. A number of countries in the region are on a course to deep crises and to a difficult transition in the politics of participation. Any major failure in this process would lead—quicker than is yet widely realized—to major disruptions in the process of economic development that is in so many ways the glue holding the region's complex societies together as they absorb the shocks of profound change.

THE SHIFT TO ASIA

The three forces driving change in the global economy are working within the border framework that provides the shift in the world economy to Asia. During the decade ahead that shift is set to accelerate. Consider the numbers. At the end of 1993, the dollar-based economy of Japan, China, and the rest of East Asia was $5.4 trillion. The North America Free Trade Agreement (NAFTA) economy was $6 trillion, and the European Union's (EU) was $6.5 trillion. The White House Council of Economic Advisers is forecasting a 2.5 percent annual growth for NAFTA over the next decade. The European Commission has forecast around a 2.25 percent annual growth for Europe. The World Bank is forecasting a 5.4 percent rate of annual growth for East Asia.

The result of these numbers is that 55 to 60 percent of growth in the world economy over the next 10 years will be created in East Asia. While Europe will expand by about $1.5 trillion, and NAFTA by some $1.6 trillion, East Asia will grow by some $3.5 trillion. That means that the shift in the world's economic center of gravity is going to accelerate during the coming 10 years. By the middle of the next decade, East Asia will have an economy of close to $9 trillion, compared to NAFTA and the EU, which will each have economies of approximately $8 trillion.

With its 7 to 10 percent annual growth rate, South East Asia will play a pivotal role in this shift. The region is set to become the economic and financial linchpin for the region from Beijing to Bombay. The region's financial and economic infrastructure, markets, institutions, corporations, areas of economic activity, and trade will be the building blocks of an emerging new dynamic of economic integration, continental in scope. As a result, the strategic importance of the region is set to increase dramatically through the decade ahead. But South East Asia can realize the promise and potential that the situation provides only if it can pool its resources, harness diversity, and focus its effort.

CONCLUSIONS

It is against this background that the new economic agenda for South East Asia taking shape. Increasingly these new issues can be best addressed from a multilateral perspective. If anything, the complexity of these issues is set to intensify. If a strong regional basis for their resolution is not set now, it will be necessary to take such an approach later. But by then the issues will be still more complex, and difficult to address.

Infrastructure

The key next step to South-East Asia's economic development is the building of an integrated, regionwide approach to infrastructure. To be most efficient, power production and distribution have to be organized in a regional grid, with common technology and performance. In this manner the region could not only achieve significant economies of scale, but would also provide for itself the means to negotiate significant spin-offs for regional economic development and investment. Such an approach would also allow it to balance the risks and financial commitments that such very large scale projects entail for individual countries of the region. A similar reasoning would apply for the establishment of regional telecommunications grid, and transportation grid out. In addition to providing a new momentum for economic development through the region, such an integrated regional which is the critical next step in its economic development.

The Ecological Environment

Much of South East Asia's development of the past three decades has occurred within what are largely traditional approaches to ecology and the environment. That is no longer enough. The environment is a regional resource. Pollution cannot be managed on a local basis alone. A regionwide effort is now required to nurture and husband critical environmental resources. Again here a multilateral, coordinated, regional approach would be the only viable manner to addressing issues of the environment. Any other approach would be either too limited to be efficient, or too broad to be effective.

Public Health

New issues of public health are being born of the region's unprecedented social surging growth, equally rapid urbanization, and the emergence of formerly unseen forms of metropolitan massification. The lightening dissemination of a disease such as AIDS is but one example of the type new issue of public health that is set to emerge. The resources to address such issues, as well as the fact that similar patterns of development appear to becoming common throughout the region, point to an integrated multilateralism as the best approach.

Trade and International Economic Policy Coordination

ASEAN was already a first and important step in the direction of economics. AFTA is the next phase. More broadly, as the stakes for South East Asia in the world economy increase, in order to make its voice felt in the such new councils as APEC with its 2020 target for free trade, and the World Trade Organization, the region must move both to overcome its own divisions, and to generate an increasingly common regional perspective. Any other approach would result in the region's interests being short changed at best, and more likely neglected.

ASEAN has provided an initial forum for the harmonizing of a regional perspective. Some have argued that the next best step for the region would be to create a body that brings together North and South East Asia into a common structure, but that would mean the region would very quickly find its interests taking second place to the inevitable power rivalry of China, Korea, and Japan. For South East Asia, it would be more efficient to develop a wider, regional structure to bring together the dozen countries of the region. It is in that structure that South East Asia could sort through its interests, work out its positions, develop a consensus, and move ahead together and hence with more authority and success. It is also only through such an approach that the region can address the international policy coordination issues now becoming increasingly important. Recent shocks to regional financial markets triggered by Mexico's payments crisis is one case in point.. As the region's stake in the world economy grows faster than that for any other part of the world, so it must employ more of its resources in dealing with such issues. Otherwise, others will make the decisions, and South East Asia's interests will not be taken directly into account.

A number of developments in this direction have already occurred. A number of the region's central banks have begun informal consultations. The Mexican crisis was occasion to take these discussions further, but a more structured, integrated, regional multilateral approach is required. The current turmoil in world financial markets is but one more reason to move in that direction.

Security of Supply

Over the past decade and a half, the world has experienced a relative commodity surplus. As a result, South East Asia, a net importer of commodities, has seen the terms of trade move very much in its favor. This situation is unlikely to last indefinitely, however. Indeed, already the forces are being set in place for a new cycle of inflation—higher and higher debt levels, new forms of regulation severely limiting the opening of new sources of supply, increased demand resulting from the rapid expansion of the world following the end of Cold War. With conditions still so favorable, now is the time for South East Asia to organize itself as a region in order to set in place programs and policies that would assure long-term security of supply when conditions become less favorable. To wait until events force the region to do so, or to believe that bilateral approaches would be adequate is to make a fundamental error of judgment with regard to the power and forces that will be at work when conditions that currently govern world financial markets are reversed.

TOWARD A NEW MULTILATERALISM

As these issues continue to move higher, and the forces driving change in the world economy continue to gather momentum, the course ahead of South East Asia will prove to be increasingly multilateral. New forms of regional coordination are set to emerge, and new types of institutional building will develop as South East

Asia's specificities, historical experience, interests, and perspectives come into play. With time these developments are also likely to extend to the broader issues of region-wide security issues. The critical key to all of these developments will be the emergence of insightful, regionwide leadership, and should there be one challenge that surpasses all others, it is here. For without the insight, the perspectives, and the will that such leadership would provide, the important next step ahead for the region will be at best halting and painstaking, and so much so that what is today close at hand would be put at risk. That is the dimension of the opportunity. It is also the measure of the challenge.

AUSTRALIAN DEFENSE FUTURES

Stephen J. Merchant

T he Australian defense futures are timely. Only late last year the Australian Government released a White Paper on Australian defense policy which provides to parliament and the community a detailed exposition of the government's approach and policies in key areas of its responsibility. It also establishes Australia's view of its strategic outlook, covering all aspects of defense policy and management in three specific areas:
- Our view of the strategic environment
- Our approach to the planning and development of our defense force
- Our international strategies to influence our strategic environment in positive ways.

On Australia's strategic environment, the starting point for the White Paper's analysis is that the conjuncture of two developments—the end of the Cold War and the economic transformation of East Asia—is fundamentally reshaping the Asia-Pacific's strategic landscape.

Stephen J. Merchant is the Assistant Secretary of the Strategic Policy and Planning Branch, International Policy Division, Australian Department of Defense. Previously, he was head of the Strategic Analysis Branch in the Office of National Assessments, Australia's national intelligence assessment organization. From 1987 to 1991 he was with the International Policy Division of Defense, where he was responsible for the management of Australia's defense relations with the United States, the ASEAN countries, and Papua New Guinea and the South Pacific.

In many ways, the Cold War sustained an artificial Asian security environment. The two major Asian powers, China and Japan, were nobbled by historical circumstances: Japan by the loss of World War II and the constraints of the peace constitution; and China by its choice of communism and subsequent estrangement from the economic dynamism of the west for 40 years.

That environment is ending. Over the next 20 to 30 years, the security dynamics of the region will be transformed dramatically by the emergence of China as a truly global power, with the world's largest economy and a modernized military. In the same period, Japan will have developed a more active and autonomous international security role, even if, as we expect, the U.S.-Japan security alliance endures. And the eventual re-unification of the two Koreas, or at least a lasting reduction in tensions on the peninsula, will lead to some significant re-shaping of the permanent U.S. military presence in the region.

Those prospective changes affecting the roles of the major powers are being accentuated by the economic dynamism of East Asia. Different rates of economic growth between the major Asian powers and the United States are changing their strategic relativities. China of course attracts most attention in this regard. I will not go into arguments about how GDPs are most accurately measured—by converting currencies to U.S. dollars using official exchange rates, or by calculating purchasing power parities against a basket of commodities—but whichever way you do it, China is on course to become one of the world's dominant economic powers over the next 20 years. The argument is not so much *if*, but *when* this might happen.

And Asia's economic growth is, of course, not confined to China. You will all be familiar with the so-called economic miracle of the North Asian tigers. More recently, most of the countries of ASEAN have also been enjoying very impressive economic growth rates, which are not only affecting the way in which countries relate to one another, but also enhancing their capacity to develop and sustain military forces. Indeed, most of the ASEAN states are modernizing their militaries, converting them from forces designed predominantly for internal security and counterinsurgency operations towards more balanced, higher technology forces with enhanced maritime capabilities.

While this obviously has consequences for our own defense policies, Asia's growth and dynamism is not something we in

Australia fear. The military modernization programs, at their present modest pace, contribute to the strategic resilience of our nearer region—improving the ability of countries to resist external pressure. And they open up new opportunities for defense cooperation between Australia and our neighbors. More broadly, by tapping into Asia's economic dynamism, we hope to provide the foundation for our own continued economic prosperity. This is the spirit in which we are so firmly committed to the APEC forum and the opportunities it offers for widespread trade liberalization in the region.

We don't regard our strategic environment as threatening—in fact, by the standards of other regions, it is decidedly otherwise—but it *is* an environment which, over the next 15 years, will become more complex and, for defense planners, more demanding. That judgement is reinforced by our expectations of the political changes which will occur in Asia over the next decade or so. These include leadership changes in China; evolutionary changes in the political structures in Japan and Vietnam; and in Indonesia, the passing of a presidency that has brought extraordinary stability to that country, and thus to the whole of South East Asia, for the past 30 years.

The response our White Paper proposes to this more demanding environment is twofold:

- First, to develop and pursue international policies which promote a favorable security environment, reducing the chance of any threat to Australia , and ensuring we have appropriate international support should any threat eventuate.
- Second, while working hard at those objectives, we aim to ensure we have the military capabilities necessary to deter or defeat any attack that might credibly be mounted against Australia, without having to rely on assistance from other countries' combat forces.

We call the ability to defend Australia without depending on the assistance of the combat forces of other countries *self-reliance,* a term that confuses some people. It does not mean we are devaluing our alliances or our relationships with regional countries. What it does mean is that at the core of our defense posture we must have a defense force able to do certain tasks on its own. We are not looking to freeload on other countries by assuming that Australia's security is so vital to them that they would commit substantial forces to our defense. Even our alliance with the United States does not mean we can expect it to provide for our defense in all circumstances. Indeed, that alliance obliges us to provide effectively for our own defense.

The White Paper's emphasis on defense self-reliance reflects our long held view that our interests are not identical to those of anyone else; that, if there were an attack on Australia, it could occur in circumstances in which our allies were otherwise preoccupied; and that we can't credibly command respect as an ally or partner if we don't demonstrably care enough to ensure our own defense.

There are obvious limitations to how far we can push this concept of defense self-reliance. As a relatively small economy with a small, capable, and professional armed force, we cannot sustain a large or comprehensive defense industry sector. We do aim to maintain industrial capabilities sufficient at least to meet our expected maintenance and basic support needs in the event of a conflict. And we recognize the wider benefits to Australia and the region of a viable defense industry, while recognizing, too, that we cannot pay unlimited premiums for building in Australia what we can acquire overseas.

Currently, in collaboration with the Swedish firm Kockums, we are building six of our own conventionally powered submarines, the most sophisticated non-nuclear submarines in the world. The government considered ordering two more, but has deferred a decision on this for the present. We are also building a new class of frigates, and our own minehunters. We produce our own variant of the Steyr rifle, as well as a range of communications and very sophisticated surveillance equipment.

As a result of all this, some 65 percent of our acquisition budget is being spent in Australia, but the White Paper points out that in terms of future capability needs, our focus will shift over the next 10 years from ships and land force equipment to aircraft. For example, our acquisition program includes AEW&C aircraft, a new lead-in fighter, probably two types of helicopters, and the replacement of C-130s. Accordingly, the White Paper points to the fact that a higher proportion of our acquisition budget will be spent overseas in the next decade or so.

In coming to these decisions about the type of capabilities the Australian defense force will need in the future, the White Paper notes that we proceed from two basic premises:

- The first is our strategic geography. We are an island nation, so that any attacker would have to cross our surrounds. Any attack could plausibly come only from our north—that's just a fact of geography. Yet most of our people and industrial infrastructure are clustered in the southeast of our continent or along its southern or eastern coasts. Our population, though small, is educated and technologically skilled. These considerations add up to a need for a force that is small, mobile, able to exploit technology, and well focused on monitoring developments in our maritime surrounds and responding effectively to them.
- Our assessment of the capabilities that could credibly be used against us should there be a marked change in political circumstances.

What is important to emphasize here is that we plan against *capabilities*, not *threats*. The term used in the White Paper to describe what we plan for, or against, is short-warning or short-notice conflict—that is, the sort of attack that could be made against us using capabilities now in existence in the region, or confidently planned to be purchased. We don't plan at this time against the possibility of a major conflict or attempted invasion because we know that no country—except the United States—has the capabilities necessary for that. Because we are confident of our ability to detect any country's move to acquire such capabilities, we don't need *now* to maintain a force necessary to respond to it. We do hedge our bets a little on this point by seeking to ensure that we would be able to adapt our force in a timely way should our security outlook begin to deteriorate, say if a real arms race developed in the region.

This concept—being prepared only for short-warning or low-level conflict but ensuring adaptability—is not new. What *is* new is our recognition that because of the changes in the nature of military technology, and in the capabilities held or acquired by countries in our region as they modernize their forces, the *scale* of the force that could be brought to bear against us even at short notice has increased. We recognize also that as countries modernize their forces and develop their industrial, technological, and educational infrastructure, their lead times for moving from present levels of capability to higher levels will shorten.

This emphasis in our force planning on the development of capabilities for the defense of Australia does not mean we are becoming isolationist. While we *structure* our force to enable it to defend Australia, we, in fact, use it for a wide variety of tasks: for U.N. peacekeeping, for coalition operations, deployments, and exercises in our region, and for support to other parts of the Australian Government. But we don't structure our force for these other purposes—rather, we continue to judge that forces structured for the defense of Australia will be sufficiently versatile to undertake these other activities. And our versatility has been amply demonstrated. For example, we have deployed forces in more than half of all U.N. operations since 1945, including, in recent times, to the Gulf, Cambodia, Somalia, and Rwanda. Closer to home, over the last 20 years Australia has built up a network of active defense relationships with regional countries. These relationships will change, indeed they are already changing, as a consequence of the economic dynamism of much of South East Asia. We have moved from relationships which had a donor-recipient, defense aid-type connotations, to relationships which reflect a greater sense of genuine strategic partnership.

We will aim to take this process further in the next few years. We are not aiming to develop a new set of military alliances, but we will look for opportunities to add greater depth and weight to our bilateral defense relationships in the region. Specifically we hope to enhance high level dialogue on strategic perceptions and take advantage of the region's military modernization programs to develop more demanding combined exercises and training activities, as well as possible joint production and support arrangements for some shared military capabilities.

The underlying objective in all of this will be to promote a regional security environment in which the threat of military attack on Australia remains remote. The White Paper's emphasis on the need for greater regional engagement proceeds from this unashamedly self-interested perspective. But we are fortunate that so many of our neighbors share our interest in a region in which countries are able to pursue their social and economic development programs free from the threat of military attack and without the consequential need to maintain debilitatingly high-levels of defense spending.

Enhanced bilateral and multilateral cooperation between Australia and South East Asian countries on security and defense issues will help to maintain that situation, but our policies recognize that it is heavily dependent on the development of a stable post-Cold War set of relations amongst the region's major powers—the United States, Japan and China. Our ability to contribute there is limited, and our contribution is indirect. We do think that continued U.S. strategic engagement—underpinned by a lasting military presence in the Asia-Pacific—is essential to the region's strategic stability.

We are confident about the staying power of the United States. Nevertheless we will work hard at our bilateral alliance and through multilateral institutions like APEC and ARF to reinforce the constructive links between the United States and the Pacific. One aim will be to provide evident and convincing reasons for the U.S. Congress and American public opinion, of why it is in America's own best interests to stay strategically engaged in the Asia-Pacific.

Nobody, however, wants or expects the United States to remain Asia's "policeman on the block." One corollary of this is its key strategic relationship in the region—with Japan—will need to become more collegial. And that in turn will require Japan to play a more active role on security issues. The artificial strategic environment sustained by the Cold War cannot last. Japan's development of a more active security role is already underway, slowly and not a little painfully, but it is happening. What is needed in the region is a better and more widely accepted set of "rules of the security game" to ensure Japan's development of such a role is a positive, not a negative, factor in the post-Cold War Asia-Pacific.

The development of these "rules of the security game," or confidence and trust building measures to use the jargon of the trade, is an important part of the work know being embarked upon through the ASEAN Regional Forum. We attach a high priority to supporting the development of a multilateral approach to these issues, and we expect ARF to yield useful returns in coming years.

Those returns could also be important in allaying concerns about China's improving military capabilities and long-term strategic intentions. In fact, we think that both APEC and ARF will serve an important strategic purpose by reinforcing China's bilateral links to the region and increasing the stake it has in the economic prosperity, and hence strategic stability, of the Asia-Pacific.

I hope that what has come out clearly in these comments is that we in Australia think effective multilateral organizations are needed if the region is to meet the post-Cold War strategic challenges. But we see those organizations complementing, not replacing bilateral relationships and alliances. For effective multilateral organizations can only be built on sound bilateral foundations.

Australia's defense policies do not represent a radical departure from those developed previously. Rather, they have evolved, and are continuing to do so, in response to changes in our strategic environment. We continue to base our defense policy around two tenets—the self-reliant defense of Australia, and the promotion of a favorable regional security environment.

We see the strategic stability of the region being enhanced through greater bilateral and multilateral cooperation between Australia and South East Asian countries, and through encouraging positive engagement of the regional powers. Multilateral forums such as APEC and ARF will be an important part of this process.

Our alliance with the United States remains absolutely central to our defense policies—we think U.S. engagement in the Asia-Pacific is essential to the development of a loose but effective post-Cold War balance of power in the region. More narrowly we recognize that as an ally of the United States we continue to enjoy privileged access to U.S intelligence, military technologies and opportunities for highly demanding exercises. That allows us to enhance and hone our own military capabilities, which in turn reinforces our attractiveness as a partner on regional military cooperation.

So we see these elements of our policy—defense of Australia, alliance with the United States, greater engagement of the regional powers and cooperation in the region—as complementary, not contradictory. We think they provide the pillars for a defense policy that will serve Australia well as we prepare to enter the 21st century.

MODERNIZATION AND STABILITY, TOLERANCE AND PRAGMATISM

Richard L. Wilson

Those of us who have worked with ASEAN over the years know that a consensus is very important, so we'll aim in that direction. What I'd like to present to you is the perspective of someone who has worked in Southeast Asia since 1983. I went to the Canadian Defense University for a year, and during that time I passed through Djakarta on a big trip throughout Asia. More than anything else, that whetted my interest in South East Asia. Lo and behold I was lucky enough to go there in 1983. In any case, based on continuous exposure as an observer of things ASEAN, I would like to give you my personal views on some values I believe are fundamental to understanding other parts of Asia as well. The two that I pick as the most important and fundamental are modernization and stability.

MODERNIZATION AND STABILITY

Stability needs to be defined in terms of family relations, of ethnic relations, at the national, regional, and international levels. It's sometimes difficult for Americans to appreciate and understand just how deeply felt this sort of anxiety about insecurity and instability is, because we in the United States more or less take it

Richard L. Wilson is Executive Director, Center for Asian Pacific Affairs, The Asia Foundation, in San Francisco. Mr. Wilson was a career foreign service officer for over 33 years. His last posting was as Deputy Chief of Mission in Jakarta, Indonesia.

for granted. From an ASEAN perspective, stability is highly prized. Of course, if you have too much stability what you really have is stagnation, and needless to say that's not of very much interest to anybody, so there's the whole question of the modernization process. The modernization process in the ASEAN context is, fundamentally at least over the last 25 years or so, related to economic growth and to education. These are both pretty revolutionary.

Historically, most countries in the good old days, or the bad old days, tended to define themselves in terms of what territory they could conquer, or as creatures of elites after their own self-benefit as opposed to the benefit of all the people. It's clear from the record that this is not the kind of modernization that ASEAN is talking about. It is also true, of course, that modernization is not shared by all levels of society. Initially it started out as a value of the elites primarily, and even today there are many segments of populations all over Asia that are highly suspicious of the modernization process. In any case, there's clearly a degree of tension between stability and modernization, and therefore we need to recognize two fairly significant mediating values. One is tolerance and the other one is pragmatism.

If you look at ASEAN's historical context or what the countries that make up ASEAN went through historically—the enormous influence out of India on early cultures and civilizations, then Islam, and finally Christian and Confucian values, mostly associated with the colonial experience—you begin to get a feel for the incredible diversity of this region. Somebody said once that ASEAN is basically the Balkans multiplied by four, and that means many more people, many more ethnic groups, many more religions and value systems. With this in mind, we need to highlight a very important point with respect to the colonial experience. During colonialism, Asian countries were, to some extent, humiliated (at least in their own eyes, in retrospect), but they also were brought into contact with the enlightenment and all the forces that lay behind liberal capitalism, liberal democracy. Those were inculcated to a certain extent, at least, among the highest levels of society or those fortunate enough to get a good education, but by no means were they spread throughout the population. So after the upheaval of World War II and all of the events that followed the war, Asian countries went through what could only be described as tremendous turmoil and instability.

The politics were politics of the elite. There was no middle class, and there was widespread poverty and ignorance. Today it's hard to believe where they began.

EFFECT OF ASEAN

There were fundamentally two models of development or modernization in contention—the more or less democratic capitalists model, with a subset of Hobbesian socialism, much more popular in the sub-continent than in Southeast Asia but with some following in Indonesia. The other was the Marxist model. Throughout the Asian countries there was at least some degree of internal insurgency because of these. Until the mid-1960s there was very little or no stability, and very little or no economic growth. Instead, there were confusion and turmoil. Then a remarkable thing happened—a group of leaders came to the fore in the ASEAN countries and said stop, what we really want is to be left alone, what we really want is stability, and we want to work on economic development for our people. A lot of this was very good fortune, one supposes, but it seems a great credit accrues to those people responsible for this extraordinary venture. Initially there was uniform pessimism in academic circles as to what was going to happen to ASEAN in the post-Cambodian situation. However, there were those who were universally positive on the subject because they had considerable confidence in what ASEAN had already accomplished and what it was likely to be able to accomplish. When one thinks about the problems and criticisms ASEAN faced initially and right into the 1980s, it is remarkable that this rather nice situation has lasted 25 years or so. During that time there has been an extraordinary transition in ASEAN, along with a great deal of stability.

INSTABILITY AND
THE POST-COLD WAR ERA

There has been an unbelievable amount of economic growth and prosperity, but with this kind of success, we also find a new set of international circumstances. With the demise of the Cold War, the prospect of instability became much more pronounced. The real problem about the end of the Cold War is that it introduced this degree of uncertainty with which we don't really know how to cope. What is the enemy? Who is the enemy? Most everyone these days really is concentrating on trying to improve the well-being of their people, but still there is mistrust and fundamental concern. There's concern about whether the United States will stay in Asia and in the Asian region. There's concern about Japan and whether it will actually integrate itself and take on the responsibilities and duties that it ought to have in the international community. And of course, overwhelmingly there's the question of China and its real intentions for the future. There are other shorter term issues, North Korea probably being the most important, but in fact there's very little that ASEAN can do about that anyway.

ECONOMICS

As we look at the future and we consider the success of ASEAN, we have to ask ourselves what kind of strategies make sense? What kind of leadership styles make sense? What's likely to be the shape of things 5 or 10 years from today? First I would like to suggest that we take a look at the economic experience because I am really impressed with the way the Asia-Pacific region, with ASEAN at the center, has gone through this exercise of designing mechanisms that seem to be appropriate to particular levels of problem solving. And this goes beyond APEC. I was fortunate enough to be in Bali in 1983 when Ali Wardona, at that time the Coordinating Minister for Economic Affairs, gave a speech to the PECC making it very clear that Indonesia was not interested in just any kind of big regional economic organization. Indonesia's priorities didn't lie in that direction. Eleven years later we have President Suharto, in large part responsible for a successful outcome in the Bogor declaration. That things have changed so far so fast is a commentary on the dynamism of the region and on the flexibility of the leadership.   Even more interesting, we have these growth triangles. At first, these look a little strange, but they turn out to be quite effective mechanisms designed to deal with a particular problem at the appropriate level. I think it's a good illustration of the pragmatism discussed earlier.

Domestic economic policy seems to be in pretty good shape. It's difficult to imagine why there should be any change necessary in the economic policies most Asian countries have been pursuing. Perhaps the only real threat to ASEAN might be a collapse in the global economy, but at this stage that is rather hard to imagine. The political side of the equation, however, isn't quite as satisfying and perhaps the prospects are not quite as good. ASEAN did realize that something had to be done on the security side if the question of instability and uncertainty were to be addressed. Some kind of a process, maybe several processes, was necessary to work on these problems as they arose, then gradually to integrate all the players into a healthy global system. So they established ARF, a good step in the right direction, but the process is slow. We can only hope they will move rapidly enough to deal with problems as they come along.

POLITICS

Another interesting aspect of stability is the effect on domestic politics. It's hard to imagine stability without good, solid, political institutions.   With the success that ASEAN countries have experienced, new sets of strains are forming. It is also interesting to reflect on the fact that, if you're an Asian country, you don't have to look to the West for models anymore; there are all kinds right in Asia. We have the Japanese one, usually described (probably correctly) as an ASEAN democracy, but everyone would agree it is a highly bureaucratic, dependent democracy at this point.   It will be interesting to follow what happens in the attempts at reform, and judging from recent literature, maybe it's slowed down again a little. There's the highly personalized style of China and Deng, and Suharto and Indonesia. There are the Korea, Thailand, Taiwan, and Philippine experiences. Only the Philippines has had any significant experience with democracy, but all are moving gradually and, one hopes, successfully toward a more institutionalized approach to politics. Finally there are the Malaysia and Singapore experiences, very interesting cases of strong one-party states.

CONCLUSION

In any case, we're in new territory and it will be very interesting to see what sorts of values will continue to hold sway. And if it continues to be the ones that have been identified—stability and modernization, with tolerance and pragmatism—our Asian friends and ASEAN friends will have to concentrate on what is going to be the best organization to accomplish those ends. It's kind of an open question, but based on my experience, I'm pretty optimistic. I believe there is a continued commitment to the well being of all citizens, not just to the elites. And that means a modernization process in which everyone has a stake and to which everyone is committed. I believe as well that there's a growing tolerance. When one reflects on the vast differences that ASEAN has managed to cope with—ethnically, religiously, and so on—one can't help but feel that it would take something quite extraordinary to roll the clock back to some less-enlightened approach.

Does that mean that everything's going to be just fine? Not necessarily, but I am fundamentally optimistic. I think some kind of an ASEAN or Asian style democracy will ultimately evolve from this process over time. There's a real possibility of a blending of ASEAN values and Western values. I predict that's the direction we're likely to take, barring some unforeseen catastrophe that, as Aristotle once said, "no one can ever rule out."

ACRONYMS

ABIT	Augmented Bilateral Investment Treaty
AFP	Armed Forces of the Philippines
AFTA	ASEAN Free Trade Area
APEC	Asia Pacific Economic Cooperation
ARF	ASEAN Regional Forum
ASA	Association of Southeast Asia
ASEAN	Association of Southeast Asia Nations
CBM	confidence building measure
CEPT	Common Effective Preferential Tariff
CER	closer economic relations
CSBM	confidence and security building measure
CSCAP	Council for Security Cooperation in the Asia-Pacific
CSCE	Conference on Security and Cooperation in Europe (now OSCE)
EAEC	East Asian Economic Caucus
EC	European Community
EEC	European Economic Community
EEZ	exclusive economic zone
EPG	Eminent Persons Group
EU	European Union
FDI	foreign direct investment
FPDA	Five Power Defence Arrangements
GATT	General Agreement on Tariffs and Trade
GSP	Generalized System of Preferences
ILO	International Labor Organization
IMET	international military education and training
IMF	International Monetary Fund
IPC	Intellectual Property Clause
ISIS	Institute of Security and International Studies
MNC	multinational corporation
MFN	most favored nation
NAFTA	North American Free Trade Agreement
NGOs	nongovernmental organizations
NIE	newly industrializing economies
NPCSD	North Pacific Cooperative Security Dialogue
NPT	Non-proliferation Treaty
OECD	Organization for Economic Cooperation and Development

OSCE	Organization for Security and Cooperation in Europe
PBEC	Pacific Basin Economic Council
PECC	Pacific Economic Cooperation Council
PLAN	People's Liberation Army-Navy
PMCs	post-ministerial conferences
PTA	preferential trading arrangement
SEATO	South East Asian Treaty Organization
SOM	Senior Officers Meeting (ASEAN)
TAC	Treaty of Amity and Cooperation
WHFTA	Western Hemisphere Free-Trade Area
WTO	World Trade Organization
ZOPFAN	zone of peace, freedom, and neutrality

APPENDIX 1.

Memberships of the Regionwide Organizations in Asia/Pacific

Countries	PECC	APEC	ARF	CSCAP	ASEAN
The United States	FM	FM	FM	FM	
Canada	FM	FM	FM	FM	
Japan	FM	FM	FM	FM	
Australia	FM	FM	FM	FM	
New Zealand	FM	FM	FM	FM	
Brunei	FM	FM	FM	FM	
Indonesia	FM	FM	FM	FM	FM
Malaysia	FM	FM	FM	FM	FM
Philippines	FM	FM	FM	FM	FM
Singapore	FM	FM	FM	FM	FM
Thailand	FM	FM	FM	FM	FM
China	FM	FM			
Chinese Taipei	FM	FM			
Hong Kong	FM	FM			
Korea(South)	FM	FM	FM	FM	
Korea(North)			FM		
Russia	FM	FM	FM		
Mexico	FM	FM			
Peru	FM				
Chile	FM				
Columbia	FM				
Papua New Guinea		FM	FM		
Laos		FM			
Vietnam	AM	FM			
India				AM	

FM = full members
AM = associate members

251

APPENDIX 2.
Trade Policy Matrix

	Japan	Canada	United States
I Trade			
A Tariffs and other import taxes	• on industrial products, about 2% • 12% average on agricultural products, will be reduced and bound	• average tariff <3.5%, but complex and multilayered system	• 5.1% weighted average for MFN countries (excluding petroleum) • <10% for 81% of items; 10.1–20% for 4% of items; high peaks on tobacco, textiles, footwear
B Nontariff barriers			
Import licensing	N/A	• restricts barley imports, dairy products	
Quantitative restrictions (QRs)	• commitment to tariffication of quotas/bans on agricultural goods, and reduction in tariffs by 2000	• cultural identity–related regulations of market access • QRs on poultry, certain vegetables and fruits	• voluntary restraint agreements (VRAs) • special arrangements for steel, shipbuilding, machine tools, textiles, semiconductors • anti-dumping and countervailing measures

	Japan	Canada	United States
C Customs procedures	• bottlenecks in import clearance procedures, and excessively high customs charges	N/A	• unpredictable interpretation of rules of origin • customs users fees not conforming to GATT • excessive invoicing requirements
II Indirect trade-related measures			
A Industrial, technical, and health standards	• overly restrictive, lack of transparency	• some criteria vague	• complex regulatory system • discrepancy with int'l standards
B Structural impediments and rules of competition	• keiretsu, lax enforcement of anti-monopoly law, nontransparent regulations, complex and rigid distribution system	• provincial-level discriminatory marketing practices	• VRA-using companies often exempt from anti-trust actions
C Government aid to industries	• close government/business relationships disadvantage those not consulted	• gov't subsidizes rail transport of agr. goods	• agricultural subsidies ($36 billion in 1990)

		Japan	Canada	United States
E	Intellectual property rights	• registration of trademarks takes time, often 3 yrs • very long time to grant patents, inviting opposition to patent before issued • moves to allow decompilation and reverse engineering of software, which would weaken current copyright protection	• patents protected for 20 years	• certain domestic legislation considered to be GATT-inconsistent
II	DFI policy			
I				
A	Barriers to entry	• investment based on cross-shareholding and long-term personal supplier & marketing relationships	• restrictions in oil & gas industry, telecommunications, transportation, mining, financial sectors	• some unequal treatment of foreign companies
B	Ownership requirements	• restrictions in a few strategic sectors	• Investment Canada Act requires review of investment to ensure net benefit to Canada	• restrictions in certain sectors including domestic shipping, airlines, and power-generating industries
C	Performance requirements	• none	• some (R&D and high tech)	• none

255

		Japan	Canada	United States
D	Transfer of profits	● restrictive screening and limitations on repatriation of earnings	● no restrictions	● no restrictions

	New Zealand	Australia	Korea
I			
Trade			
A Tariffs and other import taxes	• by 1996 most tariffs will be in the 0 to 14% range	• 7+% trade-weighted avg., with significant "peaks" • pledged to reduce most tariffs to 5% by 1996	• 7.8% average • 30+% on meat, most fruits, juices, dairy products • 28% effective rate of protection (1988)
B Nontariff barriers			
Import licensing	• completely dismantled the previously restrictive system	N/A	• required for all goods, 99% of which are automatic
Quantitative restrictions (QRs)	• monopolistic control over exports of dairy, meat, and kiwi fruit	• wide use of anti-dumping and countervailing procedures	• will begin to phase out agricultural import restrictions
C Customs procedures	N/A	• valuation treatment of royalties and buying commissions perhaps GATT-inconsistent	• sometimes very slow and arbitrary • unannounced changes in customs classifications

	New Zealand	Australia	Korea
II Indirect trade-related measures			
A Industrial, technical, and health standards	N/A	• restrictive standards on cars, elec. equip., med. and telecomm. equip, and machinery parts and equip. • phytosanitary regulations limit imports of some fruits	• nontransparent standards burdensome and in some cases unreasonable health/safety requirements
B Structural impediments and rules of competition	N/A	N/A	• excessive government regulation resulting in arbitrary treatment
C Government aid to industries	N/A	• several programs to enhance exports	• tax, duty and loan breaks to export industries
D Government procurement	N/A	• not yet a signatory of GATT Government Procurement Code • domestic preferences of 10–20% in most states	• continues to encourage local procurement • will implement GATT Government Procurement Agreement in January 1997
E Intellectual property rights	• currently engaged in full review of IPR regime	• some "bootlegging" of live performance recordings	• improved but still ineffective enforcement

	New Zealand	Australia	Korea
II DFI policy			
I			
A Barriers to entry	• few barriers to DFI	• government has broad discretion to deny specific foreign investment	• opaque and sometimes arbitrary conditions of foreign access
B Ownership requirements	• 24.9% foreign ownership in commercial fishing • conditional ownership of rural land	• only restricted in a few sectors (mining, commercial TV)	• restrictions on ownership of land and investment in areas of national security
C Performance requirements	• none	• local content for cigarette leaf production	• some local equity participation requirements and forced divestiture requirement
D Transfer of profits	• no restrictions	N/A	N/A

259

	Taiwan	Singapore	Thailand
I Trade			
A Tariffs and other import taxes	• 20–50% on some fruits and vegetables • 60–100% on cars and trucks	• 96% of imports enter duty-free	• 16.8% trade-weighted avg. (1991); 9.3% ratio of tariff collected to total imports • 60% on most agricultural products • 51% effective rate of protection (1988)
B Nontariff barriers			
Import licensing	• number of items requiring import licenses gradually being reduced • will replace with simplified "negative list"	• virtually none • rice importers required to keep buffer stock	• restrictive licensing on 47 product categories, or 4% of 4-digit HS lines (1994)
Quantitative restrictions (QRs)	• de facto bans or onerous quarantine restrictions for some meats and vegetables	• QRs or bans on amusement machines, chewing gum, and certain toys, plants and animal wildlife articles	• certain chemicals, selected food products; tariffication as part of Uruguay Round agreement

		Taiwan	Singapore	Thailand
C	Customs procedures	• approvals and documentation requirements sometimes require connections with authorities	• valuation of imports based on Brussels Definition of Value	• sometimes arbitrary valuation, long and onerous certification process • valuation of imports based on Brussels Definition of Value
II	Indirect trade-related measures			
A	Industrial, technical, and health standards	• complex, time-consuming registration procedures (pharmaceuticals, medical devices, cosmetics)	• signatory to most international standards	• many health/safety standards follow int'l standards • certification/approval of certain food and pharmaceutical products remains excessively long process
B	Structural impediments and rules of competition	• Taiwan Tobacco and Wine Monopoly Bureau	• telecommunications	• Public Warehouse Org.; Thailand Tobacco Monopoly; Forestry Industry Org.; Fish Marketing Org.; Thai Plywood Ltd.; Gov't Cold Storage Org.
C	Government aid to industries	N/A	• none	• some assistance to farmers

	Taiwan	Singapore	Thailand
D Government procurement	• public enterprises must procure locally if possible • nontransparency: invisible ceiling prices, liability requirements, pre-qualification requirements, local construction license	• open tendering system used for 85% of nondefense contracts	• tendering system is not transparent • domestic suppliers generally receive 5–15% preferential margin
E Intellectual property rights	• piracy problems, slow and sometimes arbitrary patent decisions	• software and videocassette pirating • copyright laws strengthened and enforcement is improving	• on U.S. "special 301" priority watch list since 1989; extensive piracy • new laws enacted 1991 & 1992 and situation improving
II DFI policy I A Barriers to entry	• some sectors effectively closed (agriculture, telecommunications, cigarettes)	• only few sectors closed	• no general negative clause; certain sectors closed
B Ownership requirements	• ownership limited in some industries (leasing and insurance)	• none in most industries	• export-oriented (>80%) firms or designated sectors can be 100% foreign owned; obligation for localization

	Taiwan	Singapore	Thailand
C Performance requirements	N/A	• no local content requirements	• local content for certain sectors; some export requirements
D Transfer of profits	N/A	• no restrictions	• no restrictions
E Incentives	• tax incentives for R&D and high tech	• income tax exemptions for eligible manuf. and service industries	• tax holiday; some import tariff exemptions

263

	Philippines	Malaysia	Indonesia
I Trade			
A Tariffs and other import taxes	• 4 tiers in tariff structure: 3%, 10%, 20%, 30% • 50% for about 200 "strategic" products • 32% effective rate of protection (1992)	• less than 10% average in 1990 • Australia and New Zealand enjoy preferential tariff rates on some fruits • 23% effective rate of protection (1988)	• applied tariff rates from 5% to 30% • import surcharges for about 200 tariff categories, mostly in the 5–25% range • 52% effective rate of protection (1992)
B Nontariff barriers			
Import licensing	• more than 100 items regulated through non-automatic licensing	• for about 10% of all tariff lines	• 269 tariff categories, to be removed over 10-year period
Quantitative restrictions (QRs)	• QRs/bans on ~150 items including feeder cattle, horses, certain vegetables, and gambling devices	• prohibited manufactured imports in "pioneer" industries • QRs on multicolor copying machines, certain radio receivers, and specific animal/wildlife articles	• QRs on several agriculture products including milk and rice

		Philippines	Malaysia	Indonesia
C	Customs procedures	• valuation on home-country market basis rather than invoice value, but will convert to latter (no timetable set) • valuation inconsistent on a country-to-country basis	• valuation of imports based on Brussels Definition of Value	• valuation of imports based on Brussels Definition of Value • preshipment inspections required for imports ≥ US$5,000
II	Indirect trade-related measures			
A	Industrial, technical, and health standards	• country-of-origin phytosanitary prohibitions for fresh fruit sometimes arbitrary	• signatory to many international codes	• relatively slow certification
B	Structural impediments and rules of competition	• Philippine Int'l Trading Corp.; National Food Authority	• no domestic anti-trust laws • National Paddy and Rice Authority	• BULOG, Pertamina, Krakatau Steel, Perum Dahama, and 6 other state-trading enterprises
C	Government aid to industries	• subsidy to certain export sectors	• preferential tax treatment to automobile manuf. w/minimum LCR	• subsidy to all sectors using petroleum and to farmers
D	Government procurement	• discrimination only in some sectors	• relatively low level of discrimination in gov't contracts	• preference given to "economically weaker" local groups and domestic goods & services

	Philippines	Malaysia	Indonesia
E Intellectual property rights	• inadequate laws and regulations and insufficient resources for enforcement • trademark counterfeiting and software piracy widespread	• videotape piracy prevalent • short (15-year) patent term	• on "watchlist" of US "special 301" since 1989 due to inadequate protection
II DFI policy I A Barriers to entry	• A.B.C. negative lists	• no negative clause; mass media closed	• exists in most service sectors
B Ownership requirements	• 60% Filipino ownership in order to own land • constitution limits foreign ownership of advertising agencies to 30%	• Export-oriented (>80% or >50% for specific large projects) firms can be 100% foreign owned	• DFI must be joint venture, usually at least 20% initial Indonesian share • 34-sector negative list
C Performance requirements	• local content required; export requirement to avoid localization	• local content required for tax incentives and export credits	• some export requirements and import restrictions for certain products • local content requirements to be phased out within 10 years
D Transfer of profits	• no restrictions	• no restrictions	• no restrictions

266

	Philippines	Malaysia	Indonesia
E Incentives	• 5 (4)-year tax holiday for (non)pioneer firms; export processing zones	• 70% tax holiday for 5 years for pioneer status companies	• no tax holidays; some import tariff exemptions

Sources: USTR (1994) and World Bank (1994).